The Writer's Market Companion

WRITER'S MARKET
LIBRARY

The

Writer's Market

Companion

**The essential guide
to starting your project, getting it published and getting paid**

by

Joe Feiertag, Mary Carmen Cupito

&

the Editors of *Writer's Market*

WRITER'S DIGEST BOOKS
CINCINNATI, OHIO
www.writersdigest.com

Other fine Writer's Digest Books are available from your local bookstore or direct from the publisher.

Visit our Web site at www.writersdigest.com for information on more resources for writers.

To receive a free weekly E-mail newsletter delivering tips and updates about writing and about Writer's Digest products, send an E-mail with "Subscribe Newsletter" in the body of the message to newsletter-request@writersdigest.com, or register directly at our Web site at www.writersdigest.com.

04   03   02   01   00   5   4   3   2   1

Library of Congress Cataloging-in-Publication Data

Feiertag, Joe
   The Writer's Market companion / by Joe Feiertag, Mary Carmen Cupito, and the editors of Writer's Market.
      p.   cm.
   ISBN 0-89819-930-9 (pbk. : alk. paper)
      1. Authorship—Handbooks, manuals, etc. I. Cupito, Mary Carmen. II. Title.

PN147.F43   2000
808′.02′02373—dc21   00-020341
                                                                         CIP

Editors: Kirsten Holm and Michelle Howry
Designer: Sandy Conopeotis Kent
Cover designer: Matthew Gaynor
Production coordinator: Kristen D. Heller

JOE FEIERTAG is a full-time public relations specialist who has also built a highly successful career as a freelance writer, editor and journalist. His impressive list of clients includes several multi-million dollar corporations, including Marriott, Super-Value and Furrow. In addition, he continues to write articles and is regular a contributor to the *Cincinnati Enquirer* and other publications.

MARY CARMEN CUPITO has worked as a full-time reporter for the *Cincinnati Post*, *The St. Petersburg Times* and the *Columbus Dispatch*. After leaving full-time news reporting, she moved to freelance work, writing articles for several magazines, including *American Health* and *Kentucky Monthly*.

She also writes public relations and advertising materials. As a writing instructor, she has taught journalism at Ohio State University and now teaches at Northern Kentucky University.

CHAPTER ONE

The Writer's World

The New Millennium

Americans bought 1.1 billion books last year, continuing a long trend that has seen people pick up and read increasing numbers of books nearly every year. At the same time, nearly nine hundred new magazine titles hit the shelves last year, bringing the total number of titles in the U.S. to more than 18,000—to say nothing of the 45,000 newspapers and professional newsletters now scattered across the American landscape (a number that also keeps growing each year). The trend is clear. As we step into the new millennium, more Americans are reading more books and magazines than ever. In fact, Americans are reading more of everything.

This fact is seldom realized and nearly always surprising. After all, we live in the electronic information age with radio, television, video games, cellular phones, computers and the Internet all competing for our attention. Some purveyors of these "new" communication arts have gone so far as to describe book and magazine publishing as little more than "smearing ink on dead trees." And wasn't it recently that computer experts predicted we would soon work in "paperless" offices? How could books and magazines possibly fit into this paperless world?

If technology didn't threaten the existence of books and magazines, it certainly seemed poised to threaten their importance. But just as the dawn of television was predicted to knock radio from the airwaves, the opposite has come true. There are more radio stations today than television stations. And despite the increase in electronic communication, books and magazines hold more appeal than ever. In fact, books and magazines are more important than ever. The real irony is that technology has played a part in their proliferation. And for those of us who make a living writing (and those who desire to make their living this way) there has never been a better time to be doing it.

Right Here, Write Now!

The latter half of the twentieth century has been aptly dubbed "The Information Age" because so many technologies continually shower us with knowledge and entertainment. We have to wonder how ink and paper can hold their own. The truth is, traditional books and magazines hold some key advantages. Anyone who has ever "read the book" and then seen the movie knows the limitations of what a screenplay can portray in two to three hours. What's more, it's hard to curl up in bed or relax on the beach with a computer screen, even if it's a laptop computer.

Magazines and books have filled a vital niche in this technology age, where work and entertainment have grown increasingly specialized. For example, you can't get a real overview of what television is all about by turning on the tube. For that, your best bet is a *TV Guide*. Similarly, you can't just boot up to learn about computers or log on to learn about the Internet. The best source of information is a book or magazine that is geared to your specific interests. So books and magazines have become the guides to an increasingly complex world. The proliferation of magazine titles (18,000 and counting in the U.S. alone) is a testament to this fact.

Books and magazines even hold an advantage in how we use our free time. Adults who spend all day in front of computers at work don't always want to come home and sit in front of another screen—whether it's a computer or a television. This is why a nationwide Gallup poll in 1997 found that more than half of adults had purchased at least one book over a three-month period prior to the survey. The average book buyer purchased five books during that period. Not even young people want to spend all their time with electronic gadgets. As many as one in ten Generation Xers spends most of her discretionary income on books, according to a survey by the American Booksellers Association. The study found that more young adults spend their money on books than on movies. (And the survey didn't even count books purchased for school.)

And speaking of book buying: One of the greatest commercial successes on the Internet is Amazon.com, which has carved out a hugely successful business selling books and music online. Amazon.com is not just a new way to buy books. The company's success reflects society's intense interest in reading. Every writer has to rejoice in the fact that some of the most sought-after items on the Internet are good old-fashioned books. Now there's some *real* irony.

Whatever the cause, interest in books and magazines is growing and showing no signs of slowing down anytime soon. Samir Husni, a journalism professor at the University of Mississippi at Oxford and one of the leading experts on the magazine industry, sums it up best: "There is a demand for more information today than ever before. Whether it is television, the Internet or some other technology creating the need, no one is supplying those demands more than the [print] industry. . . . The print industry has learned how to complement every other media. That is why print media are in better shape than ever before."

Magazine Market Up Close

Getting a precise handle on the number of magazines in the U.S. is nearly impossible. The Periodical Publishers Association lists 8,000, while the *Gale Directory of Publications and Broadcast Media* (Gale Research) puts the number closer to 11,000. *The National Directory of Magazines* (Oxbridge Communications) reports more than 18,000 magazines in print. Other sources put the number at more than 20,000. Much of the variance results from how you define magazines. Do you count scholarly journals, yearbooks and the publications of various institutions, clubs and associations? For a writer looking for work, it doesn't matter how magazines are defined. It's just encouraging to know there are a lot, and the numbers are growing all the time.

The last several years have been a period of tremendous growth in magazine publishing. In 1990, 557 new magazines hit the market, according to Husni. Another 553 premiered the following year, and another 679 emerged the year after that. With the exception of 1996-1997, the trend has continued with an ever increasing number of magazines appearing every year.

NEW MAGAZINE LAUNCHES
1990: 557
1991: 553
1992: 679
1993: 789
1994: 832
1995: 838
1996: 933
1997: 852
1998: 1,076

(Source: Samir Husni's Guide to New Consumer Magazines *[Oxbridge Communications])*

Of course, of the hundreds of new magazines emerging each year, not all survive. As with any business, only a small number of start-ups survive those first tumultuous years. For magazines, the survival rate is about 30 percent. Even so, the long-term trend is encouraging for writers. By the end of the 1990s there were 2,000 more magazine markets available than at the beginning of the decade.

This steady rise in new magazine titles does not necessarily mean overall readership is growing at the same pace. While thousands of start-ups have enjoyed success, many of the top U.S. magazines have witnessed declines in circulation. This suggests that the existing market continues to be fragmented into more and more small niches. This may be bad news for the larger publishing houses, but the trend is not necessarily bad for writers—particularly those who are just starting out and looking for a foothold. After all, more titles—however small—mean more prospects for selling your work.

We Are What We Read

The trends that the magazine industry goes through merely reflect society. After all, the things we choose to read about, either individually or as a group, are a clear indication of what interests us. Nearly 150 years ago, as Americans were discovering bicycles, the novelty and excitement spawned an entire new genre of magazine. New cyclists and those who dreamed of owning a bicycle were eager to learn all they could about these two-wheeled wonders. The publication industry filled that need with a wide selection of cycling magazines. This same analysis can be made today, only now the fastest growing subject areas reflect the highly specialized, highly technical society that we have become.

Medicine, business, computers, education, engineering and law are among the fastest growing subject areas today. Each has spawned hundreds of new magazine titles in the previous decade, according to *The Serials Directory* (published by EBSCO), which lists new periodicals by subject category. While none of these subjects seem similar, they all have at least one thing in common: All are career fields that require constant updates on changing technologies and trends. Magazines and trade journals have emerged as the vehicles for delivering this important information. Subject areas such as engineering and law may not inspire or even interest you as a writer, but they certainly illustrate the specialized nature of today's magazine market.

Those who are not technically minded need not worry. Art, the environment, health, history, literature, music, religion, sports, theater and travel are alive and well. Each has given rise to dozens of new titles in the last decade. In fact, if magazines are a way to measure the pulse of society, every single cultural blip is being registered somewhere in print. Take the magazine *Alive*, a lifestyle publication geared toward people who shuttle between the Arab and Western worlds. And *Wine X Magazine*, geared toward Generation X wine lovers. Or *Christian Motorsports Illustrated*. Yes, niches are being defined that narrowly. There seems to be a magazine for everyone.

Even within a seemingly broad category, such as computers, there really are very few general magazines. Most computer magazines are geared to specific segments of the market: graphic designers, game enthusiasts, network administrators, etc. Even magazines devoted to literature are broken down into niches: poetry, mysteries, short stories and science fiction. Today's markets, more than ever, require writers themselves to specialize and study the market carefully if they are to succeed. This can be good news. In the highly specialized markets of today, there is almost certainly a niche (or multiple niches) for every type of writer. A motivated writer is likely to find almost as many viable markets as there are subjects.

The World of Books

America's love of reading is perhaps most evident when we look at book sales. In the years leading up to the new millennium, book sales in the U.S. (excluding textbooks) were up a healthy 38 percent—from annual sales of 776 million books in 1991 to nearly 1.07 billion books in 1997. Some subject areas grew even faster, with gains of 75, 90, even 150 percent. The subject areas that are growing the most in popularity might really surprise you. But before we delve into the trends, let's look at what Americans like to read most, according to the American Booksellers Association.

In terms of sheer volume, nothing can touch **popular fiction**. Half of all sales in 1997 (537 million books) were popular fiction. This includes science fiction, western, romance, adventure, mystery, fantasy and thriller.

Cooking and hobbies, including crafts, home improvement, automotive and pets, was the number-two category with sales of 108 million books (10.2 percent of the market).

General nonfiction ranked third with sales of 95 million books (8.9 percent of the market), including biography, crime, true adventure, humor and history.

Religion was fourth in reader interest, with sales of nearly 92 million books (8.6 percent of the market). This category includes inspirational topics, philosophy, New Age subjects, religious history and bibles.

Psychology and health ranked fifth with sales of 67 million books (6.3 percent of the market). This category includes exercise, sex, marriage, child care, grooming and recovery. The really interesting point here is that religion outsells sex in America, at least in book form.

Technology, science and education ranked sixth with sales of nearly 60 million books (5.6 percent of the market), including topics such as computers, business, math and sociology.

Art and literature ranked seventh with sales of nearly 40 million books (3.7 percent of the market), including genres such as poetry, architecture and music.

Reference books and **miscellaneous** categories ranked eighth with sales of 28 million and 26 million books each (2.6 and 2.5 percent of the market, respectively).

Travel and regional topics round out the list with sales of 13 million books (1.3 percent of the market), including books on places of interest.

Unlike television and movies, where sex and violence reign supreme, most book buyers gravitate more toward tamer genres. This may reflect two things: Frequent book buyers tend to be better educated than the population as a whole, so their choice of topics is likely to be broader. They are also more likely to be female, and therefore more interested in romance than sex.

Trends in the Book Market

While popular fiction commands the lion's share of the book market, other genres are increasingly finding more room in the marketplace. The growing success of cooking and craft books is particularly interesting, because it appears to be driven in part by technology. It seems that people who are looking for a respite from the technology grind are gravitating toward hobbies and crafts. And they are buying books in hopes of furthering their enjoyment and learning new skills.

Noelle Backer, senior editor for *Craft Report*, explains the phenomenon to *Publishers Weekly* this way: "With technological advances comes a wave of nostalgia for what has been left behind. . . . With the mass application of computers, people have longed to return to simpler lives."

As people's lives have grown busier and more complex, armchair travel is another simple pleasure that is gaining momentum. Real travel has also grown more accessible to affluent baby boomers. This trend is rippling through the publishing business, which has seen travel books outpace the overall growth in book sales.

The market for psychology, diet and health books is growing even faster, as baby boomers wrestle with issues of aging—whether it's their own health or that of their parents and children. The market for art, literature and poetry books is also expanding rapidly, although sales overall are relatively small for this category.

You might expect books about technology, science and business to grow more popular—or at least more necessary—with each passing year, and they are. Sales of these books are increasing twice as fast as book sales in general. Yet these books are still taking a backseat to a category that is far outpacing all others: religion.

The religious and inspirational market is growing three times as fast as book sales overall. And the category is fairly large to begin with, accounting for nearly 92 million book sales in 1997. America's interest in spirituality is similar to its interest in health, according to Jen Haller, a top buyer for the Joseph-Beth chain of bookstores.

Americans have expanded their concern about health to include a "body, mind and soul approach," Haller says. "As Americans age they've gained a big interest in not only preserving their body, but preserving their mind and spirit, too."

Oftentimes, however, it's religion with a modern twist. "Religious sales are growing really quickly, but not in a conventional way. . . . We're seeing general inspirational topics and a lot of titles that cross different religious lines," Haller notes.

WHERE IS THE BOOK MARKET HEADED? (Sales Growth, 1991–1997)
Religious/Inspirational: 150 percent
Technology/Science/Business: 90 percent
Art/Literature/Poetry: 75 percent
Psychology/Diet/Health: 70 percent
Travel/Regional Interest: 45 percent
Cooking/Hobbies/Crafts: 30 percent
Popular Fiction: 26 percent
General Nonfiction: 18 percent
(Source: American Booksellers Association)

Charting Your Path

Most writers find it easier to break into the magazine market than the book market. This does not mean a book deal is out of the question for newer writers. Thousands of dedicated first-time authors are published every year in the U.S. Of the 80,000 new book titles published in 1997, more than two-thirds—some 56,000 books—were written by first-time authors.

Writing for magazines and books requires different sets of work habits, and each offers distinct rewards in both satisfaction and compensation. Whether you will do better pursuing magazine writing or a book contract depends largely on your personal style and the goals you set for yourself. For an overview of the relative advantages of each, consider the following points from Leon Fletcher, author of sixteen published books and more than seven hundred articles and a columnist for America Online's Writers Club (keyword: *Writers*).

ADVANTAGES OF BOOKS OVER MAGAZINES
Better pay
More prestigious
Spin-off benefits

DISADVANTAGES OF BOOKS COMPARED TO MAGAZINES
Harder to break in
Longer commitment
Have to hire agent

Pay for books is a lot more than that for most magazine articles. But unless you are an established author—or are lucky enough to have two or more publishers bidding against each other—the initial compensation for a book is usually in the range of several thousand dollars. Typically this pay is in the form of an advance, which is paid over the course of a year while the book is being written and edited.

A book does well if it sells even 10,000 copies. At that point a book typically earns enough to cover the writer's advance and the publisher's other expenses. For many writers, the initial advance is the only money they ever see because of poor sales. Even so, most books will probably earn you more than most magazine articles. If your book is even a modest success, the rewards can mount quickly.

Of course, a book author usually has to share a slice of his income with the agent who got him the book deal in the first place, because most book editors won't look at a manuscript unless it is referred to them by an agent. Four out of five published authors use agents, which says something about the difficulty of breaking into book publishing.

In the final analysis, books provide long-term benefits beyond the direct financial rewards. The prestige of writing a book can often boost your career. The research and expertise you gain from a book project can be spun into a variety of magazine articles or other books.

ADVANTAGES OF MAGAZINES OVER BOOKS
More opportunities
Easy to find a niche
Brief commitment

DISADVANTAGES OF MAGAZINES COMPARED TO BOOKS
Continual hunt for work
Less pay

The key advantage to magazine writing is that there are so many more opportunities, based on the sheer number of local, regional and national publications. Each publishes anywhere from eight to twenty articles per issue. Unlike books, which have a longer shelf life, magazines continually need good articles. The second advantage of magazine writing is that it usually entails a brief commitment of a few days or a week—unlike books, which require a sustained effort for a year or longer.

Leon Fletcher sums it up for many writers: "My bankbook prefers books, but mentally I prefer getting an idea for an article and grinding it out in three or four days."

Yet depending on how you prefer to work, the transient nature of magazine writing can be a disadvantage. Every few days, or every week at most, you have to hustle to find more work. You must juggle several projects at once.

Getting Started

The way to approach a magazine editor, book publisher or literary agent is through a query letter, or a lengthier book proposal, when appropriate. (Both of these will be discussed in more detail in subsequent chapters.) In either case, think of your goal not as getting your work accepted, but as keeping it from being rejected. Understanding the subtle difference can affect how well you compete in the marketplace.

To understand the difference, think of editors and agents with stacks of book proposals or query letters on their desks. Their goal is to get through the stacks as quickly as possible—a task that may seem insurmountable at times. They are looking for clues to determine whether you have what it takes. The sooner they can determine this, the easier their job becomes. In short, you are trying to keep from being rejected, because that is just what the agents and editors are looking to do. In this type of environment, every sentence should give them a reason to read the next sentence. Each paragraph should make them want to read the next. And, of course, the correct format is paramount. Clean copy with no errors is crucial.

If the task seems daunting, it really need not be. You can make yourself stand out from the stack by simply arming yourself with the right skills and the proper research. The six pieces of advice that follow are the secrets to success cited by many writing instructors and published authors. These points can go a long way toward making you stand out from the pack.

Six Keys to Success

1. Read and analyze good writing. A creative writing instructor once told Joe that writing doesn't come from a vacuum. You must read to understand what good writing is all about. You must read to inspire yourself. You should read as much as you can inside and outside of your chosen genre—books, articles, short stories, poetry, ad copy, anything that helps you develop a better awareness of style.

As important as reading, you must analyze what you see on the page. Therein lies the art of writing. Study the details: the style of language; the dialogue; the narration; the structure of sentences, paragraphs and the story itself. Ask yourself why they are written the way they are.

2. Learn the mechanics and the essentials of the business: grammar; spelling; punctuation; proper formats for manuscripts, queries and proposals; how to work with editors; and how to read contracts. (The lists of books and other resources in chapter two can help.)

3. Write every day. What you learn from reading and studying you must put into practice. "Many people want to be writers but they don't want to write. They want the name, the prestige, but they don't want the hard work—to sit down and write," Fletcher notes.

The best way to write successfully is to develop a regular writing schedule. You must find the place and the time that works best for you and stick to it. (See chapter four for guidelines.) It takes discipline, but so does any successful endeavor. Write until you know that what you are producing is at least as good as what you see in print elsewhere.

4. Study the writing markets thoroughly. It's not enough to decide that you want to write mysteries and then scan *Writer's Market* (Writer's Digest Books) or *Literary Market Place* (R.R. Bowker Co.) for a publisher who produces that kind of book. You need to know what types of mysteries a publisher wants.

Think of a type of book you enjoy reading, say, mysteries. Would you walk into a bookstore and buy any or all mystery books? Of course not. You bring specific preferences—based on your own experience—to your choice of reading. A publishing company has its own preferences based on its experience. To be successful you need to learn those preferences. You can do this by reading many books by the publisher you plan to approach. Use the directory *Books in Print* (R.R. Bowker Co.) to research what has already been published so you can differentiate your book concept. By all means thoroughly study multiple issues of any magazine that you plan to query.

5. Make sure you mean business. As writers we are very fortunate to be in a business that allows us to aspire to a form of art. But publishing is still very much a business. "When a publisher takes on a title, he or she is, for practical purposes, betting that this manuscript will generate enough income to pay the author, to market it, to pay for the services of the people who will be working to get this manuscript into publication, to cover the production costs, to promote it upon production, and to have enough left for a reasonable profit," notes Patricia Bell.

If writing professionally is a business, successful writers must give thought to the kind of service that they offer. As a self-employed freelance writer are you easy to work with? Do you make your editor's job easier by meeting deadlines and by keeping him abreast of your progress? Are you readily available to make revisions or answer questions? These are the value-added items that make editors want to do business with you.

6. Be persistent. "Persistence is the most typical, common trait of successful published writers—even more typical and more common than writing skill," according to Leon Fletcher. If, for instance, an editor rejects your proposal, that doesn't mean she is rejecting you as a writer. It could be that your idea just didn't fit her needs at that time. Try again and keep trying until you succeed.

Writing is a skill that you can hone only through practice. You can only learn

---

You're Never Too Old or Too Young

Many young people complain that they are too young to get published. Many senior citizens believe they are too old to write. The truth is neither statement is correct. Consider the following insights from *I'm Too Young to Get Published!* by Leon Fletcher:

- William Ostrow was nine years old when he wrote *All About Asthma* (A. Whitman, 1989). Twelve years later his book was still in print and the royalties were paying for his medical school studies.
- France's most respected novelist in the mid-Fifties was a teenager—Francoise Sagan, eighteen-year-old author of the top selling *Bonjour Tristesse* (Dutton, 1955).
- Gore Vidal was only nineteen when he wrote *Williwaw* (Dutton, 1946), which launched his career as one of the nation's most distinguished writers.
- Jessie Lee Brown Foveaux was ninety-eight years old when she sold her first book, *Any Given Day* (Thorndike Press, 1998), for one million dollars to Warner Books.
- Norman Mailer celebrated his seventy-fifth birthday in 1998, just after publication of his thirty-first book, *The Time of Our Time* (Random House, 1998).
- James A. Michener, author of more than twenty-two books, was eighty-five years old when he wrote his memoirs, *The World Is My Home* (Random House, 1992).

---

the business by trying. If you learn one thing from reading this book, know this: If you have talent and if you work hard enough and long enough to succeed, you will.

A Look to the Future

For much of the 1990s, companies and research organizations have been rushing to find the replacement for traditional books and magazines. The fledgling replacements have taken the form of handheld video displays that can hold more than 100,000 pages of text, downloaded over telephone lines. MIT has added a new wrinkle to the paperless debate with its development of "electronic ink." The concept involves microscopic black-and-white particles imbedded in paperlike sheets. The particles reorient themselves—forming letters and words—when an electric charge is applied. Bound into book form, these sheets could be "charged" with text, and recharged whenever you want something new to read.

Other publishing experts see consumers walking into stores and custom ordering books, which are produced on the spot using high-speed printers and bindery equipment. Another scenario has consumers buying books and magazines online, downloading the data to their home computers and outputting the finished product on their home printers.

The future course for books and magazines could take any of these routes or go in a different direction altogether. The important thing: No one doubts that books and magazines will be around in some form. Whatever way books and magazines are produced, and regardless of how consumers choose to read them, society will need writers to produce the content. The idea of books and magazines going digital is even opening whole new opportunities for writers and publishers. Once words become data they can be easily transformed into multiple products, whether these are CDs, books or some other format not yet envisioned.

"In the future, the pages may glow in the dark so you can read a book by its own luminescence," says Byron Preiss, book editor and multimedia producer, in an interview with *Publishers Weekly.* "But it will still always be a book, and reading will always be personal."

CHAPTER TWO

Your Resources

Writing is a solitary pursuit, but that doesn't mean you have to go it alone. Thousands of organizations, books, Web sites and magazines exist to assist you. The lists in this chapter introduce a sampling of places you can turn to for insight, ideas and advice.

Organizations for Writers

Some writers need a group for support or for critiquing their work. Others want advice on selling their writing, finding a job or applying for a grant. Thankfully, thousands of writers organizations exist across the U.S. to offer help in these areas and in a variety of other ways. Some are small groups of writers who meet weekly over coffee to read each other's work. Others are nationwide organizations with several thousand members and offer a broad range of services, including health insurance.

Some groups, especially national organizations, have stringent guidelines for membership. Local and regional groups usually are more open to new members and are less expensive to join. They usually emphasize feedback and interaction between members. Other organizations, such as The Authors Guild, work on the business side of writing. Still others, such as the American Medical Writers Association, serve a special niche of writers.

Your involvement with a professional organization depends a great deal on your specific needs. Whatever route you choose, you won't have to spend a lot of money to join. You'll typically pay one hundred to two hundred dollars for a yearly membership to a large group, and many local groups are free.

Evaluating a Group

Before you join a group you should compare your needs and goals to those of the group. Consider the following information:

1. What are the benefits? If you are a full-time freelance writer and need medical benefits, you'll want to look for an organization large enough to offer them. Visit a meeting before you join to determine whether or not you'll benefit from the group's programs, or talk to a few writers in the organization to determine what they like best.

2. Are your goals compatible? Some groups are organized solely to exchange business and marketing information. You must look at the group as an extension of your interests to justify your time away from the keyboard.

3. What size is the group? For some people, the most beneficial group is one that's small and allows them to participate in each session. Others value the resources of a large group. Some feel the best of both worlds is available through a local chapter of a large organization.

4. What's the experience level? If you're experienced and the majority of members are not, you eventually may feel you are wasting time. If, on the other hand, the members are very experienced, they may be unwilling to help you develop in a specific area. Many organizations have membership surveys that state the average experience level.

5. What's the cost? If you're paying for a high-service organization but are not using the services, perhaps you should look into a less expensive, local group.

For more information on writers organizations, see *The Writer's Resource Book* by Daniel Grant (Allworth Press, 1996). Other good sources include the National Writers Union and the Editorial Freelancers Association (see pages 35-37).

List of Organizations

ALABAMA

Alabama Writers' Conclave, 117 Hanover Rd., Birmingham, AL 35209.

Alabama Writer's Forum, 1014 Myrtlewood Dr., Tuscaloosa, AL 35401.

ALASKA

Alaska State Writing Consortium, 801 W. Tenth St., Juneau, AK 99811.

Fairbanks Arts Association, P.O. Box 72786, Fairbanks, AK 99707.

ARIZONA

Arizona Authors' Association, 3509 E. Shea Blvd., Suite 117, Phoenix, AZ 85028, (602) 867-9001.

Associated Church Press, P.O. Box 30215, Phoenix, AZ 85046.

Authors & Artists Resource Center, 4725 E. Sunrise, Suite 219, Tucson, AZ 85718, (520) 577-7751.

Society of Children's Book Writers & Illustrators, 2408 W. Gregg Dr., Chandler, AZ 85224, (602) 732-9842.

Society of Southwestern Authors, P.O. Box 30355, Tucson, AZ 85751, (520) 296-5299.

Writer's Refinery, P.O. Box 47786, Phoenix, AZ 85068, (602) 944-5268.

ARKANSAS

Arkansas Literary Society, P.O. Box 174, Little Rock, AR 72203.

CALIFORNIA

Alpine Writers Guild, 1878 Rancho Jorie, Alpine, CA 91901, (619) 445-5537.

Asian American Journalists Association, 1182 Market St., Suite 320, San Francisco, CA 94102, (415) 346-2051.

Association of Desktop Publishers, 3401 Adams Ave., San Diego, CA 92116.

Beyond Baroque, P.O. Box 2727, 681 Venice Blvd., Venice, CA 90291, (310) 822-3006.

California Writers' Club, 2214 Derby St., Berkeley, CA 94705, (510) 883-6206.

Christian Writers Guild, 260 Fern Lane, Hume, CA 93628, (209) 335-2333.

Computer Press Association, 1260 Twenty-fifth Ave., San Francisco, CA 94122.

Feminist Writer's Guild, 881 Coachman Place, Clayton, CA 94517.

Feminist Writers Guild, P.O. Box 9396, Berkeley, CA 94709.

Horror Writers of America, P.O. Box 50577, Palo Alto, CA 94303.

Independent Writers of Southern California, P.O. Box 34279, Los Angeles, CA 90034, (877) 79-WRITE.

Mystery Writers of America, Northern California Chapter, 710 Sinnet Court, Danville, CA 94526, (510) 837-7089.

Mystery Writers of America, Southern California Chapter, 2296 W. Earl St., Silver Lake, CA 90039, (213) 660-0040.

PEN Center USA West, 672 S. Lafayette Park Place, #41, Los Angeles, CA 90057, (213) 365-8500.

Playwrights Foundation, P.O. Box 460357, San Francisco, CA 94114, (415) 263-3986.

Plaza de la Raza, 3540 N. Mission Rd., Los Angeles, CA 90031.

Poets & Writers Inc., 580 Washington St., Suite 308, San Francisco, CA 94111, (415) 986-9577.

Sacramento Poetry Center, 1631 K St., Sacramento, CA 95814, (916) 441-7395.

San Diego Writers/Editors Guild, 3650 First Ave., Apt. 301, San Diego, CA 92103, (619) 297-3491.

Small Press Traffic Literary Center, 2215-R Market St. #447, San Francisco, CA 94114, (415) 285-8394.

Small Press Writers and Artists, 13 Southwood Dr., Woodland, CA 95695.

Society of Children's Book Writers & Illustrators, 8271 Beverly Blvd., Los Angeles, CA 90048.

Society of Children's Book Writers and Illustrators, 22736 Vanowen St., Suite 106, West Hills, CA 91307, (818) 888-8760.

Writer's Center of California, 18 E. Blithedale, No. 31, Mill Valley, CA 94941, (415) 381-1825.

Writers Connection, P.O. Box 24770, San Jose, CA 95154, (408) 445-3600.

Writers Guild of America, 700 W. Third St., Los Angeles, CA 90048, (232) 951-4000.

Writing Center, 3777 Fourth Ave., San Diego, CA 92103, (619) 297-9950.

COLORADO

Children's Book Writers, 1242 Amsterdam Dr., Colorado Springs, CO 80908.

Mystery Writers of America, Rocky Mountain Chapter, 732 Meadow View Dr., Evergreen, CO 80439, (303) 670-3654.

National Writers Club, 3140 S. Peoria St., #295, Aurora, CO 80014, (303) 841-0246.

Rocky Mountain Fiction Writers, P.O. Box 260244, Denver, CO 80226-0244, (303) 331-2608.

Society of Children's Book Writers & Illustrators, 1054 Grant Place, Boulder, CO 80308, (303) 464-1208.

Women Writing the West, P.O. Box 2199, Evergreen, CO 80437, (303) 674-5450.

CONNECTICUT

New Milford Writers Workshop, 39 Windsor Gardens, Danbury, CT 06810, (203) 744-7504.

DELAWARE

Newark Arts Alliance, P.O. Box 1085, Newark, DE 19715, (302) 266-7266.

DISTRICT OF COLUMBIA

Education Writers Association, 1331 H St., N.W., Suite 307, Washington, DC 20036.

National League of American PEN Women, 1300 Seventeenth St., N.W. Washington, DC 20036, (202) 785-1997.

National Association of Black Journalists, 8701A Adelphi Rd., Adelphi, MD 20783, (301) 445-7100.

Washington Independent Writers Group, 220 Woodward Bldg., 733 Fifteenth St., NW Washington, DC 20005, (202) 347-4973.

Word Works, P.O. Box 42164, Washington, DC 20015.

FLORIDA

Florida Freelance Writer's Association, P.O. Box 9844, Fort Lauderdale, FL 33310.

International Society of Dramatists, P.O. Box 1310, Miami, FL 33153.

Mystery Writers of America, Florida Chapter, 2201 N.E. Thirty-second Ct., Lighthouse Point, FL 33064, (954) 943-5091.

Tallahassee Writers' Association, P.O. Box 6996, Tallahassee, FL 32314.

West Florida Literary Federation, P.O. Box 1644, Pensacola, FL 32597, (904) 477-8282.

GEORGIA

Atlanta Writer's Roundtable, P.O. Box 671123, Marietta, GA 30066.

Atlanta Writing Resource Center, 750 Kalb St., S.E., Suite 104, Atlanta, GA 30312, (404) 622-4152.

Dixie Council of Authors and Journalists, 1214 Laurel Hill Dr., Decatur, GA 30033, (404) 320-1076.

Georgia Writers Inc., 2633 Foxglove Dr., Marietta, GA 30064, (770) 943-5699.

Southeast Playwrights Project, 1804 N. Decatur Rd., Atlanta, GA 30307, (404) 250-9950.

Southeastern Writers Association, P.O. Box 774, Hinesville, GA 31310, (912) 876-3118.

HAWAII

Asian American Journalists Association, 1170 Auahi St., Honolulu, HI 96814.

Hawaii National Writers Group, P.O. Box 123, Honolulu, HI 96810.

Hawaii Writers Club, P.O. Box 89353, Honolulu, HI 96830.

National League of American PEN Women, 3746 Pukalani Pl., Honolulu, HI 96816.

National Writers Club, 2419-A Pauoa Rd., Honolulu, HI 96813.

IDAHO

Idaho Writers' Archive, Hemingway Western Studies Center, Boise State University, 1910 University Dr., Boise, ID 83725.

Idaho Writers League, 1501 E. Lakeshore Dr., Idaho Falls, ID 83404.

Log Cabin Literary Center, 801 S. Capitol Blvd., P.O. Box 9447, Boise, ID 83707.

Sandpoint Writer's Project, 5706 E. Dufort Rd., Sagle, ID 83860, (208) 263-8223.

ILLINOIS

Chicago Alliance for Playwrights, 1225 W. Belmont, Chicago, IL 60657, (312) 929-7287.

Chicago Literary Club, P.O. Box 350, Kenilworth, IL 60043.

Chicago Women in Publishing, P.O. Box 268107, Chicago, IL 60626, (312) 641-6311.

Destin Asian, 5945 N. Lakewood, Suite 2, Chicago, IL 60660, (312) 275-7101.

Guild Complex, 4753 N. Broadway #918, Chicago, IL 60640, (312) 278-2210.

Horror Writers Association, 15145 Oxford Dr., Oak Forest, IL 60452.

Illinois Writers Inc., English Department, 4240, Illinois State University, Normal, IL 61790, (309) 438-7705.

Independent Writers of Chicago, 5465 W. Grand Ave., Suite 100, Gurnee, IL 60031, (847) 855-6670.

Independent Writers of Chicago, 7855 Gross Point Rd., Suite M, Skokie, IL 60077, (708) 676-3784.

National Writer's Voice Project, 1001 W. Roosevelt, Chicago, IL 60608, (312) 738-5449.

Poetry Center of Chicago, 37 S. Wabash Ave., Room 301, Chicago, IL 60603, (312) 368-0905.

Society of Midland Authors, 851 Warrington Rd., Deerfield, IL 60015.

INDIANA

Central Indiana Writers Association, P.O. Box 1502, Greenwood, IN 46142.

Mystery Writers of America, Midwest Chapter, 711 N. Ironwood, South Bend, IN 46615, (219) 289-4741

Society of Professional Journalists, 16 S. Jackson St., Greencastle, IN 46135, (317) 653-3333.

Writers' Center of Indianapolis, P.O. Box 88386, Marian College, Indianapolis, IN 46208, (317) 929-0623.

IOWA

Iowa Poetry Association, P.O. Box 374, Gowrie, IA 50543, (515) 352-5202.

KANSAS

National Federation of Press Women, P.O. Box 5556, Arlington, VA 22205, (800) 780-2715.

Novelists Inc., P.O. Box 1166, Mission, KS 66222.

Sisters in Crime, P.O. Box 442124, Lawrence, KS 66044.

Writer's Hide-Out, 118 N. Washington, Junction City, KS 66441.

KENTUCKY

Southeast Writers Association, P.O. Box 401, Bowling Green, KY 42102.

LOUISIANA

Arts Council of Greater Baton Rouge, 427 Laurel St., Baton Rouge, LA 70801, (504) 344-8558.

MAINE

Deer Isle Writers' Workshops, P.O. Box 100, Deer Isle, ME 04627, (207) 348-2791.

Maine Writers & Publishers Alliance, 12 Pleasant St., Brunswick, ME 04011, (207) 729-6333.

MARYLAND

Amherst Writers & Artists, P.O. Box 1076, Amherst, MA 01004, (413) 253-3307.

American Medical Writers Association, 9650 Rockville Pike, Bethesda, MD 20814.

Newspaper Guild, 8611 Second Ave., Silver Springs, MD 20910.

Writer's Center, 4508 Walsh St., Bethesda, MD 20815, (301) 654-8664.

MASSACHUSETTS

Freelance Editorial Association, P.O. Box 38035, Cambridge, MA 02238.

Mystery Writers of America, New England Chapter, 286 Washington St., Marblehead, MA 01945.

New England Poetry Club, 2 Farrar St., Cambridge, MA 02138.

MICHIGAN

Arts and Humanities Program, YMCA of Metropolitan Detroit, 10900 Harper Ave., Detroit, MI 48213, (313) 267-5300.

Council of Writers Organizations, 17000 Executive Plaza Dr., Dearborn, MI 48126, (313) 336-1211.

National Association for Young Writers, P.O. Box 228, Sandusky, MI 48471.

MINNESOTA

Aviation/Space Writers Association, 6540 Fiftieth N., Oakdale, MN 55128.

The Depot, 506 W. Michigan St., Duluth, MN 55343, (218) 727-8025.

Lake Area Writers' Guild, 972 Winterbury Dr., Woodbury, MN 55125.

The Loft, Pratt Community Center, 66 Malcolm Ave. S.E., Minneapolis, MN 55414, (612) 379-8999.

Minneapolis Writers Workshop, P.O. Box 24356, Minneapolis, MN 55424, (612) 922-0724.

Playwrights' Center, 2301 Franklin Ave., Minneapolis, MN 55406, (612) 332-7481.

MISSOURI

Investigative Reporters and Editors, P.O. Box 838, Columbia, MO 65205, (314) 882-2042.

Midwest Radio Theatre Workshop, KOPN, 915 E. Broadway, Columbia, MO 65201, (314) 874-1139.

Ozark Writers League, P.O. Box 1433, Branson, MO 65616, (417) 334-6016.

St. Louis Writers Guild, P.O. Box 7245, St. Louis, MO 63177, (314) 965-8195.

Writers Place, 3607 Pennsylvania, Kansas City, MO 64111, (816) 753-1090.

MONTANA

Authors of the Flathead, P.O. Box 1577, Bigfork, MT 59911, (406) 892-5704.

Billings Arts Association, 1148 Sixteenth St., West Billings, MT 59102, (406) 259-6030.

Hellgate Writers, Inc., 2210 N. Higgins, P.O. Box 7131, Missoula, MT 59807, (406) 721-3620.

Montana Author's Coalition, P.O. Box 20839, Billings, MT 59104.

NEBRASKA

Charlottesville Writing Center, 405 Third St. N.E., Charlottesville, VA 22902, (804) 293-3702.

Nebraska Poets Association, 4340 Parker, Omaha, NE 68111.

Nebraska Writers Guild, 941 O St., Lincoln, NE 68508, (402) 475-1123.

NEVADA

Silver State Fiction Writers, P.O. Box 70816, Reno, NV 89502, (702) 826-6861.

NEW HAMPSHIRE

Cassell Network of Writers, Maple Ridge Rd., North Sandwich, NH 03259.

New Hampshire Writers' Project, P.O. Box 2693, Concord, NH 03302, (603) 226-6649.

NEW JERSEY

Authors/Writers Network, Montclair State College, 34 Normal Ave., Upper Montclair, NJ 07043, (201) 754-4829.

Delaware Valley Poets, Pineknoll Dr., Lawrenceville, NJ 08648.

Mendham Poets, 10 Hilltop Rd., Mendham, NJ 07945.

Walt Whitman Center, Second & Cooper Streets, Camden, NJ 08102, (609) 964-8300.

NEW MEXICO

Southwest Writers Workshop, 8200 Mountain Rd., Albuquerque, NM 87110, (505) 265-9485.

NEW YORK

Academy of American Poets, 584 Broadway, Suite 1208, New York, NY 10012, (212) 274-0343.

American Crime Writers League, 455 Crescent, Buffalo, NY 14214.

American Society of Journalists and Authors, 1501 Broadway, Suite 302, New York, NY 10036, (212) 997-0947.

American Society of Magazine Editors, 919 Third Ave., New York, NY 10022.

Asian American Writers' Workshop, 37 St. Marks Place #B, New York, NY 10003, (212) 228-6718.

Authors Guild, 330 West Forty-second St., Twenty-ninth Floor, New York, NY 10036, (212) 563-5904.

Authors League of America, 330 West Forty-second St., New York, NY 10036, (212) 564-8350.

Bronx Writers Center, Bronx Council on the Arts, 1738 Hone Ave., Bronx, NY 10461, (718) 931-9500.

Dramatists Guild, 234 W. Forty-fourth St., Eleventh Floor, New York, NY 10036.

Greenfield Center, P.O. Box 308, Greenfield Center, NY 12833, (518) 584-1728.

Hudson Valley Writers' Center, P.O. Box 366, Tarrytown, NY 10591, (914) 332-5953.

International Association of Crime Writers, P.O. Box 1500, New York, NY 10016, (212) 757-3915.

International Women's Writing Guild, P.O. Box 810, Gracie Station, New York, NY 10028, (212) 737-7536.

Just Buffalo, 2495 Main St., Suite 436, Buffalo, NY 14214, (716) 832-5400.

Mystery Writers of America, 17 E. Forty-seventh St., Sixth Floor, New York, NY 10017, (212) 888-8171.

Mystery Writers of America, New York Chapter, P.O. Box 245, East Meadow, NY 11554, (516) 731-4537.

National Association of Science Writers, P.O. Box 294, Greenlawn, NY 11740, (516) 757-5664.

New Dramatists, 424 W. Forty-fourth St., New York, NY 10036, (212) 757-6960.

New York State Writers Institute, HU 355, University at Albany, SUNY Albany, NY 12222, (518) 442-5620.

PEN American Center, 568 Broadway, New York, NY 10012, (212) 334-1660.

Poetry Center, 1395 Lexington Ave., New York, NY 10128, (212) 415-5755.

Poetry Project at St. Mark's, Second Ave. & Tenth St., New York, NY 10003, (212) 674-0910.

Poet's House, 72 Spring St., New York, NY 10012, (212) 431-7920.

Poetry Society of America, 15 Gramercy Park, New York, NY 10003, (212) 254-9628.

Poets & Writers Inc., 72 Spring St., New York, NY 10012, (212) 226-3586.

Science Fiction and Fantasy Writers of America, 532 LaGuardia Place, 5 Winding Brook Dr., Suite 1-B, New York, NY 10012.

Small Press Center, 20 W. Forty-fourth St., New York, NY10036.

Songwriters Guild of America, 276 Fifth Ave., Suite 306, New York, NY 10001.

Writers Alliance, 12 Skylark Lane, Stony Brook, NY 11790, (516) 751-7080.

Writers & Books, 740 University Ave., Rochester, NY 14607, (716) 473-2590.

Writers Guild of America, 555 W. Fifty-seventh St., Suite 1230, New York, NY 10019, (212) 767-7800.

Writers' Center at Chautauqua, 953 Forest Ave., Jamestown, NY 14701.

NORTH CAROLINA

Greenville Writers' Group, 1609 Oaklawn Dr., Greenville, NC 27858, (919) 756-0195.

Mystery Writers of America, Southeast Chapter, 120 George Chastain Dr., Horse Shoe, NC 28742, (828) 891-4061.

North Carolina Writers' Network, P.O. Box 954, Carrboro, NC 27570, (919) 967-9540.

Society of American Travel Writers, 4101 Lake Boone Trail, Suite 201, Raleigh, NC 27607, (919) 787-5181.

Writers' Workshop, P.O. Box 696, Asheville, NC 28802, (704) 254-8111.

OHIO

Association for Applied Poetry, 60 N. Main St., Johnstown, OH 43031.

Private Eye Writers of America, 1750 Fourth St., Room 607, Cuyahoga Falls, OH 44221.

Thurber House, 77 Jefferson Ave., Columbus, OH 43215.

Writers Center of Greater Cleveland, P.O. Box 14277, Cleveland, OH 44114.

OKLAHOMA

Oklahoma Writers' Federation, 213 Telstar St., Norman, OK 73069.

OREGON

Cascade Poets, 6123 N. Commercial, Portland, OR 97217, (503) 283-3682.

Lane Literary Guild, 164 W. Broadway, Eugene, OR 97401, (541) 485-2278.

Literary Arts, 720 S.W. Washington, Suite 700, Portland, OR 97205, (503) 227-2583.

Mountain Writers Series, 1812 S.E. Twenty-second Ave., Portland, OR 97202, (503) 232-7337.

Northwest Playwrights Group, P.O. Box 9218, Portland, OR 97207.

Northwest Playwrights Guild, 318 S.W. Palatine Hill Rd., Portland, OR 97219.

Willamette Writers, 9045 S.W. Barbur Blvd., Portland, OR 97219, (503) 452-1592.

PENNSYLVANIA

American Physicians Association of Poets, 230 Toll Dr., Southampton, PA 18966.

American Poetry Center, 1204 Walnut St., Philadelphia, PA 19107.

Greater Lehigh Valley Writers Group, P.O. Box 21492, Lehigh Valley, PA 18002.

Lehigh Valley Writer's Guild, 9943 Kenrick St., Bethlehem, PA 18017.

Outdoor Writers Association of America, 2017 Cato Ave., Suite 101, State College, PA 16801, (814) 234-1011.

Philadelphia Writers Organization, P.O. Box 42497, Philadelphia, PA 19101, (215) 387-8918.

Society of Environmental Journalists, 370-D Willowbrook Dr., Jeffersonville, PA 19403.

RHODE ISLAND

Community Writers Association, P.O. Box 312, Providence, RI 02901, (401) 846-9884.

SOUTH CAROLINA

South Carolina Writers Workshop, P.O. Box 635, Irmo, SC 29063, (803) 792-2629.

SOUTH DAKOTA

Black Hills Writers Group, 1015 N. Seventh St., Rapid City, SD 57701, (605) 342-7423.

South Dakota State Poetry Society, 909 E. Thirty-fourth St., Sioux Falls, SD 57105, (605) 338-9156.

TENNESSEE

Tennessee Writers' Alliance, P.O. Box 120396, Nashville, TN 37212, (615) 292-3830.

Western Writers of America, 1012 Fair St., Franklin, TN 37064, (615) 791-1444.

TEXAS

Alamo Writers Unlimited, 10410 Country Bluff, San Antonio, TX 78240.

American Crime Writers League, 219 Tuxedo, San Antonio, TX 78209.

Associated Authors of Children's Literature, 15914 Mal Paso Dr., Houston, TX 77082, (713) 497-8028.

Association for Authors, 8880 Bellaire Blvd., Suite 326, Houston, TX 77036, (713) 465-4121.

Austin Writers League, 1501 W. Fifth St., Suite E2, Austin, TX 78703, (512) 499-8914.

Composers, Authors & Artists of America, 3828 Dexter Ave., Fort Worth, TX 76107, (817) 738-0519.

Dallas Screenwriters Association, 6858 Larmanda, Dallas, TX 75231, (214) 341-3924.

Fort Worth Poetry Society, 4508 Stadium Dr., Fort Worth, TX 76133, (817) 924-9446.

Golden Triangle Writers Guild, 4245 Calder, Beaumont, TX 77706, (409) 898-4894.

Inprint Inc., 1524 Sul Ross, Houston, TX 77006, (713) 521-2026.

Mystery Writers of America, Southwest Chapter, 5809 Dolores, Apt. C., Houston, TX 77057, (713) 781-1081.

Nightwriters of Houston, 21619 Park Brook Dr., Katy, TX 77450, (713) 578-2897.

Panhandle Professional Writers, P.O. Box 19303, Amarillo, TX 79114, (806) 352-3889.

Poetry Society of Texas, 3230 Ashwood Lane, Beaumont, TX 77703, (409) 892-3714.

Poetry Society of Texas, 5703 W. Greenbrier, Dallas, TX 75219.

Poetry Society of Texas, 8610 Jason, Houston, TX 77074, (713) 774-3598.

Romance Writers of America, 3707 FM 1960 W., Suite 555, Houston, TX 77068, (281) 440-6885.

Society of Children's Book Writers, 1908 South Goliad, Amarillo, TX 79106, (806) 353-4925.

Society of Children's Book Writers, 8826 Rowan, Houston, TX 77036, (713) 777-5394.

Southwest Literary Arts Council, 2211 Tangley, Houston, TX 77005, (713) 523-9552.

Western Writers of America, 416 Bedford Rd., El Paso, TX 79922.

UTAH

Writers at Work, P.O. Box 58857, Salt Lake City, UT 84158, (801) 649-3181.

VIRGINIA

American Society of Newspaper Editors, 11690 B Sunrise Valley Dr., Reston, VA 20191.

American Translators Association, 1800 Diagonal Rd., Suite. 220, Alexandria, VA 22314.

VERMONT

League of Vermont Writers, P.O. Box 179, South Pomfret, VT 05067, (802) 457-1637.

WASHINGTON

Christian Writers Fellowship, P.O. Box 71337, Seattle, WA 98110, (206) 842-9103.

Literary Center, P.O. Box 85116, Seattle, WA 98145.

Mystery Writers of America, Northwest Chapter, P.O. Box 1201, Port Townsend, WA 98368, (360) 765-4432.

Northwest Playwrights Guild, P.O. Box 995259, Seattle, WA 98145.

Pacific Northwest Writers, 17345 Sylvester Rd., S.W., Seattle, WA 98166.

Tacoma Writer's Club, 14710 Thirtieth St. Court E., Sumner, WA 98390, (206) 473-9632.

Washington Christian Writers Fellowship, P.O. Box 71337, Seattle, WA 98110, (206) 842-9103.

Washington Writers Info Network, (for Christian writers), P.O. Box 11337, Bainbridge, WA 98110, (206) 842-9103.

Writers' Place, 122 State St., Suite 607, Madison, WI 53703, (608) 255-4030.

WISCONSIN

Wisconsin Fellowship of Poets, 23 S. Allen St., Madison, WI 53705, (608) 233-0300.

Wisconsin Regional Writers Association, Route One, Pebble Beach Rd., Cedar Grove, WI 53013, (414) 668-6267.

Woodland Pattern Book Center, P.O. Box 92081, Milwaukee, WI 53202, (414) 263-5001.

WYOMING

Big Horn Basin Writers, 1132 N. Julie Lane, Powell, WY 82435, (307) 754-7101.

Wyoming Writers, P.O. Box 178, Lyman, WY 82937, (307) 786-4513.

Canada

ALBERTA

Writers Guild of Alberta, 305 12 Ave. S.W., Calgary AB T2R 0G9, (403) 265-2226.

Writers Guild of Alberta, Percy Page Centre, 11759 Groat Rd., Edmonton AB T5M 3K6, (780) 422-8174.

Speculative Fiction Canada, 10523-100 Ave., Edmonton AB T5J 0A8.

BRITISH COLUMBIA

Federation of BC Writers, 600-890 W. Pender St., Vancouver BC V6C 1K4, (604) 683-2057.

Writers' Union of Canada, 3102 Main St., Third Floor, Vancouver BC V4A 3C7, (604) 874 1611.

MANITOBA

Canadian Authors Association, 208-63 Albert St., Winnipeg, Manitoba R3B 1G4, (204) 947-0512.

Manitoba Writers' Guild, 206-100 Arthur St., Winnipeg, Manitoba R3B 1H3, (204) 947-3168.

NEW BRUNSWICK

Writers Federation of New Brunswick, P.O. Box 37, Station A, Fredericton, New Brunswick E3B 4Y2, (506) 459-7228.

NEWFOUNDLAND AND LABRADOR

Writers Alliance of Newfoundland and Labrador, P.O. Box 2681, St. John's, Newfoundland A1C 5M5, (709) 739-5215.

NOVA SCOTIA

Canadian Science Writers' Association, 1411 Oxford St., Halifax, Nova Scotia B3H 3Z1

Playwrights Atlantic Resource Centre, P.O. Box 269, Guysborough, Nova Scotia B0H 1N0, (902) 533-2077.

Writers' Federation of Nova Scotia, 1113 Marginal Rd., Halifax, Nova Scotia B3H 4P7, (902) 423-8116.

ONTARIO

Book and Periodical Council, 35 Spadina Rd., Toronto ON M5R 2S9, (416) 975-9366.

Black Artists In Action, 54 Wolseley St., Second Floor, Toronto ON M5T 1A5, (416) 703-9040.

Canadian Association of Journalists, Carleton University, St. Patrick's Building, Ottawa ON K1S 5B6, (613) 526-8061.

Canadian Authors Association, 27 Doxsee Ave., Campbellford ON KOL 1LO, (705) 653-0323.

Canadian Book Marketing Centre, 2 Gloucester St., Suite 301, Toronto ON M4Y 1L5, (416) 413-4930.

Canadian Literary and Artistic Association Inc., Commerce Court W., Suite 4900, Toronto ON M5L 1J3, (416) 862-7525.

Canadian Poetry Association, P.O. Box 22571, St. George Postal Outlet, 264 Bloor St. W., Toronto ON M5S 1V8.

Canadian Society of Children's Authors, Illustrators & Performers, 35 Spadina Rd., Toronto ON M5R 2S9, (416) 515-1559.

Canadian Science Writers' Association, P.O. Box 75, Station A, Toronto ON M5W 1A2, (905) 837-7600.

Canadian Writers' Foundation Inc., Box 36043, 1318 Wellington St., Ottawa ON K1Y 4Y3.

Centre for Investigative Journalism, Carleton University, St. Patrick's Building, Room 324, Ottawa ON K1S 5B6.

Crime Writers of Canada, 3007 Kingston Rd., Box 113, Toronto ON M1M 1P1, (416) 782-3116.

League of Canadian Poets, 54 Wolsely St., Toronto ON M5T 1A5, (416) 504-1657.

Literary Translator's Association of Canada, 214 Clinton St., Toronto ON M6G 2Y5.

Ottawa Independent Writers, P.O. Box 23137, Ottawa ON K2A 4E2, (613) 841-0572.

Outdoor Writers Association of Canada, RR #1, Parry Sound ON P2A 2W7, (705) 746-9440.

Periodical Writers Association of Canada, 24 Ryerson Ave., Toronto ON M5T 2P3, (416) 504-1645.

Playwrights Union of Canada, 54 Wolsely St., Toronto ON M5T 1A5, (416) 703-0201.

Writers' Circle of Durham Region, P.O. Box 323, Ajax ON L1S 3C5.

Writers Guild of Canada, 35 McCaul St., Suite 203, Toronto ON M5T 1V7, (416) 504-1645.

Writers Guild of Canada, 123 Edwards St., Suite 1225, Toronto ON M5G 1E2, 1-800-567-9974.

Writers' Trust of Canada, 40 Wellington St. E., Suite 300, Toronto ON M5E 1C7, (416) 504-8222.

Writers Union of Canada, 24 Ryerson Ave., Toronto ON M5T 2P3, (416) 703-8982.

PRINCE EDWARD ISLAND

Prince Edward Island Writers Association, P.O. Box 1204, Charlottetown PEI C1A 1H9, (902) 566-9748.

PEI Writers' Guild, Box 1, 115 Richmond St., Charlottetown PEI C1A 1H7, (902) 626-3082.

QUEBEC

Canadian Literary and Artistic Association Inc., 1981 Ave., McGill College, Montreal PQ H3A 3C1, (514) 847-4512.

Literary Translator's Association of Canada, 3492 rue Laval, Montreal PQ H2X 3C8, (514) 849-8540.

Quebec Writers' Federation, 1200 Ave. Atwater, Suite 3, Montreal PQ H3Z 1X4, (514) 933-0878.

SASKATCHEWAN

Saskatchewan Writers Guild, P.O. Box 3986, Regina, Saskatchewan S4P 3R9, (306) 757-6310.

Other Sources for Writers Organizations

Several sources of information about writers groups and organizations are available at libraries or for purchase, including the *International Directory of Writers' Groups*

& Associations (Inkling Publications) and *Literary Market Place* (R.R. Bowker Co.). State arts councils sometimes have lists of writers groups.

Power in Numbers

Two of the largest organizations for writers are the Editorial Freelancers Association (EFA) and the National Writers Union (NWU). Their services are also among the most comprehensive. One of the chief differences bewteen these two national groups is that the NWU has a couple dozen local and regional offices across the U.S., whereas the EFA offers its services from a central office in New York City.

Editorial Freelancers Association

71 W. Twenty-third St., Suite 1910, New York, NY 10010

Phone: (212) 929-5400, Fax: (212) 929-5439, Web site: www.the-efa.org

Any full- or part-time freelancer may join the EFA. Full membership costs $75 per year. (New York–area residents pay $95 beause they can take advantage of local events.) In addition to freelance writers, EFA membership is open to desktop publishers, editors, indexers, proofreaders, researchers and translators, among others.

MEMBERSHIP BENEFITS:

- **Accounting and Legal Services:** Reduced-rate accounting and tax service, free basic legal service and discounted legal advice on contracts and rights.
- **Directory:** Members listed alphabetically and by skills, specialties and geographic locations.
- **Events:** Expert panels, open-mike forums, social events, education programs and meetings (New York only).
- **Insurance:** Health insurance at group rates, including a health maintenance organization, major medical, dental insurance and disability insurance.
- **Job Phone:** Puts freelancers in touch with a wide variety of jobs, both freelance and full-time.

- **Newsletter:** Bimonthly newsletter includes reports on EFA meetings and activities, advice for freelancers, book and software reviews and regular columns on taxes and language usage.
- **Rates and Business Practices Survey:** Published every two years, this confidential poll tabulates the rates for various types of writing and editing work.

National Writers Union (NWU)

113 University Place, 6th Floor, New York, NY 10003
Phone: (212) 254-0279 or (800) 417-8114, Fax: (212) 254-0673, Web site: www.nwu.org, E-mail: nwu@nwu.org

Membership is open to all qualified writers who have published a book, a play, three articles, five poems, a short story, or an equal amount of similar work for a company, government or institution. You are also eligible for membership if you have written an equal amount of unpublished material and are actively seeking to publish your work. Full membership costs between $95 and $195 per year depending on your writing income.

Most members participate in activities through local NWU offices, whose locations include Boston; Burlington, Vermont; Chicago; Eugene, Oregon; Hadley, Massachusetts; Lawrenceville, New Jersey.; Los Angeles; Miami; Minneapolis; Oakland; Philadelphia; Santa Cruz/Monterey, California; Seattle; Tucson; Washington, DC; and White Plains, New York.

MEMBERSHIP BENEFITS:
- **Agent Database:** Database evaluating literary agents, including confidential insider information.
- **Discounts:** Substantial discounts on seminars and publications. Other discounts include car rentals, overnight delivery service and theme parks.
- **Grievance Assistance:** Members may bring specific problems with publishers to grievance officers who will try to help resolve the conflict.
- **Insurance:** Health insurance, including life insurance is available at competitive rates.

- **Job Hot Lines:** Provide technical writing opportunities and regional job banks for freelance and full-time work.
- **Magazines:** Monthly and quarterly publications.
- **Networking:** Opportunity to exchange expertise at local and national events and through electronic chats and E-mail.
- **Press Pass:** Certifies that qualified members are working journalists.
- **Publication Rights Clearinghouse:** Collects online royalties and licenses electronic material for writers. NWU members can enroll at half price.
- **Resource Materials:** Wide range of publications and resources, including the *NWU Guide to Freelance Rates and Standard Practices* and the *NWU Guide to Book Contracts*.

Books for Writers: Recommended Reading

The Art and Craft of Feature Writing by William E. Blundell (New American Library, 1988): He practiced his craft at *The Wall Street Journal*. Now Blundell gives you the benefit of his knowledge, guiding you from the very first steps of gathering information for a story.

The Art and Craft of Playwriting by Jeffrey Hatcher (Story Press, 1996): The author offers practical and creative insights, using classical and modern works to illustrate his points.

The Art and Craft of Poetry by Michael J. Bugeja (Writer's Digest Books, 1994): If poetic skill can be taught, this book can do it, or at least get you started. The step-by-step format shows you how to conceive and capture ideas. The basics of voice, line, stanza, meter and rhyme are all explored, along with forms, formats and modes of expression.

The Associated Press Stylebook and Libel Manual (Addison-Wesley Publishing): Maybe you know that "Dumpster" is a trademark and should rightfully be capitalized. But what about the other five thousand entries in this journalist's bible? Few people will ever master the AP's convoluted rules for numerals, but with this quick reference you can avoid common mistakes.

Bird by Bird: Some Instructions on Writing and Life by Anne Lamott (Anchor Books, 1995): Written in an often hilarious conversational tone, this step-by-step survival guide covers all aspects of the writer's life, from how to deal with writer's block to budgeting your time.

The Chicago Manual of Style (University of Chicago Press, 1993): A weighty reference for writers, editors and proofreaders alike. Full of essential advice, such as how to format your manuscripts to impress an editor.

The Complete Book of Scriptwriting by J. Michael Straczynski (Writer's Digest Books, 1996): This book doesn't cover a lot on technique. What it does offer is a detailed look at how to turn good writing into marketable scripts, whether it's for film, television, radio, animation or stage. With *Murder, She Wrote* and *Babylon 5* to his credit, Straczynski is an expert.

The Complete Guide to Magazine Article Writing by John M. Wilson (Writer's Digest Books, 1993): From writing compelling leads to the good use of quotes, this book is full of step-by-step instructions from an experienced writer and editor.

The Complete Guide to Writing Fiction by Barnaby Conrad (Writer's Digest Books, 1990): Whether you want to write long fiction or short stories, this book lays out what you need to know about outlining, narration, description and action.

Creating Poetry by John Drury (Writer's Digest Books, 1991): A new poet continually strives to see life from new angles and reshape language. This book understand that and can help you find your own voice.

The Elements of Style by William Strunk and E.B. White (Allyn and Bacon, 1999): One of the most essential and well-read style books ever written. It's so short, there's no reason not to read it cover to cover. Chances are your editor owns a copy, so you might as well know what's in it, too.

Find It Fast: How to Uncover Expert Information on Any Subject by Robert I. Berkman (HarperCollins, 1997): The hardest part of research is figuring out where to begin looking. This book is a road map that helps you get the most out of libraries, business sources, government documents and the Internet. This book should be the first step in any research process.

Handbook for Freelance Writing by Michael Perry (NTC Business Books, 1998): There's no need to starve while honing your creative writing skills. Perry shows you how to put together a successful freelance career that can pay the bills. He offers insights on researching markets, writing query letters and working with editors.

How to Write a Book Proposal by Michael Larsen (Writer's Digest Books, 1997): If you have the talent and a sound book idea, Larsen can show you how to get your proposal seriously considered by a top agent or publisher. An agent himself, Larsen has placed manuscripts with more than one hundred publishers. His book takes you through each step of the process.

How to Write: Advice and Reflections by Richard Rhodes (William Morrow and Company, 1995): Full of inspiring and practical advice from a Pulitzer prize–winning author. Rhodes isn't afraid to open his mind and bare his heart. Nor is he afraid to talk about his own struggles to write well.

How to Write and Sell Your First Novel by Oscar Collier, with Frances Spatz Leighton (Writer's Digest Books, 1997): This book presents the success strategies of two dozen published authors to help you navigate today's complicated market.

How to Write Irresistible Query Letters by Lisa Collier Cool (Writer's Digest Books, 1990): This is a must read for anyone who wants to enter the magazine market. Before you get to write a great article you first have to write a killer query letter.

The Insider's Guide to Writing for Screen and Television by Ronald B. Tobias (Writer's Digest Books, 1997): A practical guide that teaches how the film industry works. All-star interviews transport you behind the scenes to see how directors and actors look at scripts.

Magazine Writing That Sells by Don McKinney (Writer's Digest Books, 1994): No freelancer should bypass the advice of this former editor of the *Saturday Evening Post* and *McCall's*. McKinney shows you how to write enticing query letters and leads that capture the reader. Each step of writing and selling your work is covered.

On Writing Well by William Zinsser (HarperPerennial, 1994): Full of the principles and practices that are necessary for good writing. This book stems from a course Zinsser taught at Yale. He turns his lessons into an inspiration for anyone who writes.

The 38 Most Common Fiction Writing Mistakes (and How to Avoid Them) by Jack M. Bickham (Writer's Digest Books, 1992): Short. To the point. This book distills decades of writing experience into one easy-to-read volume. Don't write fiction without it.

The Writer's Digest Guide to Good Writing edited by Thomas Clark (Writer's Digest Books, 1994): Here you'll find dozens of columns from *Writer's Digest* that exemplify the fine art and craft of writing. Included are essays from such famed authors as Isaac Asimov, Allen Ginsberg and Stephen King.

Writer's Market (Writer's Digest Books): Probably the single greatest tool for beginning and experienced writers. Contains up-to-date lists of several thousand magazine and book publishers broken down by subject category. Articles and features lend important advice from editors, agents and published authors.

Writing and Illustrating Children's Books for Publication: Two Perspectives by Berthe Amoss and Eric Suben (Writer's Digest Books, 1995): This book offers a self-instruction writing course that guides you through the process of creating a publishable manuscript. Reading lists, editing checklists and case studies of actual experiences make this a valuable tool.

Writing for Story: Craft Secrets of Dramatic Nonfiction by a Two-Time Pulitzer Prize Winner by Jon Franklin (Atheneum, 1986): With a title this long it better live up to its billing. Unlike authors who focus on style and grammar, Franklin offers a valuable lesson in building a nonfiction story, starting with an outline.

You Can Write Children's Books by Tracey E. Dils (Writer's Digest Books, 1998): This helpful collection of guidelines will help you get your book in print. This book covers all the steps from inspiration to publication.

Web Sites for Writers

Hundreds of sites on the Internet exist to provide valuable information exclusively for writers, but nearly all are also trying to sell something. Imagine that? After all, they can't pay for computer time by giving away information. In many cases the free advice or information is a hook to draw your interest. Here's a hint to keep you from paying for more than you should: If you "shop" around enough sites, you'll find enough free information that you'll feel less compelled to pay for information that comes with the cost of a membership or newsletter.

This is not to say that you should reject all commercial offers. There are good services available online for a fee. Just be careful. More important, be selective. And look around a lot first, so you don't end up paying for something you could have gotten free.

If you are not familiar with writers' resources online, check out the sites listed below. They offer a lot of free information and advice, and most provide links to hundreds of other Internet sites.

American Society of Journalists and Authors (www.asja.org): Offers news about the latest terms and negotiations in the world of newspapers and magazines, provides information sheets on contracts, freelance tips, electronic publishing and copyright registration.

BookWire (www.bookwire.com): Features industry news, reviews, original fiction, guides to literary events, author interviews, highlights trends in book publishing and lists publishers and agents by geographic area. Sponsored by R.R. Bowker Co.

Copyright and Fair Use (http://fairuse.stanford.edu): Highlights statutes, judicial opinions and current legislation, contains articles and overviews of copyright law and fair use. Sponsored by Stanford University.

Forwriters (www.forwriters.com): Provides information about writing, getting published, markets, agents and writing conferences.

Inkspot (www.inkspot.com): Features market information, articles, interviews with authors and editors, networking opportunities and tips for improving your writing.

Sensible Solutions (www.happilypublished.com): Offers advice on marketing your work, looking for a publisher and self-publishing.

Writers Club (America Online, keyword: *Writers*): Provides a wide range of information, including the basic steps to becoming a writer, how to get the most from writers conferences, how to work with editors and how to handle rejection.

Writer's Digest (www.writersdigest.com): Features articles, interviews and a list of places to sell your writing.

Writers Toolbox (www.geocities.com/Athens/6346): Features online dictionaries and thesauri, links to genre resources (romance, mystery, sci-fi, etc.) plus resources for marketing manuscripts, managing your writing business, and finding employment.

Writerswebsite (www.writerswebsite.com): Features interviews with screenwriters, filmmakers and agents and offers copyright information.

Writers Write (http://writerswrite.com): Features articles, guidelines, interviews, and book reviews. Offers links and resources for writers, divided by genre/category (business, children's, comedy writing, etc.) and by type (agents, conferences, contests, etc.).

Writing Resources (http://owl.english.purdue.edu/writers): Offers handouts on writing skills, online resources for writers, online references, guides to style and editing, plus links to online libraries. Sponsored by Purdue University's Online Writing Lab (OWL).

WritersNet (www.writers.net): Hosts online discussions and features directories of published writers and agents.

Additional Web Sites By Genre

CHILDREN'S

Canadian Children's Book Centre
(www3.sympatico.ca/ccbc/mainpage.htm)

Children's Book Council Online
(www.cbcbooks.org)

Children's Literature Web Guide

(www.acs.ucalgary.ca/~dkbrown/index.html)

Children's Writing Resource Center

(www.write4kids.com)

Purple Crayon

(www.underdown.org)

Society of Children's Book Writers and Illustrators

(www.scbwi.org)

CRIME/MYSTERY

American Crime Writers Leagues

(www.klew.com/acwl.html)

ClueLass

(www.cluelass.com)

Internet CrimeWriting Network

(http://hollywoodshopping.com/Crime/index.html#crime)

Mysterious Home Page

(www.webfic.com/mysthome)

Mystery Writer's Forum

(www.zott.com/mysforum/default.html)

HORROR

DarkEcho Horror

(www.darkecho.com/darkecho/index.html)

Horror Writer's Association

(www.horror.org)

HUMOR

Creating Comics

(www.cadvision.com/dega/creating.htm)

Humor and Life

(www.geocities.com/SoHo/Gallery/4111/menu.html)

Satire.org

(http://www.intrepid.net/satire/)

Sitcom Format 101

(http://home.earthlink.net/~chuckat/sitcom/sitcom_101.html)

Stand-Up Comedy FAQ

(http://rampages.onramp.net/%7Estevebo/faq.html)

Writing for Television Comedy

(http://tvcomedy.miningco.com/msubwrite.htm)

JOURNALISM

AJR Newslink

(http://ajr.newslink.org)

American Society of Journalists and Authors

(www.asja.org)

Columbia Journalism Review

(www.cjr.org)

Internet Newsroom

(www.editors-service.com)

National Press Club

(npc.press.org)

PLAYWRITING AND SCRIPT WRITING

In Hollywood

(www.inhollywood.com)

New Dramatists Home Page

(www.itp.tsoa.nyu.edu/~diana/ndintro.html)

Playbill On-Line/Theatre Central

(www.playbill.com/playbill/)

Playwrights on the Web

(www.stageplays.com/writers.htm)

Playwriting Seminars

(www.vcu.edu/artweb/playwriting)

Screaming in the Celluloid Jungle

(www.celluloidjungle.com)

Screenwriters Cyberia

(http://members.aol.com/swcyberia)

Screenwriters Homepage

(http://home.earthlink.net/~scribbler)

Screenwriters.Online

(http://www.screenwriter.com)

Screenwriters/Playwrights Home Page

(www.teleport.com/~cdeemer/scrwriter.html)

Screenwriters Utopia

(www.screenwritersutopia.com)

SCRNWRiT: Motion Picture and Television Screenwriting Home Page

(www.panam.edu/scrnwrit)

Writer's Guild of America

(www.wga.org)

POETRY

Academy of American Poets

(www.poets.org)

Poetry Today Online

(www.poetrytodayonline.com)

Poetry World Home Page

(http://news.std.com/poetryworld)

Semantic Rhyming Dictionary

(www.link.cs.cmu.edu/dougb/rhyme-doc.html)

W3PX Poetry Exchange

(www.w3px.com/Index.htm)

ROMANCE

Gothic Journal

(http://gothicjournal.com/romance/gothic.html)

Romance Central

(http://romancecentral.com)

Romance Novels and Women's Fiction

(www.writepage.com/romance.htm)

Romance Writers of America

(www.rwanational.com)

Romantic Times

(www.romantictimes.com)

SCIENCE FICTION

Science Fiction and Fantasy Workshop

(www.sff.net/people/Dalton-Woodbury/sffw.htp)

Science Fiction and Fantasy Writers of America

(www.sfwa.org)

Science Fiction Resource Guide

(sflovers.rutgers.edu/Web/SFRG)

Science Fiction Writers of Earth

(www. flash.net/~sfwoe)

TECHNICAL WRITING

Business and Technical Association for Business Communication

(courses.sha.cornell.edu/orgs/abc)

Business Writing Links

(flowl.ccd.cccoes.edu/owl/links/bus.html)

Internet Resources for Business and Technical Writers

(www.english.uiuc.edu/cws/wworkshop/ww_tech.html)

John Hewitt's Technical Writing Center

(www.azstarnet.com/~poewar/writer/pg/tech.html)

Magazines for Writers

Trade magazines provide a great means of getting up-to-date information on the writer's world. A good writers magazine provides articles that inspire creativity or help us to solve problems. Some great magazine and newsletters are included with the cost of membership to the writers organizations listed on previous pages. Some of these include *American Writer*, from National Writers Union, and *Novelists Inc.*, an excellent publication from the group of the same name. Many more magazines and newsletters offer advice online.

The magazines listed below are among the most established and respected publications available to writers through subscription. All are reasonably priced, at about $15 to $30 per year. Each contains articles to help make you a better writer, or to help make your life as a writer a little easier.

American Journalism Review: Covers topics related to both print and broadcast journalism. Published monthly. University of Maryland, 1117 Journalism Building, College Park, MD 20742, (800) 827-0771 (www.ajr.org).

Byline: Presents articles on the craft and business of writing, including columns on writing poetry, fiction, nonfiction and children's literature. Published monthly. P.O. Box 130596, Edmond, OK 73013 (www.bylinemag.com).

Canadian Author: One of Canada's leading writers' magazines. Published quarterly. Canadian Authors Association, P.O. Box 419, Campbellford, ON, Canada, KOL 1LO, (705) 653-0323.

Canadian Writer's Journal: Lists markets, contests, awards and writer's guidelines, and features poetry, articles and reviews. Published quarterly. P.O. Box 5180, New Liskeard, ON Canada P0J 1P0 (www.nt.net/~cwj).

Children's Book Insider: Information for new and experienced writers of children's literature. Published monthly. 901 Columbia Rd., Ft. Collins, CO 80525, (970) 495-0056 (www.write4kids.com).

Comedy Writer's Association Newsletter: Offers help with creating and selling jokes, scripts and stories. Published semiannually. P. O. Box 023304, Brooklyn, NY 11202-0066, (718) 855-5057.

Creativity Connection: Features author profiles, how-to articles and conference/workshop listings for writers and small publishers. Published quarterly. University of Wisconsin at Madison, Department of Liberal Studies and the Arts, 610 Langdon St., Room 622, Madison, WI 53703, (608) 262-4911.

Cross and Quill Newsletter: Advice for Christian writers. Published bimonthly.

Rt. 3, P.O. Box 1635, Clinton, SC 29325, (803) 697-6035 (members.aol
.com/cwfi/writers.htm).

The Editorial Eye: Specializes in standards and practices for writers, editors
and publication managers. Published monthly. 66 Canal Center Plaza, Suite
200, Alexandria, VA 22314, (800) 683-8380.

Fiction Writer: Advice on how to develop and sell fiction. Published quarterly.
1507 Dana Ave., Cincinnati, OH 45207, (800) 289-0963 (www.writersdigest
.com).

Food Writer: Marketing advice and other resources for freelance writers, authors and editors. Published quarterly. P.O. Box 156, Spring City, PA
19475-0156, (610) 948-6031.

Freelance Success: Marketing and management strategies for veteran freelance
writers. Published monthly. 801 N.E. Seventieth St., Box IK, Miami, FL
33138, (305) 754-8854 (www.freelancesuccess.com).

Gothic Journal: Geared toward writers and publishers of suspense, mystery and
gothic romance novels. Published bimonthly. P.O. Box 6340, Elko, NV
89802, (702) 738-3520 (gothicjournal.com/romance/gothic.html).

Hellnotes: Your Insider's Guide to the Horror Field: The name says it all. Published
weekly. 27780 Donkey Mine Rd., Oak Run, CA 96069 (www.hellnotes.com).

Hollywood Scriptwriter: Offers practical advice and guidance from working
professionals. Published monthly. P.O. Box 10277, Burbank, CA 91510,
(818) 842-3912.

Locus: The Newspaper of the Science Fiction Field: Offers insight and news of
interest to writers and publishers in the science fiction field. Published
monthly. P.O. Box 13305, Oakland, CA 94611, (510) 339-9198.

Network: Specializes in news about women writers. Published bimonthly. International Women's Writing Guild, P.O. Box 810, Grand Station, New
York, NY 10028, (212) 737-7536 (www.iwwg.com).

The New York Screenwriter: Offers insight on how to get scripts produced.
Published monthly. 655 Fulton St., Suite 276, Brooklyn, NY 11217, (800)
418-5637. (www.nyscreenwriter.com).

On Second Thought: Offers insight on professional writing. Published quarterly. Center for Professional Writing, 200 University, ON, Canada, N2L 3GI, (519) 725-0279.

Papyrus: The Writer's Craftletter Featuring the Black Experien. umns, publishing guidelines and information of special in writers. Published quarterly. P.O. Box 270797, West Hartfor\ (www.readersndex.com/papyrus).

Poets and Writers Magazine: Offers commentary, interviews with authors, information on grants and lists of awards. Published bimonthly. 72 Spring St., New York, NY 10012, (212) 226-3586 (www.pw.org/mag).

Publishers Weekly: The leading news magazine covering book publishing and bookselling worldwide. 245 W. Seventeenth St., New York, NY 10011, (800) 278-2991 or (310) 978-6916 (www.bookwire.com/pw/pw.html).

Script: Presents articles on the craft of screenwriting, plus interviews with screenwriters. Published bimonthly. 5638 Sweet Air Rd., Baldwin, MD 21013, (410) 592-3466.

Science Fiction Chronicle: Offers market listings and news about science fiction and fantasy writing. Published bimonthly. P.O. Box 022730, Brooklyn, NY 11202-0056, (718) 643-9011 (www.sfsite.com/sfc/home.htm).

SFWA Bulletin: Offers insight and news from the Science Fiction and Fantasy Writers of America. Published quarterly. Department H, Wildside Press, 522 Park Ave., Berkeley Heights, NJ 07922 (www.sfwa.org).

Small Press Review: Contains book reviews, columns, tips for getting published and news on the small press and small magazine industry, including start-ups. Published bimonthly. P.O. Box 100, Paradise CA 95967, (800) 477-6110 (www.dustbooks.com/sprinfo.htm).

Speechwriter's Newsletter: Practical advice on speech writing in the business, government and education sectors. Published monthly. Ragan Communications, 212 W. Superior St. #200, Chicago, IL 60610, (800) 878-5331 (www.ragan.com/pubs/order_SN.html).

Talking Agents: Examines the world of literary agents from a writer's point of view. Published monthly. Department WS, 334 E. Thirtieth St., New York, NY 10016 (www.agentresearch.com/services.html).

Write On Newsletter: Presents writing techniques, ideas, market information and writers guidelines. Published bimonthly. Box 66064, Heritage PO, Edmonton, AB, Canada T6J 6T4, (403) 438-6335 (www.duban.com/writeon/help.htm).

The Writer: Features inspiring articles by established writers, plus information on how and where to submit manuscripts. Published monthly. 120 Boylston Street, Boston, MA 02116, (888) 273-8214 (www.channel1.com/thewriter).

Writer's Digest: Features interviews, expert instruction, inspiration and information on every aspect of the writing life. Published monthly. 1507 Dana Avenue, Cincinnati, OH 45207 (www.writersdigest.com).

Writer's Guidelines: News and insight to help writers get published. Published bimonthly. P.O. Box 608, Pittsburg, MO 65724, (417) 993-5544.

Writers Guild of America East Newsletter: News and information on the broad range of activities and services of interest to writers, including advice on contract negotiations. Published monthly. 555 W. Fifty-seventh St., New York, NY 10019, (212) 767-7800 (www.wgaeast.org).

Writer's Journal: Contains author interviews, desktop publishing advice, information on the business of writing, plus poetry, book and software reviews. Published bimonthly. P.O. Box 394, Perham, MN 56573 (www.sowashco .com/writersjournal).

Writing That Works: Offers techniques on business writing, editing, publication design, production and marketing strategies. Published monthly. 7481 Huntsman Blvd., Suite 720, Springfield, VA 22153, (703) 643-2200 (http://writing thatworks.com).

Written By: The Journal of the Writer's Guild of America West: Information on the art, craft and business of script writing in Hollywood. Published monthly. 7000 W. Third St., Los Angeles, CA 90048, (888) WRITNBY (www.wga.org).

CHAPTER THREE

You, the Writer

If you write, there's really only one place to start. Look inward.

Consider first what you know and care about, and look there for stories to tell. Without some level of personal engagement, writing becomes drudgery.

"Ask yourself, what do I know, what am I good at?" advises Jim Gorman, senior editor of *Backpacker* magazine. "There are five magazines for everything you like to do in this world—for installing bathroom fixtures, baking things or whatever it is. Go get them, study them and come up with story ideas from your personal experience."

While there is plenty of room on this planet for intimate personal essays, don't take this advice to mean that you should write only about yourself. Although the world's bountiful stories are any writer's to tell, all the stories in the world aren't right for every writer. So start with what you know and love when writing.

As Betsa Marsh, who was a newspaper and magazine writer and editor for twelve years before becoming a freelancer, put it: "It's just following what you really want, what your key interests are. Because we all know journalism doesn't pay very well, so you better do something you like."

Writers are storytellers. Discovering your own stories is an intensely personal process, like recognizing an old friend's face in a crowded waiting room. But some of us have more old friends waiting to be recognized than others. In "An Idea Is

Only the Bait," in the 1998 *Writer's Handbook* (Writer, Inc.), Madonna Dries Christensen notes that writers know how to grab the bait and develop it into a magazine article, a poem, a book. She tells how her mother cooked supper for Henry Fonda in a cafe in 1951, which later became the bait for a nonfiction story and a fictionalized account. A visit to an Iowa library inspired a published reminiscence about the library and its librarian. Two short obituaries sparked a fictionalized story about the death from a lightning bolt of her great-grandfather and his daughter. She also has used guidelines for authors as inspiration, noting that she would not have written any of the ten stories she had published in the journal *Thema* had it not first set out a theme for each issue.

The Great Idea

Marcia Thornton Jones, a children's book author and elementary school teacher, says that she and her writing partner, Debbie Dadey, never fear running out of ideas. "What we have trouble with is finding time to pursue them all," Jones says.

Ideas, of course, are everywhere; recognizing them is the trick. At a book signing, for example, Jones and the mother of one her young readers named Jack were chatting about how many people they knew by that name. "Jacks are wild," the mother commented. "That sounds like the name of a children's book!" Jones exclaimed, pulling out her journal and jotting it down.

Part of the recognition process involves knowing where and when ideas are most likely to be spotted. "I do my most productive thinking about writing in the shower and emptying or loading the dishwasher," says Jim Kraft. At those moments, says Kraft, who began writing children's books after a career writing greeting cards, the story often comes to him just out of the line of vision of the mind's eye. Approaching the topic obliquely "seems to work better than sitting at my desk thinking about it," he says.

Chance remarks rouse ideas as well. Once, on the way to basketball camp with his two sons and their friends, suddenly they all fell silent. Kraft's younger son commented, "Suddenly silence." The next minute, Kraft had an idea for a book.

INSIDER REPORT

A Christian Writer Finds Her Niche

Karen H. Whiting knows her roles, and their priorities, in her life: a Christian first, a wife and mother second, and a writer third. But putting writing in third place doesn't mean it finishes last.

Since this mother of five decided to pursue a writing career in 1994, she has had at least one story idea accepted at Christian publications every month and has earned five book contracts. Still, she puts aside her writing when the children come home from school and picks it up again after they go to bed.

A trained puppeteer, Whiting has combined her faith and her hobby to create a writing career. It began when she helped her daughter start a puppet ministry at their church. To raise money for supplies, Whiting tried to sell a puppet script. It was rejected. But with the rejection came a checklist of what was wrong with the script. Only one item out of twenty was checked, but Whiting thought, "If I write another puppet script and make sure none of the reasons for rejection can be checked, it might sell."

So she wrote another and within two months sold it to One Way Street, Inc., which included the script in its booklet *Bible Puppet Scripts*. In the meantime, she wrote and sold two short pieces, a puppet monologue about a homeless woman finding hope after picking up a dirty old penny on the street, and a child's curriculum activity using an engraved penny as the focus.

Whiting's bedtime reading choice became the *Christian Writers' Market Guide* (Harold Shaw Publishers). Scanning the listings helped her think of ideas. "I also became familiar with the publishers and the editors' names this way, as well as any denominational affiliation," she says. "It helps when you later meet editors at conferences that you know something about them."

She learned about the breadth of publications in the magazine market. She learned which use fillers, how to get samples and guidelines, how to submit items. She looked up magazines according to the category of her interests—parenting and scripts. "I discovered Standard Publishing bought individual scripts, with one-time rights, for drama booklets, and sold to them," she says.

In the guide, she learned of a writers conference in Titusville, Florida, realized it was at her sister-in-law's church, and attended. "From that conference I've sold dozens of magazine articles, fillers and curricula and received book contracts," she says.

When targeting an idea to a new magazine market, she will find an article similar to her idea in that magazine and read it—up to fifty times. Her goal is to make her story match the style, tone and structure used in the magazine. "There's so much

continued

to learn in reading an article—its title, placement, style, etc. Some people probably learn faster, and as I write more, I think I read a few less times," she says.

She also studies the letters to the editor as a source of possible story ideas. In the *Church Library Magazine*, for example, a reader wrote asking about how to help young readers, which Whiting turned into an article idea that sold that same week.

Whiting often writes personal-experience pieces, devotionals, puppetry and crafts how-to articles and books, and parenting articles, "often with a related craft for spiritual development," she says. She's written profiles, children's stories and book reviews. "All have a Christian theme," she says. "That's my niche market."

"I find it easier to break in with shorter pieces," she noted. For these, she often skips the query letter and sends in the piece itself. For example, she enjoyed reading columns about activities for children in *Christian Parenting Today* magazine and noted that the magazine's guidelines say it wants 'tried and tested' ideas. So Whiting wrote a piece about a spiritual treasure box she had made with each of her children when they were preschoolers. After Whiting sent in the article, the editors liked it enough to make it into a cover article, rewriting it into a longer feature and adding artwork.

"I consider myself a creative writer. I often just let the piece flow out first," she says, "then I will rewrite and rewrite until I feel it's a good match for the structure, voice and style of a target publication. I think that's why it will sell."

It became "Night Noises," a children's story about what happens when all the normal noises of the night suddenly stop.

The process isn't very different for nonfiction writers. Freed from the obligation to invent an interesting reality, they are nonetheless obliged to view reality from a fresh perspective. Pat Crowley, a newspaper reporter and freelance magazine writer, says ideas rush at him everywhere he goes. On the way to talk to a journalism class, the radio prompted two freelance story ideas. One was about whether lowering the legal blood alcohol limit, as lawmakers were proposing following a rash of drunk-driving accidents, would really make any difference. The other idea was on the sometimes-alarming side effects that advertisers calmly list in their commercials for drugs—an idea that hit him while listening to an ad for an anti-hair-loss product, which sounded great until the announcer mentioned it could cause inconveniences such as dry mouth, blackouts or sexual dysfunction. "Anyone would rather lose every hair they have than have sexual dysfunction," Crowley says, "and that's the way I'll sell it."

What follow are some prompts to help you analyze your interests and expertise and generate your own stories from them. Then, we've included some steps to help you match those ideas to markets.

As with any idea-generating exercises, you'll probably come up with some unworkable notions. But the point of any creativity activity is to knock that interior editor who's always telling you what you do wrong off her perch for a while, so that the ideas percolating inside can tumble out. Don't criticize, don't revise. Just allow the ideas to flow. Only after you've jotted down some story ideas do you let the editor crawl back up and peer over your left shoulder to search for the gem that will become your story.

What Do I Write About? Eight Easy Steps

1. Read. The importance of this step can't be overrated. Good writers start with knowledge and then move to understanding, even wisdom. While creativity exercises can help generate ideas, there is no substitute for real, solid information in devising a story. Professional writers are also great readers, and their stories are grounded with information. Fiction writers can be inspired by history books and newspaper articles as easily as nonfiction writers can.

Reading keeps you informed about what is going on, but also, if you read carefully, you'll begin to notice what's *not* covered in stories. A story in a local newspaper about plans to build a new museum downtown, for example, mentions the location would be where a well-known hat shop has stood for decades. The fate of the hat shop, and the reaction of some of its loyal customers, might make a short item for your local city magazine. Read anything—posters, flyers, freebie publications, junk mail—because it's a wonderful world, and information seeds stories.

2. Write. A writer should keep a writing instrument handy. Whether you like notebooks and pencils or electronic gadgets, keep *something* to record ideas wherever they strike. Into this record, jot those stray notions that otherwise would evaporate and be lost. You really don't know when or where an idea will strike you, and you should never trust your memory to record it for you. Ideas are like dreams: You can recall them with clarity while supine, but they retreat into the ether when you get up to face the dailiness of living. Write them down.

3. Listen. The next time you're waiting in line, watching your daughter's soccer game or waiting for the waiter to bring your dinner, listen—really listen—to the people around you. What concerns them? Parents at the soccer game may grumble about a coach's ill temper. Could there be a story on how parents can tame a fractious coach? They may joke about the child on the field who is more interested in hunting for a four-leaf clover. Is there a story about pushing young children into sports too soon? They may talk about how one of their daughters has suffered yet another injury—a story on coaches' need to know about the importance of stretching and warm-ups? About sports injuries increasing among girls?

While you're at it, make notes on the incident that sparked an idea—the appearance of the people talking, the sounds of their voices, the way they interact. Describe the day, its light, its warmth, its breezes. You never know when you'll need an anecdote.

4. Watch. On a tour of the local observatory with your kids, for example, you'll probably be spending a lot of time watching and listening to the tour guide. Allow yourself to wonder about him. Does he stay up nights watching the stars? Does his wife mind? Does he seem more enthusiastic about this nocturnal occupation than the kids do? Would he—or his job—make a good story? Colorful people, and ordinary people with colorful or unusual occupations, are everywhere. Mary once interviewed a man whose job was to analyze concrete. Her immediate reaction was pity—until he told her of the time his analysis had helped prove a man had murdered his wife and buried her beneath the basement floor, patching it with concrete from another house.

5. Observe relationships. With everything you see, remember to ask yourself, Is there a story here? Let's say you're watching the neighborhood kids. You see ten-year-old Anita commandeering a crew of children, some older than she, into playing school. She is the teacher. They switch to a new game of exploring, and she is the fearless scout. They switch to kickball, and she's the coach, the referee and the star player. This girl could spur ideas for several articles: teaching children to stand up for themselves, what to do if your child is bossy (or a bully), or looking at childhood leadership as a sign of giftedness.

6. Talk. Bat around your story ideas with friends—preferably writer friends.

Sometimes you come up with the raw ingredients of an idea, but it doesn't quite cook until you talk it over. Such informal brainstorming, especially when warmed by good company and food, can generate far more ideas than you can dream up in your lonely room at night. Join a writers group. There's nothing like peer pressure to force you to come up with ideas and write about them.

7. Keep an idea file. Clip stories from newspapers, newsletters, junk mail, advertorials, the World Wide Web. Rip out the pages from your writer's notebook. Put these all in one place. Take them out periodically and look at them. Can any be expanded into a good story for a particular audience?

8. Ask. Allow yourself the freedom to wonder about things. The next time you hear something, see something or read something that could be worth writing about, you'll probably have questions. Ask them. The conversation might produce a story idea.

Idea-Generating Exercises

Narrow Your Ideas

Take the slice-and-dice approach to idea generation. For example, don't plan on writing 2,000 words on teenagers' drinking habits. Slice it into more manageable, focused ideas. How about warning signs of alcohol abuse among preteens? The failure of alcohol-abuse prevention programs among teen boys? The trend among parents to convene groups to prevent their children from drinking?

Robert Frost once said, "An idea is a feat of association." Bounce two topics off each other, combine several thoughts together and watch what happens. You can use a grid to formalize this approach, as Cheryl Sloan Wray suggests in her book, *Writing for Magazines: A Beginner's Guide* (NTC Publishing Group, 1997). Down one side of the grid, list topics you're interested in—items in the news, hobbies, activities. Along the top, list some of the magazine categories, from *Writer's Market* (Writer's Digest Books), that appeal to you. (Other books suggest listing events in the news along the top and human needs, such as shelter and companionship, on the vertical bar.) Combine the topics in the rows and columns to create possible ideas. Look at the chart below to see what we mean.

	Juvenile	Retirement	Career
Violence	Crimes committed by young girls	Abuse of the elderly	Employee assistance programs for victims of crime
Education	When children become the teachers	Returning to college following retirement	Planning a career in the sixth grade
Job Insecurity	Requiring students to sign ethics pledges before entering the workforce	Planning for retirement in an uncertain world	Employees' lack of loyalty and the bottom line

A Day in the Life

Wray and other writers also suggest reflecting on the seemingly mundane events of your life as story possibilities. Wray suggests writing down a few things that happened to you in the past few days. Then consider, what can you tell others about these events? Unless you live an exceptional life, you will not produce stellar ideas for every event in your day. But if you practice looking for stories in ordinary places, you may well find them. What this exercise really does is helps you grow antennae to sound out everything as a potential story, as many a professional writer does. An example follows.

Event	Idea
Spent twenty minutes arranging car-pooling for kids after school	Time management for parents
Daughter forgot homework—again	How to teach young children responsibility
Displayed our tacky plastic Christmas decorations	Decorating with natural items
Watched daughter in full regalia and makeup perform at dance recital	Have parents subverted childhood?
Stayed up late helping daughter with homework while son finished his homework in fifteen minutes	The debate on how much and what type of homework is best
Fell asleep before my kids did	Changing sleep patterns with aging

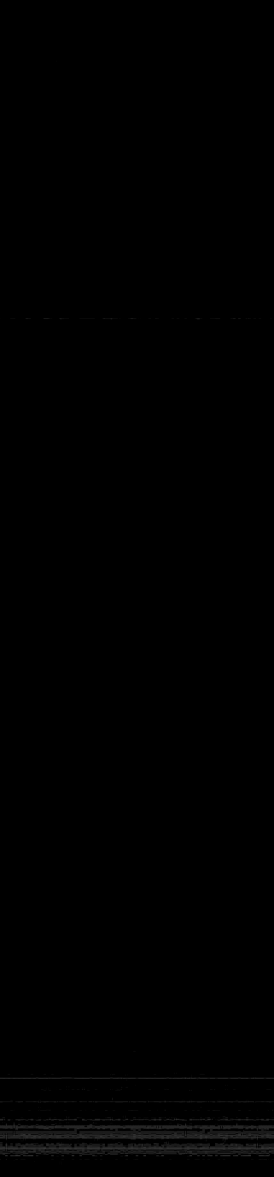

Write Short

Beginning writers have a better chance of breaking into the magazine market by writing short pieces of about 100 to 500 words. You can find descriptions of such short items and fillers by reading through *Writer's Market* or scrolling through the writer's guidelines at www.writersdigest.com.

Use the following chart to help you think of a topic you want to write about and to match it with one of the categories of shorter pieces. Look in *Writer's Market* for categories of magazines that might suit your topic and focus. Fill in the blanks below to devise an idea and target category. For example, if you enjoy writing about cooking, you could write for retirement magazines helpful tips focusing on cooking quick dinners for one person.

Topic	Story Category	Focus	Magazine Category
	first-person essays		
	inspirational essays		
	travel briefs		
	short profiles		
cooking	helpful tips	dinner for one	retirement
	humor		

You can make a more targeted list of shorter story ideas by analyzing the front-of-the book pieces in your favorite magazine over several issues. What tone do they use? How many sources are used? Are they informational? Do they perform a service for readers? What topics are typically covered?

Also look at the magazine's preferences for its columns and departments, where stories typically run from several hundred to 1,500 words. Read the writer's guidelines for descriptions of appropriate column or department topics, and study the style of these pieces in the magazine you are targeting. Then, come up with some ideas.

The 30-Minute Writer: How to Write and Sell Short Pieces by Connie Emerson (Writer's Digest Books, 1996), is a good source of advice for anyone interested in writing shorter pieces.

Look Inward

Think about ways to turn your personal experiences into stories—even if you don't write in the first person. Michael Bugeja, in his *Guide to Writing Magazine Nonfiction* (Allyn and Bacon, 1998), shows writers how to start with their own characteristics to come up with stories. For example, Mary's mother immigrated to America from Italy, and her father was born here of Italian immigrants. She grew up on a street populated by aunts, uncles and cousins, but it was in a solidly German-American neighborhood that now has become home to many races and ethnic groups. This experience suggests several possible stories: "Preserving Ethnic Cooking" (for a food or women's magazine); "How to Make Homemade Wine" (for a culinary magazine); "The Immigrant As Entrepreneur" (for a business magazine); "The Changing Face of America's Neighborhoods" (for a general-interest magazine).

Look also at the expertise you possess. Most of us, even those who think their only hobby is reading books in comfortable armchairs, probably have wide interests and skills. Use the following prompts to examine what you have to offer.

- My family's heritage
- My (and my family's) health problems
- A crisis weathered
- Changes in my community
- My exercise habits (or lack of them)
- My volunteer activities
- My career goals
- My hobbies
- My expertise at work
- A celebrity or unusual person I know
- My passions
- Five things I wonder about

Be Alert for News

Fill in these blanks:

- The last time I thought to myself, *I didn't know that*, was _____ .

- The last time I just had to tell someone something was ＿＿＿＿＿＿ .
- The last time I was really surprised was ＿＿＿＿＿＿＿ .

Then ask yourself, Would other people think the same way? Could you tell them something new?

Freewriting

Often touted as a cure for writer's block, freewriting also can help you think creatively. The notion is simple. Sit down and write for a set length of time, say ten minutes. Don't edit. Forget what your English teachers told you. Ignore syntax, style, grammar and spelling. Don't even worry much about content. You're not creating a piece for publication here. You're just allowing your thoughts to spill out and lead you where they will. Sometimes, this can create a story idea. Other times, it just feels good and limbers up your fingers and your mind for the real work of writing.

Following is an example on the topic "your biggest problem growing up," from one of Mary's journalism students. This process got him thinking about a story on how teens learn self-esteem by saying no to peer pressure:

> The biggest problem I had growing up was that I didn't stand up for myself. Not that I don't just stand up for myself, but let people talk me into things easily. When I was 14 my friend Henry and I were arrested for shoplifting. I wasn't brought up that way because my mom would do anything to get me what I wanted. He could talk me into everything that he wanted to do. He has lured me into everything from shoplifting to egging houses. There was another time we egged a house and then tried to swim back across the river. But halfway across we got tired and had to float down a little ways. In the end it was a very good life experience.

SOME PROMPTS FOR FREEWRITING

- You've discovered you suddenly have no appointments, no duties, nothing to worry about for the next fifteen minutes. What do you do with your time?
- What do the people at your son's or daughter's sports games talk about on the sidelines?

- What do you like most about yourself? Least?
- What was your mother's most recent ailment?
- Do you remember an important first—first kiss, first car, first publication?
- What was your last argument about?
- Look at an old photograph. What does it make you think about?
- What bothers you about your family?
- What do you love to eat and why?
- Have you ever experienced a life-changing event, when you knew that things would never be the same for you or your family? What lessons did you learn from it?
- What was the biggest problem you had growing up?
- What is the biggest problem you face today?

Ideas Online

The Internet is a bonanza for writers, with Web sites and information at every click. It also offers many sites designed to help people write, often affiliated with universities. One of the best is sponsored by the Purdue University Online Writing Lab. While much of the advice has to do with writing academic papers, a lot more has to do with simply writing well. For some ideas about getting ideas, type these URLs into your browser: owl.english.purdue.edu/Files/101.html and owl.english .purdue.edu/Files/65.html.

Using Emotions As Prompts

Emotions can spur ideas. If the emotions are strong, they also help guarantee you'll remain committed to finishing a writing project. Think about some of these emotions when considering what to write.

- What do you like most about where you live? Least?
- What story in the newspaper recently made you angry? Glad? Sad?
- What is your favorite possession and why?
- What was the most recent thing you cried about?
- What was the most recent thing you laughed out loud about?

- When was the last time you were embarrassed?
- What scares (worries, angers, gladdens) you? Your children? Your spouse? Your parents?

Lists

Sometimes lists can help you generate story ideas. If you keep a to-do list, analyze it. What do you spend most of your time doing? Is it the most important thing in your life? If not, maybe there's a story in how we squander our free time.

To Market

Finding Magazine Markets for Your Ideas

To get the nod to write for a magazine, you must match your idea to a specific market. This requires you to read the magazine before pitching an idea for it. In fact, many writers start with the magazine rather than the idea. (See chapter eight, "Selling Your Articles and Other Short Nonfiction," for more details on this process.)

Reading through the letters to the editor can generate ideas targeted to readers' concerns. Scanning several issues' table of contents helps you look at stories as the magazine's editors do. Looking at the ads gives you a good picture of who reads the magazine. Reading the stories gives you an idea of their tone, sourcing, style, slant and organization.

Find a magazine you love, then request the writer's guidelines to learn what types of stories the magazine wants. Write away for the magazine's writer's guidelines or get them online. After you do this, ask yourself what you have to offer. Then call the magazine and ask for the name of the editor for whichever section appeals to you, and send a query with your idea.

Or, if you're a person to whom ideas flock like squirrels to a birdfeeder, take your ideas to *Writer's Market*. In the table of contents, find the magazine category that matches your idea (Romance and Confession? Personal Computers?), and flip to the individual listings to find publications that seem to be suited to the idea. Once you find them, read each magazine—preferably several issues of it. If a magazine has covered the topic before, think about a new slant you can take that matches the tone and style of the magazine.

To find online magazines, visit The Gebbie Press site (www.gebbieinc.com/mag url.htm) or The Internet Public Library (www.ipl.org/reading/serials).

Use the Internet as a marketing tool. Freelancer Pat Crowley says when he has a story idea, he just types the subject into a favorite search engine, "and there are twenty magazines and one hundred Web sites for every idea." Read through the hits, looking for places that might be suitable markets. But check the site or the *Writer's Market* to see if the publications accept E-mail queries. If they don't, you'll have to take a trip to the post office, but at least you've located a potential market far more quickly than you could have in the past. Remember to send a stamped, self-addressed envelope if you want a reply.

Finding a Market for Book Ideas

To find a publisher for your book, turn to the back of *Writer's Market* for the Book Publishers Subject Index. There, you'll find lists of books arranged by topic, from adventure to young adult for fiction, and from agriculture to young adult for nonfiction. Then read the listing about each publisher for such vital information as how it prefers to be approached, what percentage of books it publishes from first-time authors and contact information. Write away or visit the publisher's Web site for catalogs and submission guidelines. Also check the subject guide to *Books in Print* (R.R. Bowker Co.), available at libraries, to find which houses publish books like yours and to get an idea of the competition.

Then, advises children's book author Debbie Dadey, browse a bookstore to see what's selling. But seeing what's *not* on the bookstore shelves can also be a useful marketing exercise as well, as Dadey's experience attests. "You've got to write what you want to write, what really is important to you," she notes. Writing a series called The Adventures of the Bailey School Kids was important to her and coauthor Marcia Thornton Jones. Both educators, they saw a need for books for primary school children who were reluctant readers— children who wanted to read but weren't yet ready for a novel and scorned picture books as "for babies." They realized there weren't many books filling that need, and their series became immensely popular with those very children.

While you're at the bookstore, note which houses publish books similar to yours. Call the publisher and ask for the name of the person who edited the books. While you're on the phone, double-check the name and address of the publisher. See chapters nine, "Selling Your Nonfiction Book," and ten, "Selling Your Fiction," for details about approaching a publishing house about your book manuscripts.

Writer's Market and its sister publications probably are the most popular books for beginning writers to use to learn about markets. But if you can't find what you need there, more information about book publishers is contained in numerous catalogs and directories from R.R. Bowker, a unit of Reed Elsevier. *The Publishers' Trade List Annual* (R.R. Bowker Co.), for example, is a compilation of publishers' catalogs. Browsing through this book, available at many libraries, gives you a sense of who publishes what.

Although the Internet is supposed to be multimedia, it has most often been a medium for reading, which is good news for writers. To find books similar to yours, visit an online bookstore and simply type in a subject.

Magazines, such as *Writer's Digest* and *The Writer,* offer help with the craft of writing and offer advice about finding markets for your work. You also can find thousands of sites devoted to writing and publishing on the Web, a few of which are listed below.

Resources

BOOKS/DIRECTORIES

Bacon's Newspaper Directory and *Bacon's Magazine Directory* (Bacon's Information, Inc.). Lists magazines, newsletters, newspapers and news syndicates.

Books in Print (R.R. Bowker Co.) The subject guide to this comprehensive annual compilation describes books according to topic (www.bowker.com).

The Canadian Writer's Market (McClelland & Stewart, 1998). Lists markets in Canada.

Christian Writers' Market Guide (Harold Shaw Publishers). Lists more than 1,000 markets. Includes publishers of books and periodicals, arranged by subject, as well as a host of other publishing information, including writers conferences, editorial services and market analyses.

Gale Directory of Publications and Broadcast Media (Gale Research). Lists more than 37,000 newspapers, magazines, journals and other periodicals. Markets are arranged geographically and indexed by subject (www.gale.com).

International Directory of Little Magazines and Small Presses (Dustbooks). See www.dustbooks.com. Lists editors' names and addresses and descriptions of topics published at thousands of small publishers. Listed by subject, region and area of specialization.

Literary Market Place (*LMP*) (R.R. Bowker Co.). The definitive resource for the publishing world. More than 15,000 entries listing names and contact information for book publishers, electronic publishers, literary agents, direct mail promoters and more. Searchable online by subject area (for a hefty fee) at www.literarymarketplace.com. *LMP*'s *Industry Yellow Pages* is a directory of names, addresses, phone numbers and E-mail addresses of people listed in (LMP).

Ulrich's International Periodicals Directory (R.R. Bowker Co.). This huge directory includes information on more than 156,000 serials, arranged in 973 subject headings. Volume 4 of this multivolume set cross-indexes publisher information by subject. It also indexes online serials. A Web site (www.ulrichsweb.com), available by subscription, features a database of more than 235,000 active and ceased periodicals, serials, annuals (regular and irregular) and newspapers.

Working Press of the Nation: Magazines and Internal Publications Directory (National Register Publishing). This multivolume set includes brief descriptions of consumer magazines and internal publications of various industries, including data on deadlines and freelance rates. It is cross-indexed by subject.

Writer's Digest Books' Market Book series (Writer's Digest Books). These books include *Children's Writer's and Illustrator's Market, Guide to Literary*

Agents, Poet's Market, Science Fiction and Fantasy Writer's Sourcebook, Romance Writer's Sourcebook and *Writer's Market.*

The Writer's Handbook (Writer, Inc.). A comprehensive guide including how to write various genres, interviews with established authors and listings of markets to sell your writing.

WEB SITES

To learn about the business of book publishing, news, events, writers associations, online publishers and more, start with BookWire online (www.bookwire.com) and the Book Zone (www.bookzone.com).

For links to publishers around the world and their catalogs, try the Publishers' Catalogues home page (www.lights.com/publisher). Another wonderfully comprehensive site for librarians, the Directory of Publishers and Vendors (www.library.vanderbilt.edu/law/acqs/pubr.html), includes links to a publishers' E-mail address directory and Web sites.

For links to magazine markets, see the Internet Public Library (www.ipl.org), which links to thousands of magazines' Web pages, Writer's Digest (www.writersdigest.com) or the Inkspot (www.inkspot.com), a site that gives advice on writing and marketing online. Writers Write (www.writerswrite.com), a terrific site for anyone who writes, has links to other useful sites.

Finally, two university sites offer lots of help with writing in general: Purdue University's Online Writing Resources (owl.english.purdue.edu/writers) and the University of Illinois at Urbana-Champaign's Writers' Workshop (www.english.uiuc.edu/cws/wworkshop/index.htm).

CHAPTER FOUR

Your Writing Plan

Sharyn McCrumb had always wanted to write a novel. But when a publishing house accepted her first book proposal, McCrumb was working full-time, teaching a night class in fiction, taking two graduate English courses and trying to raise an eight-year-old daughter. She was married to a man who was working and was also a graduate student. In addition, she was six weeks pregnant. The publisher wanted the book in just six weeks.

So McCrumb wrote *Bimbos of the Death Sun* (TSR, 1987) in six weeks. It won the Edgar Allan Poe Award for Best Paperback Novel in 1988 and was still in print more than a decade later. So she remains skeptical when people complain about not having time to write. "Each time someone blames his unwritten masterpiece on a lack of time, I smile sympathetically and nod," McCrumb, now a full-time writer, wrote in *Writer's Digest.* "I am thinking: 'Crap.' "

The fact is, as McCrumb points out, that nobody has time to write a book. It's

> **I insist on being at my desk at 7:30 A.M. I rush just as if I were a commuter.**
>
> —Maeve Binchy, author of *Evening Class* (Delacorte Press, 1996),
> quoted in September 1997 *Writer's Digest*

even hard to find time to write magazine articles, short stories or poems. Yet, successful writers do find the time every day to meet their writing obligations, whether those obligations are external, from editors, or internal, from an incontestable desire to write.

While few writers will ever have to face a deadline as onerous as McCrumb's, professional writers also know that there's nothing like a deadline to make you focus on your work. In fact, the real problem for beginning writers is usually not scrambling to meet a punishing deadline, but simply organizing your time efficiently enough to find time to write at a productive pace. As other commitments encroach on our days, writing is pushed aside like an unpleasant chore. Instead, it is a promise unfulfilled.

Accomplishing your writing goals requires making a writing plan, a time schedule that lists what you need to do and when. This chapter will explore some ideas on managing your time to *create* the best time for you to write. It will give you tips on how to best use the time you have to produce a finished piece. It includes checklists of steps that should be taken to research, write and rewrite.

Choose to Write

Everybody has the same amount of time every day. How we choose to use that time makes some of us writers and others of us short-order cooks. If you are a short-order cook who wants to write, however, you should probably think about how you use time—which is, after all, the stuff of your life.

The Silent Cradle **was written while I practiced OB/GYN full-time. I had to write whenever and wherever I could. Before work, during lunch, after work, on the labor deck, inside the on-call room, in the hospital's library. My handwriting's terrible; I switched from pen and paper to a typewriter, then to a laptop. I closed my medical practice when I sold the book. Now I write at home, at the Berkeley City Club, the UCSF library, and in hotel rooms when my husband and I travel.**

—Margaret Cuthbert, author of *The Silent Cradle* (Pocket Books, 1998), quoted in June 1998 *Writer's Digest*

Writing for publication demands a sincere commitment of time and effort to the craft. You have to want to do it, and you must be as dedicated to it as you are to the other priorities in your life.

Sandra Felton has written ten books on how to get organized, targeted to the naturally messy. In fact, Felton has included the word *mess* in the titles of her books, her latest being *Stop Messing Around and Organize to Write* (Messies Anonymous), for people who haven't the slightest idea how to organize their writing, or who lose manuscripts and research materials and sometimes even contracts. ("This is not theoretical," she notes.) "I think the whole answer is focus," Felton says. "I think what focus means is you have to decide what you want to do and lop off other stuff that you also want to do. Because you want to write *more*."

Note that the choice is not between writing and doing something else that you don't want to do. The choice is between a nearly overwhelming array of things that seem appealing: reading, visiting friends, going to movies and theater and the opera, family get-togethers and trips, and watching way too much television. Faced with so many options, people tend to choose too many and feel short of time.

Some people actually can use stray snippets of free time to write, penning novels on the backs of envelopes while waiting in the checkout line at the grocery store. Such people need not read this chapter. For most of us, writing for publication requires time to research, time to ponder, time to draft, time to rewrite and time to polish.

Make Writing a Habit

Finding time to write requires a modicum of organization, but using it productively demands dedication to writing. The theme of virtually every article about getting organized to write is straightforward: Just do it. Wanting to write and writing itself are cousins, not identical twins. Psychological research indicates that writing every

---

Begin at the beginning . . . and go on till you come to the end and then stop.

—Lewis Carroll

General Tips on Time Management for Writers

Even people who write and publish regularly can have trouble finding time to write. When Joe signed a contract to write this book within one year, he was also working full-time in public relations and running a freelance writing business in his spare time. He would come home from a full day at the office, then work into the early morning hours. After a couple months on this schedule, he grew tired and increasingly nervous about the project, with the vast amount of work the book demanded depriving him of time with his two young children.

So Joe asked Mary, a neighbor who had worked on freelance assignments with him, to help write the book. He immediately felt relieved, and settled down more comfortably into a regular writing and researching pattern.

Mary agreed to write the book instantly, gladly. Then she panicked. She was teaching four writing courses at Northern Kentucky University, writing an article a month about computers for a trade magazine, writing short features for an educational newsletter, serving on her children's school council, editing and laying out the school's monthly newsletter, and trying to spend precious time with her two young kids, too.

A naturally disorganized creature, Mary still felt as if she were suffocating every time she approached the computer in her shambles of a study to work on the book. The filing cabinets full, she had resorted to keeping papers in semicircles around her chair, as well as spread in piles on the oversized desktop. The study was a cluttered, chaotic, wholly unpleasant place. To make things worse, she shared this space with her husband, a newspaper editor with tendencies toward neatness. He would periodically gather all her piles of papers into one pile, where she couldn't find anything.

She needed help getting organized enough to write, setting up a writing plan and controlling time so that her writing would not be shunted off like the pile of papers kicked into the study's corner. Web sites, books and experts on organization helped her figure out how to get more organized, to find more time to write. These tips may be useful to you, too.

- **Publicize your writing goals.** Tell your friends, your spouse, your kids. Post them near your desk to remind you of them daily. This serves two purposes: It encourages people who love you to give you support and time alone to write, and it puts subtle pressure on you to perform.

- **Do the hard jobs first.** Nothing is worse than having walked ten miles in a blizzard to find Mount Everest blocking the end of your path. Imagine how good you'll feel when you've reached the top of the mountain and can see your path wending downward before you. So start with the hard things.

continued

"People tend to go to the easiest things first," notes Stephanie Denton, a professional organizer and writer. "But that's a short-term reward." It may feel great to cross off lots of little items from a to-do list, but if your goal is to submit an article in a month and you spend a week doing ten unrelated, little tasks, then you'll feel little gratification—you're really just wasting time.

- **Keep a time log for a week.** (See chart page 87.) If you cannot figure out where your time goes or how you could possibly find time in your busy life to write, the log will help you to look closely at how you live and the commitments you've made to things other than writing.

If you think this process sounds like a perfect nuisance, rest assured, it is. But it is also useful in helping you pinpoint which activities you treat as priorities (Mary, for example, found she spent more time with her children than she thought she did) and which ones are time wasters (checking your E-mail five times a day, for example).

- **Make sure you do something every day to help you reach your writing goal,** no matter what else is on your to-do list.

- **Be flexible.** Nothing in a writing project, possibly nothing in life, goes entirely according to plan. People you want to interview leave town, or die. The report you wanted to read is available only in an archive in Toledo. Somebody you love gets sick and needs your attention. So adjust your plan. (That's why you write it in pencil.) Kick items off one day's to-do list onto another's; do something that was scheduled for tomorrow today. Expect some shuffling of items, and don't berate yourself for falling off your writing schedule. Just climb back on at the earliest opportunity.

- **Consider space as well as time.** Some people can write anywhere, in any conditions. They probably are already doing so. Many others need a quiet place, free from disturbances, with a door that can close out noise, distractions and even the thought of other responsibilities. When the place where you write disturbs you with its clutter, its noise, its lighting or whatever, you're probably grumpily wasting time and energy when you're there. So change it to suit your writing preferences.

After deciding her study was oppressively messy, Mary, for example, bought a new filing cabinet, picked up the papers off the floor and filed them. She cleaned up the area after every work session. She bought a day planner and filled it in faithfully. She considered it all a big pain. But these simple steps ultimately improved her mood, and she became more productive because that first sight of the office no longer made her want to flee.

- **Set your priorities.** As important as writing is to most of us, other things rejuvenate us and make life worthwhile: family, friends, rest and leisure. Set aside time for writing and for work, but leave time for people and play.

continued

- **Listen to your body.** Humans live by diurnal rhythms. If you're a night person, work when everyone else in the house is asleep. If your IQ diminishes with the lateness of the hour, get up and work as the sun rises. Work with your nature, not against it. Don't try to change what works best for you just because somebody (even us) gave you different advice.

- **Just say no.** Being busy has become a status symbol of sorts, but it's one that is ultimately debilitating to many of us. Joe asked Mary for help when he became too busy. And Mary soon realized that she could not perform well if she continued trying to work at all the jobs she'd taken on. So she set priorities: her family, her teaching job and the book. She told the computer magazine she couldn't write monthly articles for at least six months. She finished the short features for the educational newsletter well before their deadlines, because they distracted her from focusing on the book. She asked for help on the school newsletter. Your own capacity for work will differ from a fellow writer's. Many of us are multitasking to the point of exhaustion, and many would benefit from learning to say, "No, I can't fit that into my schedule right now."

- **Feel free to ignore some or all of these tips.** The way a person finds times to write is as distinctive to the individual as the sound of the voice, the style of the gait. What works for one person, or even for many, may not for you.

"I'm a loosely knit person. Schedules drive me crazy," says Sandra Felton, who writes about organizing for messy people. Felton believes she finishes writing jobs because she makes commitments to her writing and then is obliged to keep them. For example, she accepted a speaking engagement to discuss her latest book on getting organized to write—before she had written the book. That deadline looming, she then simply had to focus on the book. And focus, she believes, Is the real key to getting writing done. "I don't know what method I use, but whatever method it is is based on focus," Felton says. "I just am focused on getting the work done because I believe in my message. I have something I really think is important for people to know."

day, whether your muse is whispering in your ear or has deserted you, produces not only more writing but more ideas for future writing. The writing habit, like the exercise habit, is its own reward. When you don't do it, you feel as if you're cheating yourself.

"The only thing I can tell you I do that's inviolate is when I have to write: I get up in the morning and literally go straight to the typewriter," says Stephanie Culp, who has written books on organization and time management. "Any little distraction that takes me away from my desk kills it. When I'm writing something large, it takes about three fitful days, and then I'm in the rhythm of it, and I write it. I can still write a book in three weeks."

Get into a writing habit. Start by setting aside an hour, or even a half hour, every day to write. Or set a goal to write a certain number of words every day. Try to write at the same time every day so it will feel peculiar to do something else at that time. Write even if you feel uninspired, even if you don't feel ready to write. If you would be a writer, you must write. Just do it.

Your Writing Plan

Often, getting started on a writing project is the hardest part.

Most writing jobs, however, can be viewed as a sequence of doable tasks that follow the same general path from beginning to end. If you accomplish each task, in order, you can follow this plan to a finished piece.

The planning guidelines on pages 71-73 are designed to help you write a nonfiction magazine article, but they can be modified to suit many writing projects. A book, for example, is made of chapters that are similar to magazine pieces. Break the book down into individual chapters, and break the chapters down into component parts. Schedule your writing project into your day at specific times, and, with a little luck but more hard work, you'll finish your pieces on time.

For people who resent and resist scheduling, remember that creating a writing plan is meant to relieve some stress, organize your life and make your writing process more efficient. "Organizing is not meant to be uncomfortable," notes Stephanie Denton, a time management consultant who writes for *Family Circle* magazine. Meeting even mini-deadlines can lift your spirits and bolster your confidence.

> **I never finish work for the day. I stop working in midparagraph or midsentence, so that I don't have to face a blank screen in the morning.**
>
> —Malcolm McConnell, author of *Inside Hanoi's Secret Archives* (Simon and Schuster, 1995), quoted in September 1997 *Writer's Digest*

Conquering Writer's Block

You've closed the office door. The phone has stopped ringing. The kids are in bed. This is your time to write.

You sit before your computer, staring at the screen, fingers on the keyboard, waiting for inspiration. You feel nervous. You type a few words. The sentence lurches across the screen. You wanted perfection; you created a blot on the page. You start over. Words stumble onto the screen. You read it, thinking it's abominable. You know it will never be accepted for publication. You delete it. Whatever made you think you could write? You'll never be a writer. You cannot write. You're a failure. You despair.

Such are the thoughts and feelings of a person with writer's block. Few things are as frustrating as setting aside time to write and then finding, suddenly, you just can't.

Psychologist Robert Boice has studied fluency in writing and writer's block for more than two decades. He believes writer's block is a manifestation of irregular work schedules and lack of patience, not a desertion of the muses.

Much of his research on writer's block has focused on academic writers, but "as much is based on 'real' writers," Boice says. People with writer's block, he found, either over- or underestimate how much they can write each day. He believes in short, regular writing times to help overcome blocks. In one study in the 1980s, Boice asked blocked academic writers to prepare five $15 checks. If a writer didn't meet his writing goals, a check would be mailed to an organization that he said he hated.

Within six months of completing the study, seventeen of the twenty writers had at least one article or book chapter accepted for publication. Most continued to write productively at least six months following the experiment.

In another study, Boice used the same regimen of writing daily to meet goals and the same contingency if they failed—the threat of sending checks. This study found that people who met their writing goals under these conditions not only wrote more each day, but they also generated more new ideas for other writing projects than people who wrote spontaneously.

Boice, who has retired from academia but still writes from his North Carolina home, has since adopted a gentler approach to helping people write. Sending those checks to despised groups can make writing unpleasant, so he advises instead using small rewards to encourage yourself to write regularly—if a contingency must be used at all. "I've softened my approach because I want people to be productive and happy as writers," he says.

Boice doesn't believe in the common idea that true writers suffer a kind of creative madness, feeling euphoric while writing in long, inspired binges, but suffering bouts

continued

of depression and writer's block between binges. His studies indicate that new professors who wrote in brief, pleasant, daily sessions wrote more, published more, scored lower on depression tests and had more creative ideas for future writing.

Believing the myth has terrible consequences for many who want to write, he thinks. It implies that mental health and efficiency "actually get in the way of creative productivity," he writes. "So it is, presumably, that only a minority of us, perhaps those with the right genes or muses, are already doomed to write well or not."

The concept that regular writing in short bursts produces more publishable work and induces more creative ideas is hard for people to believe. "I think most people strongly object to what I write about," Boice says. "They say they just don't believe the data. English and composition teachers generally don't like the psychological approach, don't like controlled experiments, and don't even like rules. A lot say you can't teach writing. I love writing and I love helping people."

One of Boice's books, *How Writers Journey to Comfort and Fluency: A Psychological Adventure* (Praeger Publishers, 1994), discusses his thirty-two Rules of Practice to help people use pacing and calm constancy to become "fluent" in writing. "It's more about learning to wait patiently, before plunging into writing, by preparing preliminaries," he says. It's also about doing prewriting tasks, such as conceptual outlining to generate ideas.

A few of his writerly rules:

1. Wait. Don't passively wait for inspiration or impending deadlines. Instead, observe what is being written in your genre, collect information, note the tone and content of published works, consider what is in print and what you can add to this "conversation" between already published writers.

2. Be patient. Impatience leads to writer's block—because people associate writing with rushing and with expecting perfection. It leads to stress, fatigue and thinking of writing as unpleasant.

3. Practice writing regularly. Like many skills, writing becomes easier with practice. And Boice believes regular writing leads to motivation to write more.

4. Stop. Learning to stop is as important as starting. Writers who write in brief, daily sessions often produce more than those who write in long binges.

Simply crossing items off to-do lists feels so good that it rewards you for working toward your writing goals and keeps you writing.

Use these guidelines to help you fill in the charts in this chapter—to organize your time for writing—and finish your writing projects. There are seven general steps to take with any writing project, followed by a set of many smaller tasks that must be done to reach your writing goal.

The General Steps

1. Set reasonable, measurable goals. Let's say a magazine has expressed interest in your idea for an article and wants you to write it on spec (the publisher will only pay you the full fee if the editors like the article enough to publish it). The magazine has given you a month to write the piece. (If you're writing without such an offer, give yourself your own deadline and treat it seriously.) Because you understand the power of the written word, you should write down a specific goal, complete with due date: "Finish article by [due date]."

2. Divide and conquer. View your writing project not as an overwhelming monolith, but as a compilation of many smaller tasks. The reason hard jobs get bypassed is that they're often not written manageably on your list of goals. "Write a book in the next year" is not only huge, it's a nebulous goal, notes Denton. The scope of the project is daunting and the deadline is so far away that it seems unreal. So focus on smaller tasks you must do today, tomorrow, this week and this month to help you reach that goal. You're likelier to accomplish many tasks in the near future than one vague goal in the faraway beyond; the specific tasks help you reach that distant goal step-by-step.

3. Create a plan of ordered tasks. "Figuring out the order of things you need to get done is a priority," Denton says. Writing down these jobs in the order in

---

I find that I need to go to my desk every day, even if I don't feel particularly inspired. Because otherwise on the days when I am inspired, nothing will happen. . . .
I think it's easier, more comforting, to be disciplined about writing than to wait for inspiration to strike. If you wait for inspiration, then you can become so nervous, so insecure—Is it going to happen today? Is it going to happen tomorrow? Why isn't it happening today?—You can fret yourself into a kind of paralysis while waiting for the gods to descend. So it makes more sense to me to be regular—businesslike, even—about it: Go to your study, close the door, invent your confidence.

—Diane Ackerman, poet, essayist and naturalist, quoted in September 1997 *Writer's Digest*

which they should be done keeps you focused, as well as frees your mind to concentrate on the important things—rather than wasting mental energy trying to remember all the niggling details that must be done each day.

4. Set a starting date on your calendar for your writing project. Make it today.

5. Work backward to make a schedule. The most important step in planning the time for your writing project is this one. On your calendar, mark the story's final due date. Then, figure out when each of the specific items, in reverse order, must be completed if you are to meet that deadline with a finished piece. For example, if the story is due June 30, then the mailing deadline might be June 26, the final fact checking and polishing might have to be done by June 25, the second draft may have to be done by June 20, etc.

6. Make a daily to-do list to accomplish the tasks. Next to each item on your list, write the time you think it will take to accomplish it and the deadline for completing it. People commonly put far too many items on to-do lists and, as a result, feel defeated when they have to copy uncompleted items from day to day. As William James once wrote, "Nothing is so fatiguing as the eternal hanging on of an uncompleted task." So jot down what you can reasonably expect to accomplish in a day.

7. This writing plan is likely to be forgotten in the pace of most hectic days unless you also formally make it part of your life. Transfer all your due dates to whatever organizing system you use to remind yourself of your other daily duties. Remember that even primary school children use day planners these days. Whether you think that's a good development for civilization, it's a fact of life that many grown-ups need them, too. Mark your writing deadlines on the daily planner to make them an official part of your day, as important as your other work and your personal commitments. Also mark them on a central calendar in your home or office.

I lacked time and energy. Then I read that a person writing two pages a day could write a book in one year. Anybody, I reasoned, no matter how tired, could write two pages a day. At the end of the year, I had the novel written, and the first publisher I sent it to bought it.

—Dorothy Boone Kidney, author of *Portrait of Debec* (Moody Press, 1972), quoted in April 1994 *Writer's Digest*

Scheduling Refined

Depending on the complexity of your project, you may want to subdivide your writing project. Consider scheduling these mini steps toward your writing goal.

• **The first interview.** Finishing the first interview usually boosts your confidence. After that, the remaining interviews just seem easier to handle. So schedule the first one as early as possible.

• **The note analysis.** Some people wander around in their thickets of notes for hours, getting lost and confused. Consider setting a deadline for having studied your notes and for having important parts highlighted.

• **A rough outline.** Scribble a rough outline as an exercise to start yourself writing something. You can always revise it after you've started work.

• **A deadline for writing the lead.** Deciding the beginning of your story also can help you plan the ending, so this step helps you accomplish two writing tasks at the same time.

• **A second draft.** Many stories benefit by being revised and revised again. If you have time, use it for this.

• **The halfway point.** Breaking a longer piece in half can keep you focused and give you an earlier sense of accomplishment. Ah, half finished already!

The Specifics

Here are some specific tasks you need to do, in the general order you need to do them, to finish many writing pieces. You can use this checklist to help you fill in the chart on page 83 to set up a writing plan to suit you.

1. Read. Take notes. Make copies. Read for content, but also read for what's not there—questions that you need to answer. Read for insight and understanding. Read for new ideas.

Do research in the library, on the Internet and/or at the scene. If you're writing a complex, informational magazine piece, you'll probably need many hours for research and interviewing. If you're writing a personal-experience essay, you may not need any (but you do need time for reflection). Remember, most topics can be researched forever, especially if you use that great time-waster the Internet. Stay focused on your idea, and stop researching it when the information begins to sound repetitive.

2. File your notes immediately, labeling them for easy retrieval later. Don't skip this boring but crucial step. Nothing is more frustrating than spending hours looking for an article you know you've copied.

3. Make a list of people you must interview. Depending on your story, you might want to subdivide this list into (1) official sources, who usually work in government or regulatory agencies; (2) expert sources, who know the topic better than most people; (3) academic sources, who study your topic and may teach others about it; and (4) "real people," whose lives are affected by your topic.

4. List your interview questions. Usually begin with open-ended questions that the source will find easy to answer and will make him warm to the subject—and to you. End with questions that might annoy or even anger the source, but must be asked.

5. Set up interviews. This step is often most difficult to manage, because your schedule must defer to those of your sources. So call people early to set up interviews. But don't be surprised if a source says, "Let's do it now." If that happens, pull out your question list and shoot. Tell all your sources that you may need to talk with them again to check facts to make sure your article is accurate. Most people welcome such follow-up calls.

6. Conduct interviews. You will get better information, and far more descriptive notes, by interviewing people in person. But doing so eats up great quantities of time. Budget according to your time and your story's needs.

7. Read and reread your notes. Highlight important parts. Think about what you've learned. This requires time, too, so budget for it.

Much of *Invisible World* was written in hotel rooms, trains and airplanes across South America and China, but now I'm confined to a dingy little office with a desk, chair, computer and no telephone. I write chronologically, making up the plot as I go along, but I don't hesitate to skip ahead or back as the mood hits me. I have tried to make outlines in advance, but I find it impossible. During the rewrites, though, I make a map of the entire book, page by page, so that I can look objectively at which segments might be disproportionately long. I do the same with dialogue, but on a smaller scale.

—Stuart Cohen, author of *Invisible World* (ReganBooks, 1998), quoted in July 1998 *Writer's Digest*

---

8. Make an outline. Complicated stories probably require formal outlines, with main points and facts to bolster them. One easy way to do this is to write main points on index cards, along with their sources, and rearrange the cards into a logical sequence. Simpler pieces may need only a rough image in your head showing where you want the story to go.

9. Write a first draft. Don't put absurd pressure on yourself by expecting to write a lyrical masterpiece as soon as your fingers hit the keys. It's often easier to write if you get a draft down and tell yourself you'll rework it later to make it sing.

10. Edit or rewrite as often as necessary (or until time runs out). Often, the first draft is too long. Rereading it, or giving it to someone else to read, presents options for tightening it. Work at polishing the ideas, the structure and the language.

11. When you're satisfied, check all the facts in your piece—twice. When it gets published, you can bet a reader will know if you've made a mistake.

12. Mail it. E-mailing pieces to your editor may give you a few extra days to work on a story. But if your publisher wants paper, you must allow a few days in your schedule for the post office to deliver it on time.

13. Work with editors to polish the piece. Editors are paid to ask questions, and they *will* ask questions. Build in time for working with them to make changes on one piece as you're beginning this process again for another.

Resources

BOOKS

How Writers Journey to Comfort and Fluency: A Psychological Adventure by
   Robert Boice (Praeger Publishers, 1994).

Get rid of the family for a while—it worked for me. My husband had a two-week business trip planned, so I sent my young children to their grandparents' house. Then I set myself to a fourteen-hour-per-day writing schedule and stuck to it. I was amazed at how much writing I got done without the usual distractions. (But I have to admit it got a bit lonely at times.)

—Megan V. Davis, coauthor of *Victoria Johnson's Attitude* (Penguin, 1993),
quoted in April 1994 *Writer's Digest*

The Messies Superguide: Strategies and Ideas for Conquering Catastrophic Living by Sandra Felton (Fleming H. Revell, 1991).

Stop Messing Around and Organize to Write by Sandra Felton, Messies Anonymous, 5025 S.W. 114th Ave., Miami, FL 33165.

You Can Find More Time for Yourself Every Day by Stephanie Culp (Betterway Books, 1994).

Checklist for Completing Writing Projects

Use this checklist to set up a writing schedule. Start with the due date and work backward, filling in deadlines that must be met. Transfer all deadlines to a central calendar or organizer so they become part of your daily work plan.

Often the hardest part of writing is simply facing the typewriter each day. Sometimes you're tired, uninspired or just plain scared. Whenever that happens to me, I say to myself: "OK, Ann. Just for today you only have to write two sentences." Once I've written those two sentences, I find that I'm on my way, and before I know it, I've written my daily quota (or more!).

—Ann Herrick, author of *Practice Makes Perfect* (Harlequin Retail Inc., 1988), quoted in April 1994 *Writer's Digest*

WRITING CHECKLIST	Date
Story title:	
Publisher:	
Final due date	
Mailing date	
Final draft due	
Grammar/spelling/punctuation checked	
Fact checking completed	
Polishing/tightening completed	
Second draft completed	
First draft completed	
Lead written	
Final outline completed	
Draft outline completed	
Rereading notes completed	
Interviews completed	
Half of interviews completed	
First interview completed	
Interviews scheduled	
Interview questions listed	
Source list compiled	
Reading completed	
Research completed	
Research begins	

Interview Source Log

Once you've done some research, you'll be ready to list people you need to interview. Include each person's expertise (for example, physician, race car driver, politician, minister) and/or category (official, expert, academic, real people). Use this list to track whom you'll interview and when. Remember to transfer interview times to your daily calendar.

INTERVIEW SOURCE LOG

Story Title:

Publisher:

Interview Date	Interview Time	Source's Name and Phone Number	Source's Expertise/Category

Weekly Activity Log

Fill in this chart if you want a good estimate of where you really spend your time. Under "Clock Time," write the time that you begin an activity. When you start something else, note the new starting time (round it off to the nearest quarter hour). Subtract one from the other and put that answer under "Total Time," how much time you spent on each activity. At the end of the day, rate each activity as 1 (most important), 2 (medium importance) or 3 (not important). Then, ask yourself if you can delegate or simply not do the 3s.

WEEKLY ACTIVITY LOG

Clock Time	Activity	Total Time	Priority Rating

ACTIVITY SUMMARY SHEET

Activity	Time	Activity	Time	Activity	Time	Activity	Time
sleeping		eating		hygiene		drive time	
Totals							

Activity	Time	Activity	Time	Activity	Time
personal		writing		other	
Totals					

SAMPLE: WEEKLY TIME BAR CHART

Divide the total hours spent in each activity by 168 to get a percentage. Then fill in the bar chart below with your percentages to see how you spend your time.

```
     100% _____
      90% _____
      80% _____
      70% _____
      60% _____
% TIME 50% _____
      40% _____
      30% _____
      20% _____
      10% _____
       0% _____
                        ACTIVITY
```

Weekly Time Bar chart

```
     100% _____
      90% _____
      80% _____
      70% _____
      60% _____
% TIME 50% _____
      40% _____
      30% _____
      20% _____
      10% _____
       0% _____
                        ACTIVITY
```

CHAPTER FIVE

The Paper Chase

Writers can go to great lengths to understand their subjects. This may be best exemplified by James Thom, a former journalist who has written a number of acclaimed and best-selling books about the American frontier experience. When Thom decided to write the story of Mary Ingles for his book *Follow the River* (Ballantine Books, 1981), he actually retraced parts of the route Ingles followed when she escaped Indian captivity in 1755.

In an interview following the completion of the book, Thom said he could only write Ingles's story after he had walked in her steps. Thom couldn't trace Ingles's entire six-week trek through the woods along the Ohio and Kanawha rivers, but he made five separate trips to key spots along her route. At times Thom even ate what Ingles had eaten, and at one point he fasted for a week.

For the rest of his research Thom visited Ingles's descendants, read detailed family accounts of her life and studied historic documents. In the long run Thom's research only made his job easier, and it made his account more believable.

This kind of dogged pursuit of authenticity can make your work stand out from the pack, whether you are writing a historical novel or an article on historic cars. To convince readers—and editors—that you know what you are talking about, you must first spend the time to understand your subject.

As you outline your book or article, the idea of research may sound like drudgery, a necessary evil you must go through before you can get to your real work—the writing. Yet what many of us would consider drudgery is actually the most important step in the writing process. Consider, for a moment, that good research is what makes your finished work come alive with realism and truth. Each interview, each trip to the library is what adds excitement and authenticity to your finished piece. Research enlightens you and enables you to enlighten your audience. Research is nothing less than the heart and soul of what we do.

In reality there are only so many subjects you can write about from personal experience. And there are only so many subjects that you can learn firsthand, as Thom did. Fortunately, to learn about other subjects you can rely on others' expertise through interviews (as discussed in chapter seven). The Internet has made millions of information sources available to anyone who can afford a modem (see chapter six). For the rest of this chapter we will focus on how to do paper research, whether at a library, through the government or through some other source.

Whether your research is based on personal experience, interviews, document searches, the Internet or any combination of these, you should approach it with the same dogged professionalism. In the end, the quality of what you write will be based on the quality of what you know and learn. This is true whether you are writing novels, nonfiction books or magazine articles. In all these cases research adds the critical element of realism.

The Right Mind-Set

The quality of what you learn is determined not just by the quality of your source material, but by the mind-set you bring to the project. Approach your research with a real desire to learn. Find enough sources to obtain as many points of view as possible. But do not merely accept the things you read or hear. Ask questions and make your judgments based on factual information. At the same time, challenge your own assumptions. Be willing to consider other ideas and opinions even if it means reevaluating your work or redoing what you have done to date.

How Much Searching?

While thoroughness is important, don't let your research become an end in itself. In Thom's case his book required detailed accounts of events from another century. His reward was a lucrative book deal. You must tailor your research, and the amount of time you spend on it, to the size of the job at hand. To do this keep these simple questions in mind:

- Who is your audience, and how much do they already know?
- Where can the material be located most easily?
- How much time do you have and how much space will you be given?
- How much are you being paid to complete the project?

Where to Look

The task of research is somewhat like the task of writing. More important than where to start is the act of starting. You can't know exactly what an article or book will be until you write it. Similarly, you can't know all the information you need or where your search will lead you until it is underway. You can, however, narrow your choices with some foresight and good planning.

For most topics the best place to conduct paper research is a library. After all, libraries hold the cumulative written knowledge of our entire history and civilization. Practically nothing that is known cannot be found in a library somewhere. Best of all, there are guides (research librarians and reference librarians) to point you in the right direction. Thanks to interlibrary loans, virtually no volume is beyond your reach. With many directories now on CD-ROM and the Internet, searching has never been easier.

There are three types of libraries: public libraries, college libraries and specialized libraries maintained by industries or special interest groups. The federal government is another leading source of information, but many of its publications are also available in larger libraries.

Main Public Libraries

The best places for conducting research are usually main public libraries. The selection of material is unmatched by any suburban branch location (though if you know what you want you can often have it sent from the main library to the branch near you). The reference librarian at your local library is a fine source of information. Many accept phone calls from patrons asking research questions, so long as the questions are specific and can be answered quickly.

Colleges and Universities

A library at a large institution will have more resources available than most branches of your public library. College and university libraries are usually open to the public, though you may not be able to borrow books unless you are affiliated with the school. In addition to the central campus library at most universities, many of the academic departments have their own specialized libraries, which may be open to the public.

Specialized Libraries

There are more than ten thousand special libraries throughout the U.S. While their collections may be limited to certain subjects, many offer an unparalleled amount of information on those subjects, whether medicine, engineering, law, history or art. Most are open to the public at least on a limited basis, though you will probably need permission in advance to gain access. Even those that aren't normally open to the public will likely allow you access if you explain the nature of your research. You can find out about special libraries in the *Directory of Special Libraries and Information Centers* (Gale Research) or in the *Subject Directory of Special Libraries and Information Centers* (Gale Research). Both volumes are available at larger public libraries. The Special Library Association may also be of assistance at 1700 Eighteenth St. NW, Washington, DC 20009, phone: (202) 234-4700, fax: (202) 265-9317 (www.sla.org).

Business Sources

Businesses routinely make information available through their public relations offices, customer service departments and sales staffs. Many trade associations can also provide you with valuable material, including chambers of commerce and tourism offices at the state and local levels. In fact, many of these outlets exist primarily to disseminate information. They are often eager to provide writers with information. The *Encyclopedia of Associations* (Gale Research) and its accompanying volumes *International Organizations* and *Regional, State, and Local Organizations* list thousands of viable information sources.

Federal Government Information

There are several sources for government publications. You can contact the authoring agency directly or use any number of government outlets that serve as information clearinghouses. In many instances the cost to purchase government documents can be prohibitive. Fortunately, many documents are available for free viewing at public libraries or at thousands of other depositories throughout the country. The *Monthly Catalog of U.S. Government Publications*, published by the Government Printing Office (GPO), is one way to find what you need. The GPO's Subject Bibliography Index lists thousands of publications by category. To inquire about government documents try the following agencies:

- The **Federal Information Center** serves as a single point of contact for people who have questions about any federal agency. Its information specialists can also help you locate government documents and publications. Contact at (800) 688-9889 (fic.info.gov).
- The **Census Bureau** has thousands of reports about the U.S. population and economy. It offers statistics on such diverse subjects as fertility, education, mining, ancestry, income, migration, school enrollment, construction and international trade. You can access data through more than two thousand libraries and other locations that serve as data centers and federal depositories. Contact Public Information Office, Room 2705, FB-3, U.S. Census Bureau, Washington, DC 20233, phone: (301) 457-3030, fax: (301) 457-4714 (www.census.gov).
- The **Consumer Information Center** may be the best known distributor of federal documents through its facilities in Pueblo, Colorado. It specializes in consumer-oriented materials, and many of it documents are free or avail-

able for a minimal charge. Contact Superintendent of Documents, Dept. WWW, Pueblo, CO 81009, (888) 878-3256 (www.pueblo.gsa.gov).

- The **General Accounting Office** is the investigative arm of Congress and compiles reports on all aspects of government. All of GAO's unclassified reports are available to the public. Contact U.S. General Accounting Office, P.O. Box 37050, Washington, DC 20013, (202) 512-6000 (www.gao.gov).

- The **Government Printing Office** is the largest distributor of government documents. The GPO provides information to designated libraries and other locations throughout the country, where you can view the information for free. Contact Superintendent of Documents, U.S. Government Printing Office, Washington, DC 20401, (202) 512-1800 (www.access.gpo.gov).

- The **National Technical Information Service** distributes scientific, technical and engineering documents. The staff can perform searches by subject. Contact National Technical Information Service, Springfield, VA 22161, phone: (703) 605-6000, fax: (703) 605-6900 (www.ntis.gov).

Devise a Strategy

A research strategy will save you time and frustration by focusing your attention on the most important information sources, and by ensuring that you don't overlook important information. Depending on your topic you should adapt the following steps to best suit your needs.

1. Develop Your Topic

State your topic as a question. For example, if you are writing about the effect of a food additive on the health of fetuses, pose your concept in the form of a question: "What impact does chemical XYZ have on fetal health?" Next identify the keywords in your question. In this case they are *chemical XYZ* and *fetal health*.

Test the keywords by looking them up in the library catalog and in periodical indexes. Be flexible. If you find too much information and too many sources, narrow your topic. Finding too little information means you may need to broaden your subject.

Narrow your subject by asking yourself questions that better define it:

- Do you want to focus on a specific country?
- What years should you cover?
- Are you more interested in the medical or social consequences?

Expand your subject by asking questions that broaden the scope:

- How safe are food additives in general?
- What are other safety concerns facing expectant parents?
- Are there any related topics to explore, such as food-labeling requirements?

2. Learn Background Information

Reading entries in encyclopedias and articles in newspapers or magazines can give you a quick overview of your subject. This can save you time in the long run by helping you understand the broader context of your subject matter.

Use an online index or newspaper for an overview of more current topics. Use an encyclopedia for topics that are less current or for general background information. Better still, find an encyclopedia or similar source that focuses specifically on your area of study, such as *The Oxford Illustrated History of Medieval Europe* (Oxford University Press, 1992). You can find specialized encyclopedias and reference books in the library catalog or in a reference bibliography (a bibliography of reference sources broken down by subjects).

Don't overlook useful sources that may be listed as further reading at the end of the encyclopedia entry. These can be good starting points for further research.

3. Find Books

You can use the library catalog or a bibliography to find books on your subject. Bibliographies are lists of works on a given subject. They can save you time, especially when they include annotations (descriptions of the works listed). When searching a library catalog, use keywords for a narrow or complex topic. Use subject headings for a broader search.

The subject guide to *Books in Print* (R.R. Bowker Co.) is another great resource for finding books by subject.

To find additional sources, scan the bibliography in the back of each book you use.

4. Find Articles

Periodicals are good sources for keeping up with the latest developments on a subject, because articles are usually more up-to-date than books. Finding articles is a two-step process. You must first look in a periodical index to find listings of useful articles. You can search by subject, author, title, keyword or date. Next check the library's catalog or its list of periodicals to see if it stocks the publication that contains the article you need.

Periodical indexes may be in print or computer-based formats. The printed index *Readers' Guide to Periodical Literature* (H.W. Wilson) is one of the most common and covers popular magazines from 1900 to the present. There are many others, such as the *Business Periodical Index* and *Periodical Abstracts*. Ask at the reference desk if you need help figuring out which index is best for you.

Prior to searching through a periodical index, develop a list with more than one keyword to describe each idea (for example, *atomic energy* and *nuclear energy*).

Another way to find useful articles is to ask an expert on the subject. She should know of useful articles and publications.

Select the Right Source

To make the best use of your time, think ahead about which sources of information are best suited for your type of research.

Books offer the most in-depth coverage of a topic, but the information may be more dated. The author is usually an expert, but the bias may be that of a single individual—the author.

Newspapers offer the most up-to-date coverage and cover a wide range of subjects, but most reporters are generalists with limited expertise in the stories they cover. Try a newspaper for local statistics and current events.

Magazines are similar to newspapers for offering current information. As with newspapers, the writers are not usually experts in the subjects they cover. Magazines are, however, more specialized, assuring that you are more likely to find the information you need. Magazines are more apt to openly represent an editorial bias (conservative or liberal, pro or con) depending on the readership they target.

Journals are highly specialized, offering detailed case studies and analyses. Articles are written by scholars in the field or by others who have done research in the field. Scholarly or scientific journals are less likely to contain bias, but the material may be harder to digest due to technical language.

Quick References

BIOGRAPHY
- *Biography and Genealogy Master Index* (Gale Research)
- *Biography Index* (H.W. Wilson)
- *Contemporary Authors* (Gale Research)
- *Current Biography* (H.W. Wilson)
- *Dictionary of American Biography* (Scribner)
- *Dictionary of National Biography* (Oxford University Press)
- *Dictionary of Scientific Biography* (Scribner)
- *Encyclopaedia Britannica* (Encyclopaedia Brittanica)
- *Who's Who* (St. Martin's Press)
- *Who's Who in America* (A.N. Marquis)

BUSINESS
- *ABI/Inform* (University Microfilms International)
- *Business Dateline* (University Microfilms International)
- *Dictionary of Business, Finance, and Investment* (Drake Publishers)
- *F&S Predicasts*

CURRENT EVENTS
- *CARL Uncover*
- *Keesing's Record of World Events* (Longman)
- *Periodical Abstracts*

EDUCATION
- *Education Index* (H.W. Wilson)
- *The Encyclopedia of Education* (Macmillan)
- *Encyclopedia of Educational Research* (Macmillan)

HUMANITIES (Architecture, Art, Drama, Film, History, Literature, Music, Mythology, Philosophy, Religion)
- *Encyclopaedia Britannica*
- *Humanities Index* (H.W. Wilson)

INTERVIEWS
- *Biography Index*
- *The New York Times*
- *Periodical Abstracts*

MAPS
- *Demographics USA*
- *Information Please Almanac, Atlas and Yearbook* (McGraw-Hill)
- *The Times Atlas of the World* (Times Books)

SCIENCE AND TECHNOLOGY
- *Applied Science and Technology Index* (H.W. Wilson)
- *Biographical Encyclopedia of Scientists* (Marshall Cavendish)
- *Dictionary of Scientific Biography*
- *General Science Index*
- *Handbook of Current Science and Technology* (Gale)
- *How It Works* (Grosset & Dunlap)

- *McGraw-Hill Encyclopedia of Science and Technology* (McGraw-Hill)
- *Milestones in Science and Technology* (Oryx Press)
- *Science and Technology Desk Reference* (Gale Research)
- *Van Nostrand's Scientific Encyclopedia* (Van Nostrand Reinhold)
- *World of Scientific Discovery: Scientific Milestones and the People Who Made Them Possible*

SOCIAL SCIENCE (Economics, Government, Political Science, Psychology, Social Work, Sociology, Urban Studies)
- *A Dictionary of the Social Sciences*
- *Encyclopedia of American Social History* (Scribner)
- *Encyclopedia of Social History* (Garland)
- *Social Sciences Index* (H.W. Wilson)
- *Social Sciences Ondisc*
- *World Quality of Life Indicators* (ABC-CLIO)

SPEECHES
- *Vital Speeches of the Day*
- *Weekly Compilation of Presidential Documents*

STATISTICS
- *America's Top-Rated Cities: A Statistical Handbook* (Universal Reference Publications)
- *The Gallup Poll*
- *The Information Please Almanac, Atlas and Yearbook*
- *Statistical Abstract of the United States* (GPO)
- *Statistical Masterfile*
- *The World Almanac*

Tips and Tricks

- Work from the general to the specific. Look for general background information first. Use that to better define your search for more specific information.

- Develop a rapport with the reference or research librarians at your local library. They live to help people find information.

- A quick check of an encyclopedia (for less current topics) or an online source or newspaper (for current topics) can provide a quick overview of your subject—saving you time in the long run.

- To get a quick overview of a large book or document, check the index for a list of illustrations, charts, tables or graphs. Lengthy, complicated subjects are often summarized with charts and graphs. This is especially true of government and scientific documents. If you find a graphic that is of particular interest, scan the text pages around it for related details. Also look for an executive summary at the front of the document and conclusion statements at the end of each section.

- If you have trouble finding information on your subject, it could be you are using the wrong search words. For instance, instead of *Afro-American* try *African-American*. Check your words against the subject heading list in the directory you are searching, or use a thesaurus to come up with alternate words.

- When retrieving your books from the library shelves, browse nearby books to see if any others might be useful. Library shelves are arranged so that books about the same topic are generally kept near each other.

- Keep a list of what you find and where you found it. You may need to go back to it later.

- A volume number usually refers to the year that a periodical was published. Volume 10 refers to a magazine in its tenth year of publication.

- When you need facts, assume there is a reference source that has what you need. There nearly always is.

- Most books and many articles themselves have bibliographies that list additional sources of information. By following these leads you can amass a body of information quickly.

- A local college or university may have a professor who specializes in your subject area. If so, he will likely have a list of recommended reading on the subject. Call the public information office and inquire.

- Don't overlook that most ubiquitous of books, the yellow pages. Doing a story on home improvement and need an expert source? Open your yellow pages to *Remodeling* and start dialing.

Evaluate Sources

As important as finding information is finding good information. The author's credentials as well as the timeliness of the book or article are factors to consider in evaluating the quality of the material you find.

Book Review Index (Gale Research) and *Book Review Digest* (H.W. Wilson) are good sources for checking whether a book is well respected. *Who's Who in America* (A.N. Marquis), *Biography Index* (H.W. Wilson) or the biographical information in a publication itself are also useful in checking the author's expertise.

Also note whether the author or publication is closely aligned with an organization. If so, ask yourself what biases that might create.

Subjects such as medicine and computers require timely information because they are easily affected by changing technology. Is the source current enough for your topic?

With the above help, it's fairly easy to write out a list of places to get information. What to do when you get to those places is another story. There is more than one path to the same point, and some are quicker than others. Think of unique ways to get the information you need, and think of unique ways to use the information you get. In other words, be as creative in your research as you are in your writing.

CHAPTER SIX

The Cyber Chase

Like much of the technology we rely on in our daily lives, the Internet started as a military defense project. In fact, the Internet might not have evolved when it did if not for the specter of nuclear destruction that loomed over America in the 1960s.

As America sank deep into the Cold War, traditional forms of communication—telephones, televisions and radios—were considered too vulnerable. After all, they relied on switching centers and broadcast points that could be easily targeted. The Internet was envisioned as a way to tie thousands of computers together in a web of communication, with no single point being any more important than any other. Knock out any part of the system, and the rest could still function.

Universities and military contractors were among the first to link their computers together in the early 1970s, and a curious trend developed. The network quickly evolved into a high-speed, electronic post office. People began to collaborate on projects, transfer notes and just gossip.

As personal computers grew abundant in the 1980s, more and more systems were added to the growing phenomenon that came to be known as the Internet. In 1991 the government opened the communication web to individuals who, like their predecessors, began using the system to collaborate on projects, transfer notes and just gossip.

Understanding the evolution of the Internet is critical to understanding its makeup today. Unlike radio and television, an open-ended system quickly takes on the character of its users. In this way the Internet has more in common with the U.S. mail than most forms of electronic communication. Like the mail, the system contains whatever words or pictures its users decide to put into it.

The amount of information available on the Internet is mind boggling. There are millions of Web pages maintained by government agencies, universities, libraries, companies, organizations and individuals. Some experts estimate that the amount of information online is expanding at several pages per second. You can read and download government reports, newspaper and magazine articles, research studies, even the full text of some books. While the Web can't supplant libraries and other sources of detailed information (at least not yet), using it for research is like one-stop shopping.

The World Wide Web is also like a flea market. In the vast array of information, each item is useful to someone. But finding what is meaningful to you often requires you to sort through a lot of junk. Knowing the shortcuts to get what you want can save you a lot of valuable time.

Three Ways to Search

The Web has no comprehensive directories or indexes because it is constantly changing. There are, however, several hundred sites that serve as search points or partial directories. Using these sites as a starting point can save you valuable time and help ensure a successful search.

1. Search Sites

There are two types of basic search sites: those that offer subject directories and those that offer search engines. (Some sites offer both.)

Subject directories are set up to help you browse through general information on a topic. Subject directories feature lists of topics, such as art, business, computers, education, government, health, recreation and science. Under each of these topics are layers of subtopics. The subtopics are in fact hyperlinks. Point at them and click and they take you to other Web sites that deal specifically with their topics. Subject guides, then, are like subject headings in the library. They direct you to a spot where more information is available. While far from comprehensive, they can give you an overview of the information available on your topic.

Search engines help you find more specific information on a subject. They constantly scan the Web to create indexes of information. When you enter a word or phrase and hit the search button, the search engine creates a list of Web pages that relate to your subject. That list can include thousands of sites. Many of these have also incorporated subject guides.

AltaVista (www.altavista.com)

Excite (www.excite.com)

Google (www.google.com)

HotBot (www.hotbot.com)

InfoSeek (www.infoseek.com)

Lycos (www.lycos.com)

WebCrawler (www.webcrawler.com)

Yahoo! (www.yahoo.com)

2. Metasearch Sites

These sites send your search request to several different search engines at once, giving you a consolidated report of what is available. This can increase your results. It also increases the chance that you will be deluged with thousands of sites. Thus, these are best used for searching obscure topics. Metasearch engines can also save you time by giving you a quick overview of what is available using certain keywords or phrases.

alltheweb (www.alltheweb.com)

dogpile (www.dogpile.com)

Internet Sleuth (www.isleuth.com)

MetaCrawler (www.go2net.com)

ProFusion (www.profusion.com)

3. Specialized Search Sites

Some search engines are subject specific, like News Index (which indexes articles and publications around the world), AskERIC (education) and Thomas (govern-

---

Words of Caution

There are thousands of Web sites filled with credible information. While the Internet is a great research tool, it is far from perfect. Consider the following points to steer past some of the pitfalls.

1. While the Web opens the door to galaxies of information, you don't always know the level of expertise of the provider. Cross-check information if you are not sure of the source.

2. Hyperlinks are handy, but they can be distracting. It's easy to spend hours searching the Web only to have little information to show for it when you are finished. One way to keep yourself disciplined is to set a time limit for your search. Don't forget, sometimes the best and quickest source is a plain old encyclopedia, book, magazine or, better yet, a real live person.

3. Web searches are good at uncovering snippets of information buried deep in a document. Then again, many Web pages only contain excerpts and overviews. And since the Web is relatively new, much of the information only goes back several years. Be careful not to miss the broader context of the information you encounter.

---

ment). These types of sites are good places to start your research because they focus your search on Web pages more likely to cover your topic in detail.

AskERIC (www.askeric.org)

Medline (www.nlm.nih.gov)

News Index (www.mwsearch.com)

Thomas (www.thomas.loc.gov)

Improve Your Results

You can greatly improve the results you get from a search engine by the way you use keywords and various symbols that can act as search tools. Although every search engine is different, most allow you to use the following methods to refine your search.

Connect the Thoughts

Conducting a search with the words *New York Times* would generate a list of any site that contains either the word *times, York* or *new.* You might get a site about

Times Square. The solution is to place *AND* or a plus sign (+) between each word, for example, *New AND York AND Times* or *New+ York+ Times*. This ensures that any site listed will at least contain all three words.

To find sites that contain your string of words in the same order that you type them, enclose the set of words with quotation marks (*"New York Times"*).

Be Exclusive

Conversely you can further define your search by using *AND NOT* or a minus sign (-) to exclude certain words. *Indy AND winner AND NOT Unser* would generate a list of sites containing *Indy* and *winner*, but not the name *Unser*.

Parentheses can sometimes be used for more complicated searches. For example, to find documents that contain the word *Indy* and either the name *Unser* or *Foyt* you would type *Indy AND (Unser OR Foyt)*.

Feast or Famine

Most search engines provide a list of search results ranked in order of relevance. Sites at the top of the list are most likely to have the results you seek. It is not unusual to get hundreds of thousands of responses to an Internet search. Instead of feeling like you hit the jackpot, you may be left looking for the proverbial needle in the haystack— no better off than when you started. Whether your search produces too many results or not enough, the frustration is the same. The solution is to refine your search strategy.

If your problem is too few results, you were probably too specific in your search. If you use five keywords in your search, try using the three or four most probable words. Or try redefining your search with new words. For too many results take the opposite tack: Be more specific; add keywords to better define your target.

If you use the Web long enough you will eventually encounter a search that produces no results. In this case double-check that you are spelling your search words properly. You may also need to pick different words altogether.

Search Tips
- Read the help menu of any new search site you visit.
- Use search words that are as descriptive and specific as possible.

- Most search engines pull their information from the same sources. The only difference is in the way you operate the search engine. Your best bet is to pick a couple of them to use routinely and learn how those particular search engines work.

- As a general rule use singular forms of search words to increase your chance of success. For instance, most search engines will list sites containing the words *children* and *child* if you type in the singular word *child.*

- Capitalization is sometimes important when searching for proper names.

- There is no single source. You have multiple options for finding the same information, but you may need to look at multiple sites to get a complete picture of your subject.

- Don't expect everything you find to be fact. Anyone can publish anything online. Even respected sites are sometimes put together quickly. Verify information by checking multiple sources.

- Correct spelling is important. Your search results are only as good as the information you provide.

- Enter multiple spellings if more than one correct version exists, such as *Huck Finn* and *Huckleberry Finn.*

- Be creative. Think of multiple words or phrases to define your search. For example, *automobile history* may produce different results than *automotive history.*

- Look to these parts of Web site addresses for clues about the site owners or operators: .com (commercial business), .org (nonprofit organization), .gov (federal government) and .edu (university).

Play It Safe

Once you find your information you may want to download a file to your computer. There are millions of downloadable files on the Internet, including sounds, graphics, text and computer software. There are also times when you may want to purchase information or products that you find. On the Internet this usually means sending

---

Web Jargon

ADDRESS: (e.g.: www.writersdigest.com/bookclub) The first part identifies the actual site (www.writersdigest.com), also known as the domain name. Any part after the domain name refers to a subsection within that site. In this case, the address directs your computer to the bookclub section of the *Writer's Digest* Web site.

BOOKMARK: A placeholder that you activate with the click of your mouse to store a Web address on your computer. This allows you to jump back to the page later.

BROWSER: A program that displays Web pages on your computer.

HYPERLINK: A word or picture that links you to other places on the Internet. Clicking on a hyperlink is like pushing the button on your car radio. Your computer takes you to another page on the same Web site or to an entirely different Web site.

PAGE: The basic unit of a Web site. Think of each Web site as layers of pages through which you navigate by clicking your mouse.

WORLD WIDE WEB (WWW): The part of the Internet that you navigate by pointing and clicking a computer mouse to activate words or pictures.

---

credit card information to the provider. In both cases—downloading or purchasing—keep in mind safety and security issues. You need not be afraid, only cautious.

Computer Viruses

Any file downloaded from the Internet can contain a virus. A computer virus is a destructive code hidden within a file and can damage existing files stored on your computer. While it cannot harm your computer hardware, it can damage or erase data, which may be even more costly.

Few if any files that you encounter will contain a virus. Yet a good antivirus program is a sound investment. Think of it this way: Your home will likely never be targeted by a burglar, but you certainly consider locks a sound investment. Antivirus programs are relatively cheap and easy to use. You should install one on your system and always scan new files for viruses before opening them.

Antivirus software can only protect you against viruses that it recognizes. As new viruses are created, antivirus publishers provide updates for their software (often for free). Acquiring these updates keeps your virus protection current.

ANTIVIRUS TIPS

- Don't open files received from strangers.
- Routinely create backup copies of important files.
- Use an antivirus program and keep it up-to-date.

Security Issues

Purchasing items or information on the Internet can also be quite safe, but you must exercise due caution. Giving someone your credit card number always carries an element of risk. To protect yourself, only do business with established vendors whose names or products you know and trust. Fortunately, reputable Internet merchants have incorporated software into their Web sites that encodes the information that travels between you and them. This encryption technology makes it extremely difficult for third parties to steal the information.

If you are concerned about privacy, remember that you are sitting at home, or some other protected place. In most cases no one will know anything about you that you don't tell them. You won't see anything that you don't choose to see. As with television you can change the "channel" or flip the switch at any time. Any E-mail that arrives unsolicited can easily be trashed. Is sending your credit card number over the Internet any more dangerous than giving the same information to an unknown store clerk or to someone on the other end of the telephone?

Research Sites

American Medical Association (www.ama-assn.org) contains information on health and fitness, including access to the *Journal of the American Medical Association* (*JAMA*). This site also has links to other medical sites.

Argus Clearinghouse (www.clearinghouse.net) offers a collection of Web sites and directories searchable by subject. Categories include art, business, engineering, health and science, just to name a few.

Britannica Internet Guide (www.britannica.com) indexes and reviews thousands of Web sites to provide a searchable directory of information sources.

Census Bureau (www.census.gov) maintains detailed information about the U.S. population and economy, much of which is accessible through this Web page.

Central Intelligence Agency (www.odci.gov/cia) offers a publication section with maps and statistics for hundreds of countries, including information on heads of state.

Consumer Information Center (www.pueblo.gsa.gov) specializes in consumer-oriented materials. Many of its guides are available free online.

Department of Health and Human Services (www.hhs.gov) allows you to browse through information on health and medicine, including such topics as disease prevention, pediatrics, elderly care and health care fraud. It also has links to libraries, databases, online journals and medical dictionaries.

Editorial Freelancers Association (www.the-efa.org) has links to dozens of government, medical and library sites.

Electronic Text Center (etext.lib.virginia.edu) offers thousands of humanities texts in multiple languages. Many are available to the general public.

Encyclopedia Mythica (www.pantheon.org/mythica) maintains a database of myths, legends and folklore with more than five thousand definitions of gods and goddesses and legends from around the world.

555-1212.com (www.555-1212.com) provides telephone and Web directory services, including area codes, phone numbers, yellow pages, reverse lookup, Web sites, international directories and E-mail addresses.

General Accounting Office (www.gao.gov) is the investigative arm of Congress. Many of the GAO's unclassified reports are available to the public online.

InfoSpace (www.infospaceinc.com) provides a global directory of telephone numbers, E-mail addresses, fax numbers and mailing addresses.

Internet Public Library (www.ipl.org) provides library-type services via the Internet, including a comprehensive list of online texts, a ready-reference collection plus links to search engines and more than two thousand newspaper and magazine sites around the world.

Legal Information Institute (supct.law.cornell.edu/supct) provides information about Supreme Court decisions.

Library of Congress (lcweb.loc.gov) presents American history in pictures, sounds and text.

Medscape (www.medscape.com) includes medical articles and a comprehensive database of articles in medical journals.

National Political Index (www.politicalindex.com) contains thousands of links to political Web sites at the local, state and national levels.

National Writers Union (www.nwu.org) offers hundreds of links to search engines, Web directories, libraries, government sites, reference collections, newspapers and databases.

Search.Com (www.search.com) allows users to browse popular Web sites by category or browse Web directories and specialty databases.

Internet Mailing Lists

Forget what you normally think about mailing lists. On the Internet they have nothing to do with ads. They are, in fact, great sources of information. To understand them, think of them as communities of people who share an interest in a topic and enjoy discussing it by E-mail. Unlike the disjointed discussions that take place in chat rooms, where dozens of people talk back and forth at once, mailing lists lend themselves to thoughtful discussions.

Another type of mailing list operates in a newsletter format, where a single writer or moderator publishes an E-mail to an interested audience. A good example is Keith Dawson's "Tasty Bits from the Technology Front" (TBTF).

If you specialize in a certain subject, a mailing list can be a good place to keep up-to-date on a particular issue. But beware, mailing lists groups are not good places to drop in uninvited and begin asking questions. They are forums for members to bring something valuable to the discussion.

A Few Words to the Wise

Many lists are not meant for the general public, so you must do some research before you can join in. For example, a list that goes by the name "Poets" may have nothing to do with poetry. It could be a group of friends who just happened to pick that name for reasons known only to them.

Always research a group before joining. Barging in, however easy it may be, is no way to be accepted by a group of strangers—no more than if you barged in on a group of strangers having lunch in a restaurant. Even if the group is open to the public, it will have many longtime members who have developed their own sense of community—complete with their own sensitivities. The best way to join in is to watch quietly for a few weeks to learn how the members act. Then maybe you can E-mail one of the experienced members and introduce yourself. Certainly read the list of frequently asked questions before you converse. This can save you a lot of time and keep you from wasting someone else's.

Keep in mind that as you "converse" online no one can see your facial expressions or body language. They can only judge you based on your words. You may not think this makes a difference until you experience how people react, or don't react. A funny remark you might make in person loses its meaning when you strip away body language and facial expressions. Courtesy is of the utmost importance whenever you communicate via the Web. If in doubt, don't "say" it.

Use sites like Liszt (www.liszt.com) or Deja.com (www.deja.com) to find mailing lists of interest to you.

CHAPTER SEVEN

The People Chase

Part One: Popping the Questions

It's been said that a good interview is just like a good conversation. That's not so.

In a good conversation, it's polite for the folks involved to ask questions of each other and to listen with equal interest to the answers. It's a time for *mutual* discovery and communication. But an interview is by definition a lopsided interaction. The interviewee probably doesn't care much about the person popping the questions, and the interviewer is probably doing more than simply enjoying himself. Interviewing is, after all, work.

But it shouldn't feel like work, and that's what the interviews-are-conversations theory is all about. If a person being interviewed feels as if she is talking to an old friend, the interview is more likely to produce powerful anecdotes, colorful quotes and revealing information. Yet, before a source feels comfortable with an interviewer, the interviewer has to relax—a tough trick for many beginners, for whom antacid is as essential for an interview as pen and paper.

In an effort to calm your nervous stomach, we've included in this chapter resources for finding people to interview for your stories, tips on how to interview people, and some mix-and-match, interview-starting questions.

But be forewarned: Nothing can take the place of doing your homework before an interview. There's no excuse for asking someone who's just earned a Pulitzer prize whether she's won any awards lately. Before doing the interview, head to the library or go online and look up background on the topic and your interview subject, if possible. Research will help you devise questions.

Don't think you have to know everything about the topic prior to interviewing someone. It's perfectly OK to tell a source that you've read his latest report on waste-water treatment options, but you need him to explain the finer details. (In fact, sometimes playing dumb is the best way to get people to open up to you.) Most people are grateful that an interviewer has taken time to try to understand their business, and many enjoy assuming the role of a teacher to an interested pupil. Still, the more you learn about the topic, the less likely you are to be confused by a source's statements or bamboozled by someone who wants to evade controversial issues.

Figure out who you'll need to interview, what you hope to get from them, and what approach you'll need to take. Despite what you see on certain television interview shows, being unfailingly polite when requesting interviews and thanking your source at the start and end of the interview is the professional approach.

Jot down a list of questions that pertain specifically to your topic before the interview. You will probably need to ask yes-or-no questions, designed to gather information or provide verification ("Did the dress really cost $10,000?"), as well as open-ended questions, designed to encourage the source to describe events, processes, thoughts and emotions ("How did you know she was the woman for you?"). Start with the easy questions and end with the explosive ones. That way, if the source ends the interview after a touchy question, at least you'll have something in your notes from this source.

> **In the final analysis, the best way to get an interview is to have faith in yourself and your purpose. This sense of professionalism and self-confidence will communicate itself to the respondent, even over the phone. It's in your voice. Too many novice interviewers feel that they are so worthless and miserable that no one could possibly want to talk with them. That, too, communicates itself, making it a self-fulfilling prophecy.**
>
> —Ken Metzler, *Creative Interviewing* (Prentice Hall, 1977)

Don't overwhelm the source with questions. You want the source to do most of the talking. Just ask questions then listen. National Public Radio's *Morning Edition* anchor Bob Edwards once said his two favorite interview questions were "Oh?" and "No!"

Don't rely entirely on the questions in this chapter for your interviews. Think of them as catalysts. Add your own to the mix. Or, after you devise a list of questions based on your research, scan the list below and include those that you think will help flesh out the interview. Then turn to part three of this chapter for help in finding people to interview.

Finally, relax. Interviewing can be the most fun part of the writing process, as you're free to approach people you never could hope to meet under ordinary circumstances. So bring your notebook, pen and tape recorder, and leave your antacid tablets at home.

Personality

"Who" is the foremost question in the sextet of journalistic queries, followed by what, when, where, why and how. When you write profiles, *who* is paramount, along with *what* that person did. However, finding out more about who you're interviewing is quite useful for many other types of stories. It's often a good idea to observe the person, as well as ask questions, to gather color to add to your stories. Try out some of these questions to help you learn about a source's personality.

- How did you decide to go into your profession/avocation?
- How long have you been doing this?
- What did your parents think of your decision? Your friends?
- What is a typical day like? (Or for the reticent: How does a typical day start for you, how does it progress, and how does it end?)
- Why do you think people believe your work is important? Why do you believe it is?
- When did you know that you would become what you are today? How did that knowledge change your life?
- What have you accomplished that makes you most proud?

- What mistakes have you made and what have you learned from them?
- How did you end up in this town?
- How did it feel when you reached your goal (or lost the battle)?
- How did you meet your spouse?
- How many children do you have?
- Do you own pets? What kind? How many?
- How do you juggle the demands of career and family life?
- What do you wish you could change about your life (career/cause)?
- What do you do to relax?
- Who was your mentor? What did you learn from him or her?
- Who are your best friends? Enemies?
- What do you read for work? For fun?

Emotions

Some TV journalists have rightly earned contempt for pushing a microphone in the face of a grieving parent of a dead child and asking, "How does it feel?" Yet, our emotions tie us together; they draw readers deeply into stories and books and reward them with a rush of recognition and understanding.

Observation and description can be better than quotes in conveying emotions in your writing. It's more powerful to write that tears trickled into the wrinkles in the elderly woman's face and dripped steadily on the bedclothes of her comatose husband than to quote her saying, "I felt sad." But if you're not there at the moment of turmoil, you'll have to ask how it felt. When you do, show respect for your sources who have experienced pain, and ask your questions gently.

> If you go in there with a laundry list of questions and you've got blinders on and you don't observe what's going on, you really are going to miss the guts of the story. You keep your eyes open. . . . I hate the laundry list approach. Sometimes I'll use it if all I'm interested in is a factual response. But most of the time I'm interested in an emotional response and I'm trying, even in the half-hour interview, to get a little closer to this guy than might ordinarily be possible.
>
> —William E. Blundell, reporter, *The Wall Street Journal*

Asking about positive emotions is easier and much more fun. Just smile or laugh with your source, and ask how good it felt.

Skim through the list below for some ideas on wording difficult questions about emotions. You'll notice that some aren't questions at all—they're exclamations designed to elicit a response. These can be less intrusive than a question.

- I know this might be painful for you to talk about, but it will help people to understand your story. Can you describe what you were feeling at the moment when _____?
- What was your _____ (your friends'/your family's) reaction? How difficult was it?
- Can you please tell me about the emotions that you felt?
- How did you recover?
- How long did the feeling last?
- What an awful time it must have been for you.
- I'm so sorry.

Anecdotes

Little stories within stories add depth and interest to your writing. The problem is that the surest way of creating amnesia in another person is to ask, "Do you remember any good stories about this?" You can always leave your card and ask the person to call you if he does remember any scintillating anecdotes, but getting the stories at the interview is more efficient. Sometimes questions beginning with *when* help people remember good anecdotes.

- When did you realize that you were going to become a _____?
- When did you first meet?
- When did you make up your mind? How?
- When was there a turning point?
- When did it all begin?
- When did you decide to go ahead (or turn back)?
- At what point did things begin to go your way (or against you)?
- At what moment did you know that this organization (or cause) was special (or not worth your trouble)?

Information

You will rely on people to give you information, not just to describe emotions and reminisce about anecdotes. Often, the substance of the story can be broken into four steps, suggested some years ago by Professor LaRue Gilleland of the University of Nevada. They are known as GOSS, for goals, obstacles, solutions and start over.

- What were your (or your organization's) **goals**?
- What **obstacles** did you face?
- How did you find **solutions** to those obstacles?

The last *S* means that you often need to **start over** and probe for details and background. Ken Metzler, author of *Creative Interviewing* (Prentice Hall, 1977), suggests adding *EY* to the GOSS formula: *E* to ask the source to **evaluate** the information and *Y* as a reminder to ask **why**. Using these questions as the scaffolding, it's easy to sprinkle your own probes among them.

- If you had known then what you know now, what would you have done differently?
- What mistakes did you make and what did you learn from them?
- Would you advise others to do it that way?
- Was it worth it?
- Who are the experts in this field (or the leaders in this endeavor or this industry), so I can contact them?
- What journals cover this field the best, so I can go read them?

People on Personalities

People enjoy telling stories about other people. These anecdotes make profiles and other articles come alive. Here are some questions to help get people started.

- When did you meet? How?
- What was your initial impression of this person?
- How has that changed?
- If you were to describe this person to your next-door neighbor, what would you say about him?

- Does he remind you of anyone (or anything)?
- When were you ever angry with this person?
- When did this person make you glad to know him?
- Why is this person's work (or actions) important?
- How will this person's work (or actions) affect the lives of others?
- How has this person's work (or actions) helped you? Hurt you?
- Who else should I talk with about this person?

Going Fishing

Often, interviews help you discover new story ideas. If you find yourself finished with an interview for one story and your source is friendly and willing, try fishing for a few other ideas.

- What types of things concern you (or your group) most right now?
- What new projects are coming up?
- What trends will affect your business?
- How will the future bring changes for you (or your group)?
- If you could, what would you change about your organization?
- When people talk to you about this group, what do they complain about most often?
- What do they praise?
- Has your group won any awards lately?
- If something new happens on this, would you please call me?

Follow-Ups

It's not clear whether novelist Gustave Flaubert, architect Ludwig Mies van der Rohe or art historian Aby Warburg first said, "God is in the details." But whoever said it knew what he was talking about. And even though the saying has become corrupted to "The devil is in the details," the meaning remains the same. Big things merely sketch an outline; little things make it living color. After reading a story about a man who killed another during an argument about a bag of potato chips, a newspaper editor once asked the reporter, "How big was the bag?"

Few sources volunteer all the details you will need to make readers feel as if they are *in* your story. You'll have to prompt your sources with follow-up questions, a few of which are listed below. You'll have to make a point to look for the telling detail. Because these questions can become pesky, it's a good idea to let sources know what you're up to by stating first, "I'd like to know about that in much more detail because it's so interesting. Let me ask you some specific questions."

- At what moment did you know that this organization (or cause) was special (or not worth your trouble)?
- Exactly when did the problem start?
- How did it start?
- Can you describe everything in the room (at the scene)?
- Who was there?
- Where were they standing?
- What were they wearing?
- How did they behave?
- What did they (she, he) say?
- What did they do next? And after that?
- How many? How much? How long? How soon?
- What was the weather like? (Weather often makes a good metaphor, and you'd be surprised how many people remember the weather at important moments.)
- What color was it?
- What did it feel like? Smell like? Sound like? Taste like? Look like?
- What were you thinking at the time?
- How much did it cost?
- How much did it weigh?
- Where was it?
- Exactly when did it end?

Part Two: Interviewing Tips

Why?

The peerless follow-up question is, of course, "Why?" But the problem with asking why is that its single syllable can seem abrupt and provoking. It can jab the source like a poke in the ribs, inducing defensiveness. Try softening the thrust of this necessary monosyllable by cushioning it inside other words: "Do you remember why you made that plan?" or "What an interesting idea. Why do you say so?" All those words really mean, "Why?" They just sound nicer.

When Redundancy Is Good

Prepare for interviews by assuming something will go wrong. Your tape recorder will tie the tape in bows. The batteries will die a silent death. Your pen will run dry or unleash a flood. These things don't always happen . . . but eventually, they all will. So, to borrow a term from computer systems people (who know a thing or two about backing things up), *create redundancy.* Bring two tapes, three pens, spare batteries, and several notebooks to every interview. You may not be ready for any-thing—a reporter at *The Cincinnati Post* once had to interview a man in a sauna, sans everything. But you'll be ready for most.

The Silent Treatment

Some people just aren't garrulous. You'll ask a question designed to encourage a person to expound on a life-altering event, and she'll answer in a five-word declarative sentence and stop talking. You have two options if this happens: (1) probe for details, asking multitudes of follow-up questions, or (2) simply remain silent, pen in hand, a half smile on your expectant face. Such silence can be so uncomfortable that reluctant sources may start talking again.

Beware of Body Language

For a class assignment at Northern Kentucky University, students had to interview a teacher. Several of them talked with teachers who shared a large office space with Mary, who noticed that most of these nervous, first-time interviewers exhibited the same body language. They hunched over their notepads, scribbling furiously and never looking up. After the first question, the interviewees saw only the tops of the students' heads.

Remember, an interview is a form of interpersonal communication. Look at the person you're interviewing every now and then. Smile. Nod. Appear interested.

You also can use facial expressions instead of questions. Often, a confused or doubting look on your face will prompt the interviewee to try to explain more without even being asked.

Bring a wandering interview subject back to the point by waving a finger to get his attention, without speaking to interrupt him—which feels rude.

Notice your source's body language, too. Did a question make him squirm? Laugh out loud? Stand up and pace? Describe his reaction in your writing.

The Waitress Routine

Asking questions is not enough. Listening to and understanding the answers is the whole point of an interview. So, particularly for complex interviews, adopt the technique most American waitresses have used for years: After one hears your order she asks, "So you want a burger with mustard, pickles and no onions, super-sized fries and a Diet Coke?" Turn your source's answers into reflective questions: "So let me see if I got this right. Are you saying . . . ?" If you get it wrong, the source is usually grateful for the chance to set you straight.

Ask for Help

Unless you're writing an investigative piece that could send people to jail, the people you interview are likely to be friendly—or at least not hostile. Most of their mothers brought them up right. It's OK to exploit those two facts. Few people find it easy to turn down someone who says, "Could you please help me?" If you need help in understanding a complex subject, be direct and ask for assistance.

Be There

The best interviews are done in person. It's far easier for someone to cut short a phone interview, or worse, to work on something else as he absentmindedly answers your questions. E-mail interviews solve the problem of taking notes. But you can never be quite sure who has typed those marvelous responses, or terrible ones—some people just can't communicate well in writing. It's also easier to ignore electronic questions than spoken ones, and it's harder for the interviewer to probe for details electronically. So try to do your initial interview in person, and then ask if you can follow up via phone or E-mail to check facts or pose questions that may occur to you later.

Admit That You Don't Know

You're interviewing a source and she uses a term that, despite your research, you've never heard before. Not wishing to display your ignorance, you decide to let it pass. She uses it again, and then later, again. In fact, you discover that this topic is of utmost importance to her. It's often painful for beginning—and experienced—interviewers, but sometimes you simply have to admit your ignorance. Do so, apologize, and ask her to explain.

But don't let sources intimidate you. Sometimes, people use jargon and multi-syllabic words in an effort to impress or evade. One of the best interviewing questions ever asked is simple: "What does that mean?" One of the best final questions to pose is: "Have I forgotten to ask something important?"

Part Three: Getting to the Source

You'd be surprised who is willing to talk with you. Famous people, people who have just had the worst experiences of their lives, people who don't like your profession or your looks, people who are tired of being interviewed, people who are busier than anyone ever should be. The big surprise is often how nice people are to interview.

When you think about people to interview, think first about the people you already know and the people they know. Somewhere in that network of folks is somebody who might be willing to give you background on your topic. Ask for a chat, and remember to ask him for the names of other people to talk with and experts in the field. Also ask librarians, those marvelous people whose vocation is to find information for others.

Remember, too, that important people employ other people to arrange interviews. Organizations, universities and businesses have public relations people—also called community relations people, marketing communications people or public information officers—who want to get publicity for the people in their organizations. Call them.

Your library or Internet research will inevitably lead you to sources; simply call the people who wrote the encyclopedia entries, research papers or government reports that you find. Often, the best route to finding a local source is to use the yellow pages to find companies or groups in your area. If you're unsure which state agency handles your topic, call the governor's office and ask for the name and number of the public information officer who can help direct you. Call the mayor's office for help finding city personnel.

Many books and millions of Web pages can also help you find sources. You can post requests for interviews on electronic mailing lists or search the Net for people you'd otherwise not be able to reach.

We've listed here some of our favorite sources for finding people. Many of these books are available in libraries. Of course, a few people will turn you down or won't return your calls, but frankly, if one person says no to an interview request, usually others will be happy to talk with you. Few sources are irreplaceable, and persistence is the key to getting to the source.

Resources

BOOKS

The Almanac of American Politics (National Journal Group). This book is an oxymoron: It's an interesting reference book. It gives brief biographical information about senators, representatives and governors, and it includes their records and election results and often fascinating information about their states and districts. It also includes office locations, telephone numbers and E-mail addresses.

The College Blue Book (Macmillan). This lists almost 3,000 colleges in the U.S. and Canada and degrees they offer. It gives main telephone numbers, which you can call to ask for the public relations department for help in finding professors who are experts in various fields.

Congressional Directory (GPO). This federal government publication lists members of Congress, from the vice-president on down, with addresses and phone numbers, brief biographies and committee information.

Current Biography Yearbook (H.W. Wilson). This is a compilation of biographies about important people, often well written and interesting. It also includes contact information.

Encyclopedia of Associations. This three-volume tome, indexed by subject, is a wonderful compendium of descriptions of groups of all types, with contact information. For example, the thirty-third edition lists five associations dedicated to the mouse, including The Rat Fan Club and the American Fancy Rat and Mouse Association. The encyclopedia lists about 23,000 national and international organizations, trade and business groups, fan clubs and other associations, and it seems as if every possible topic is represented—from the Screen Actors Guild to the National Association for Holocaust Education, from the American Heart Association to the American Dehydrated Onion and Garlic Association. Association officials or members often make good sources.

Lesko's Info-Power III (Visible Ink Press, 1996). This helpful book lists experts in government and some organizations, along with good advice on how to find information through interviews. Matthew Lesko believes that it often takes seven phone calls to get the information you need, and he encourages people to not give up with call number three or four. Among the information included are lists of about 11,500 experts, descriptions of government agencies and offices and their functions, and contact information for governor's offices, state libraries and federal public information officers.

If you're not getting a successful interview after careful preparation, then look inside. Were you sincerely interested in the person you interviewed? Dogs, horses, and kids know when someone dislikes them, but they warm up with people they know they can trust. People being interviewed do, too.

—Joy Parise, *The Writer*, February 1999

Newsmakers (Gale Research). This annual book gives short biographies of people in the news, indexed by nationality, occupation and subject. It includes information about how to contact them, such as the names and phone numbers for celebrities' agents or publicists.

Politics in America (Congressional Quarterly). This guide to senators and representatives touts itself as "primarily a book about people." Short biographical sections include key votes, committee assignments and offices and phone numbers.

Polk City Directory. These terrific books give people's names, occupations and telephone numbers, along with street addresses, in virtually every city in the country. They also list the names of key officers at businesses. You also can look up who lives in each house on a street, which can be useful in finding neighbors of someone you're writing about.

Student Contact Book (Gale Research). Don't be put off by the title if you're not a student. Each chapter in this small but useful book starts with ideas for research topics, such as the "attractions of young persons to cult organizations." Its chapters start with broad categories, such as Cults and Sects, and then break them down into smaller categories, such as New Age or Occult. Then it lists contact information for organizations dealing with that topic, such as the Parapsychology Institute of America, and names of free or low-cost publications of the groups.

Thomas Register of American Manufacturers (Thomas Publishing). Volumes 24, 25 and 26 list alphabetically 152,000 companies and their capabilities, with names of company executives, phone numbers and office locations.

Washington Information Directory (Congressional Quarterly). This book divides information sources into agencies, Congress and nonprofit organizations. Chapters are arranged by broad topic, such as Environment and Natural Resources. It includes names, addresses and phone numbers of people and the places they work. A section on Congress gives extensive information on members, their committee assignments and their staffs. Reference lists give information on federal regional offices throughout the country and top state officials. A subject index can help you find the department that handles that topic—where your sources work.

Who's Who in America (A.N. Marquis). Here's the venerable resource for finding important people. The ninty-ninth edition includes brief bios and contact information 105,000 people chosen for their positions or noteworthy achievements. It has geographic and professional indicies. There are several other similar titles, not all published by the same firm, such as *Who's Who Among African Americans* (Gale Research) and *The International Who's Who* (Europa Publications).

The Yearbook of Experts, Authorities and Spokespersons (Broadcast Interview Source). This book lists sources for thousands of topics, arranged alphabetically and by topic and geography.

WEB SITES

We have listed exact pages at Web sites to help you find people. But Web sites are often updated and changed, so these URLs may no longer be valid. If any of the following addresses do not work, try trimming everything but the main page name and searching from there. For example, if www.access.gpo.gov/congress/browse-cd.html doesn't take you to the Congressional Directory, start at www.access.gpo.gov to begin your search.

Associations: Several sites give contact information for associations on the Net, often searchable by topic or geographical region. Sometimes the *Encyclopedia of Associations* is faster and more comprehensive; sometimes the Net will be. Here are some searchable sites:

Associations on the Net (www.ipl.org/ref/aon)

The Union of International Associations (www.uia.org/website.htm)

World Directory of Think Tanks (www.nira.go.jp/ice/index.html)

Education World (www.education-world.com) Clicking on a topic in the database box pulls up a variety of links, including associations and directories of people.

Census Data: (www.census.gov/contacts/www.contacts.html) Find out census experts' phone numbers. Census experts can be publicity shy, but a government Web site lists public information officers for vast quantities of census data. Sometimes, if you E-mail the public information officers with a question, they respond. (The census site also has a fun section called Facts for Features, which includes news releases with statistics for various holidays. For example, the Mother's Day release lists stats on working mothers, the number of children women are having and where births are taking place.)

Expert Sites: Several sites on the Internet offer ask-an-expert services. ProfNet .com (www.profnet.com), a subsidiary of the PR Newswire, allows you to find an expert by typing in a topic. It pulls up experts' names, phone numbers, E-mail addresses and URLs. Another good site is the Yearbook of Experts, Authorities and Spokespersons (www.yearbooknews.com), where you can search more than fourteen thousand topics to find experts. The paper version of this book is available free to working journalists; call (800) 932-7266 for information or try Nedsite (www.nedsit e.nl/search/people.htm) for E-mail addresses, phone numbers and fax numbers.

Government Contacts: The Congressional Directory is online, with brief bios and contact information for members of Congress (www.access.gpo.gov/congress/ browse-cd.html). Another good starting point for phone numbers and Web pages— and much more—about members of Congress is the Office of the Clerk's page (clerkweb.house.gov/mbrcmtee/mbrcmtee.htm). For links to federal departments and agencies, go to ecs.rams.com/wwwlinks/.

To find state pages, type the state name into a search engine or start from the Library of Congress's State and Local Governments page (lcweb.loc.gov/global/ state). In addition, Tammy Payton, first-grade teacher and Web editor at Loogootee Elementary School West in Indiana, has posted a Web page that lists dozens of government and politics sites (www.siec.k12.in.us/~west/sites/govt.htm). The site offers links to federal agencies on the Internet, the National Association of State Information Resource Executives and E-mail addresses for members of Congress.

The Mother of All Lists: Read electronic mailing lists and discussion boards to understand what people are thinking and talking about. Before posting a request for an interview on a list, however, check the frequently asked questions to see if it's proper "netiquette." To find lists on every topic, try a terrific list of lists at www.neosoft.com/internet/paml/sources.html or Deja at www.deja.com. If you do an E-mail interview, check out who is responding; make sure the teen mother from Philadelphia you think you're interviewing isn't in fact a hairy male bus driver from Paducah. Ask for names of other people who know this person, check out their addresses and phones in the *Polk City Directory* and ask for resumes to verify information.

People Locators: Most search engines can find people's addresses and phone numbers. Try People Finder (www.databaseamerica.com/html/gpfind.htm) or PeopleFind (www.lycos.com/peoplefind/). Many telephone and E-mail directories are available online, and some offer help in contacting celebrities. Try Metacrawler's Ultimate Directory (www.infospace.com/), or Yahoo's People Search (www.people.yahoo.com), for white pages listings. Other sources include The Global Yellow Pages (www.globalyp.com/world.htm), 555-1212 (www.555-1212.com) and the Internet 800 Directory (inter800.com).

Universities and Colleges: Universities and research organizations have a strong presence on the Web and are chock-full of experts. You can reach these people by contacting the institutions:

Four-Year Colleges (cnsearch.collegenet.com/cgi-bin/CN/year4page)
Scholarly Studies Project (www.lib.uwaterloo.ca/society/guidelines.html)
University Pages (isl-garnet.uah.edu/Universities)

CHAPTER EIGHT

Selling Your Articles and Other Short Nonfiction

The wonderful thing about magazines is that there are just so many of them. Those eighteen thousand magazines constitute eighteen thousand markets for a writer's work.

The terrible thing about magazines is that there are just so many of them. Those eighteen thousand magazines each have different audiences, different styles and different voices—and different writer's requirements.

The trick to selling your short nonfiction to any of these magazines is matching the article to the magazine. In other words, to sell an article to a magazine, writers have to do a little marketing. Now before you argue that you are a writer and not a marketing professional, consider this: The skills you use in marketing your story are not very different from those you use in everyday life.

Say you're seated at a dinner party next to a woman in an evening gown, high heels, pearls and a coiffure of perfection. Would you initiate a conversation by leaning her way and inquiring, "Hey, what'dja think about that wrestling match on TV last night?" Rather than assuming she's a WWF fan, you'd probably invest

---

Querying Checklist

Before sending queries, ask yourself:

- Have I addressed the query to the right person at the magazine, and have I double-checked spellings, particularly of all proper nouns?
- Is my query neatly typed and free of errors?
- Is my idea to the point?
- Have I outlined the story or given at least a good idea of the direction the story will take?
- Have I included sources I have interviewed or plan to interview?
- Do I know which department or section my piece best fits and have I told the editor?
- Have I included clips that show my talent?
- Have I noted why I'm the right writer for this story?
- Have I included a self-addressed, stamped envelope (SASE) for reply?
- Does my letter note my address, telephone and fax numbers and E-mail address?
- Have I recorded the query's topic, the date and the target publication in a log? (If I don't hear back in six to twelve weeks, I can follow up with a letter reminding the editor about my query or a postcard withdrawing the idea.)

---

a bit of time to learn her interests before plunging into such a conversation.

Yet would-be writers commit such gaffes with magazines every day. They try to sell stories on canoeing to backpacking magazines. They offer fiction to magazines that publish fact. They view themselves as writers whose work will be appreciated by whoever reads it rather than as someone whose job is to figure out whom they're talking with and tell those people a story they'd be interested in hearing.

Professional magazine writers recognize that magazines are as individual as people are. They hold conversations with their readers every month, discussing their topics of mutual interest in their own styles of language. Magazine editors know the people who read their magazines. They know their ages, their sexes and their incomes. They know what stirs their interests and what bores them. So if you go to the trouble of learning about the magazine and its audience, you improve your chances of joining its conversation with its readers.

Avoiding Rejection

Most editors expect to be approached by professional writers. And professional writers do not write 2,000-word feature articles and ship them off to a magazine. A professional first writes a letter—the query letter—that proposes a story idea and that proffers himself as the perfect person to write it.

Queries are letters of introduction and sales pitches combined. While your query must explain in some detail what your story will be about, it also must be concise. Editors are busy people, and many figure that if you can't boil the story idea down to a page or so, it probably doesn't have a point.

In theory, querying doesn't sound hard. But ask editors to describe the actual queries they receive, and you're likely to hear sorrowful sighs. They often receive what they delicately call "inappropriate" queries. And the single biggest reason for the inappropriateness is writers' ignorance of the publication. Again and again editors complain that most people who write queries haven't bothered to read the magazine.

If you were to read through most of the fifty query letters that cross his desk any week, says Jim Gorman, senior editor of *Backpacker* magazine, "you can tell that person has never seen the magazine, hasn't studied it, has an idea that's square and is trying to fit it into our circle. I'm a former freelancer with a little bit of a marketer's instinct. You've got to know who your audience is."

"People haven't taken the time to study the publication to know what we're doing," says J.D. Owen, editor in chief of *Boys' Life* magazine. "Queries that this magazine rejects are often not kid appropriate; they're too adult. The best advice for anyone wanting to write for us would be to look over some of our issues, see what we're doing and focus in on the kinds of things that are going to ring our chimes."

"That's really the crucial thing," says David Heim, executive editor of *The Christian Century*. "The one thing somebody could do that would make me give a query a second look is an indication that they've not just found our address somewhere, but they have a pretty good idea of the kind of articles we print and who our audience is."

From *Beer* and *Pizza Today* to *Ms.*

It's a great time to be a writer, Pat Crowley says.

"If I get an idea, I know I'm going to sell it," says this full-time political reporter for the *Kentucky Enquirer* and virtually full-time freelance magazine writer for online and paper publications. "Because with the Internet, with cable channels, with twenty-four-hour news, there is such a thirst for information."

The Net is a vast marketplace, a terrific tool for querying and a research resource for writers. Seldom these days does Crowley have to make copies of clips, then bundle them with a query letter and SASE and trek the package to the post office. Today, he just shoots off E-mails to multiple online publications; usually one responds.

Freelancing has never been easier for the writer. "Even if you don't want to do it full-time, it's a good way to make money part-time," he says. "A lot of these Web sites aren't the most sophisticated in the world, and they are looking for ideas. If you have an idea, they'll take a chance on you."

In addition to writing more than a dozen stories a week in his day job as a reporter, Crowley also writes about seven freelance pieces each month for online publications. He also writes for trade publications, such as *Beer*, *Pizza Today* and several RV magazines. He is determined to crack the larger markets, having just sold a piece on Kentucky's "Bitch Caucus" to *Ms.* magazine.

Although Crowley is an experienced writer, writing for *Ms.* was not easy. *Ms.* was interested in his query about the group of female legislators who were openly called the Bitch Caucus by their male counterparts. But after he turned in the piece, the editor sent him a two-page memo, criticizing his writing and his take on the story. It hurt. But he says, "It was the best thing that ever happened to me."

While the *Ms.* editor was tough, she also was willing to work with him, asking for a total rewrite and some later changes—and Crowley was glad for the chance. The piece improved with her guidance, and he says he has a clip he's proud of.

But he also takes pride in his work for trade publications, magazines that typically are "homework reading" for workers in a particular industry. While the pay is usually far less than for a national magazine and the subject matter is considerably narrower, these publications still demand good writing and reporting.

To break into writing for trade or consumer magazines, Crowley encourages beginning writers to do more than write. He tells them to read.

Writing is just like playing basketball, he says. If you want to play basketball well, you watch how Michael Jordan plays and then try it yourself. If you want to write,

continued

you read the best in the business and then try it yourself. He has a stack of magazines beside his computer, and he reads them as pages download. He reads every chance he gets, and it inspires him. Consequently, Crowley is never at a loss for ideas. "I can't keep up with them," he says.

Crowley tinkers with a single idea to tailor a single idea to multiple markets. His first article on the Corvette museum in Bowling Green, Kentucky, for example, was an informational piece for a travel magazine, explaining what the museum is and why people might want to go. A later story focused on a museum visitor who adored the cars. ("I asked, 'If you could drive out of here with any car, which one would it be?'" Crowley says. "I thought he'd say one of these real cool ones from the fifties. He says the 1983 because they only made two.") Even when the museum fell on hard times and resorted to installing dinosaur exhibits beside the cars in an attempt to lure visitors, Crowley managed to get a story out of it—for a magazine covering the travel industry. This story explained the museum's problems attracting visitors and how it was working to correct them.

"There's a magazine for everything," he says. "I always pitch my idea more than one place. I figure I'll sell to whoever wants to buy it."

Understanding the Audience

Knowing who reads the publication is crucial if you want to write for magazines. That's why many magazine writers study a magazine to devise ideas appropriate to its readers rather than thinking up ideas first. "I almost always start with the magazine," says freelancer Sarah Bewley. Any time she's near a newsstand, she makes a point of buying a magazine that she's not seen before or hasn't seen in a while. She'll then scroll through her idea file and ask herself, What do I have that might work?

Bewley credits "the magic of the Internet" as initiating her career of full-time magazine writing. When she was getting started in 1994, Bewley found electronic forums online in which publications were looking for writers. She pitched a couple ideas to a new magazine in England, which accepted them. Bewley wrote regularly for this magazine until it went belly-up—but then she got another job with its sister publication in the U.S.

In the meantime, she kept querying other magazines, earning enough to live by

Glossary of Magazine Terms

BOOK: Another word for magazine. Thus, *front of the book* means front of the magazine.

CLIPS: Copies of published material; to be sent with a writer's query letter.

COPYRIGHT: The legal right of a creator of a work to reproduce, distribute, publish and earn fees for his work.

DEPARTMENT: A standing section of a magazine, such as Nutrition, Your Health, etc.

EDITOR'S INTRODUCTION: (also called a letter, preface or foreword) A note from the editor commenting on that issue or the magazine's philosophy or goals; speaks directly to readers.

FILLER: A short piece, often 25 to 250 words, used to fill in a small space in a column or on a page.

KILL FEE: Money paid to a writer if an assigned article is rejected after it's written; often 25 to 33 percent of the original pay rate.

MANUSCRIPT: A typed, double-spaced copy of a written work; abbreviated *ms.* (or *mss.* for plural).

MASTHEAD: A list of the names and titles of a magazine's staff; also may include publication, advertising and Web site information.

MEDIA KIT: A packet of information for advertisers describing the magazine audience's demographics.

MULTIPLE SUBMISSION: Sending several ideas or pieces of work to an editor at once.

PAYMENT ON ACCEPTANCE: The writer is paid when the magazine agrees to buy the work.

PAYMENT ON PUBLICATION: The writer is paid when the material is published.

QUERY LETTER: A sales letter pitching a story to a magazine editor; usually one page and pointed to a particular target audience.

RESPONSE TIME: The time it takes for an editor to accept or reject a writer's idea or manuscript.

RIGHTS: (see also **work-for-hire**) Magazines and other periodicals can purchase the rights to publish written material in a variety of ways:

- All rights: All rights are signed over to the publisher and the writer forfeits the chance to resell the work.
- First serial rights (First North American Serial Rights): The right to be the first to publish a work. The periodical buys the right to print it before any other publication, and then the copyright reverts to the writer, who may resell it.

continued

- Electronic rights: The right to publish a piece electronically, such as in an online database or electronic database or on CD-ROM; usually set for a specific time period.
- One-time rights: A periodical buys the right to publish a work once, but the author may simultaneously sell it to other publications, usually in a different area.
- Reprint or second serial rights: The right to publish a piece after it has already been published elsewhere.

SASE: Self-addressed, stamped envelope.

SERVICE JOURNALISM: How-to pieces, meant to explain in step-by-step fashion how to create or accomplish something.

SIDEBAR: A shorter piece containing information that accompanies and complements the main article.

SIMULTANEOUS SUBMISSION: Sending the same idea to multiple magazines at the same time.

SPEC: Working "on spec," or speculation, means the magazine will not pay the writer unless it determines the manuscript is suitable for publication. No kill fee is offered if the piece is rejected.

TARGET AUDIENCE: Readers of a particular magazine.

THEME: A unifying idea tying a story together and adding meaning.

WORK-FOR-HIRE: A work whose rights are owned by the publisher, not the writer, from the moment it is created; this covers employees of publications and freelancers who sign a work-for-hire contract with a publisher. An author gets no royalties, but typically gets a larger advance or a salary.

WRITER'S GUIDELINES: A written document provided by a magazine describing appropriate types of writing, the submission policy, pay rates (sometimes) and other information for freelancers.

her words. "The key is just querying everybody all the time," she says, noting that at the start of her career she would send five to ten queries each week. Today, the pace of querying has slowed since she writes regularly for three magazines and has won a commission to write a play.

Bewley also makes simultaneous submissions—sending the same query to multiple magazines. "I think anybody that doesn't is being foolish," she says. While editors often prefer having the exclusive right to accept or reject an idea, magazines are targeting ever narrower audiences. So it's likely each publication would want a story with a different angle anyway, she notes.

Before you submit queries to one magazine or many, do some market research. Here are a few steps to help you:

1. Analyze the magazine's style. When reading, don't allow yourself to be swept in by the stories or distracted by the content. Study the magazine to discern its style. Is it light or weighty, serious or flip? How do the features, the longer pieces, differ from the shorter departmental pieces in the front of the book? Does the magazine just report the facts or encourage writers to comment on them? Does it only use first-, second- or third-person accounts, or does it use all of them in different parts of the magazine? Are sidebars typically used? Are experts quoted, or is the author the voice of authority? Who reads this publication, and how does the magazine slant its stories to them?

"Make sure to read the three or four most recent issues of that magazine," says Betsa Marsh, a freelancer who specializes in writing travel articles. "Don't just skim." Particularly on the shorter pieces for the front of a magazine, Marsh not only reads but also studies them. She asks herself, How are those things structured? How long are they? Is it a really breezy tone, and does what I'm suggesting to them lend itself to breeziness? Or is their front of the book more serious?

2. Read more than just the articles. The table of contents in many magazines will show the topics that are covered. Note the angles that are taken for each topic, often explained in subtitles. Look carefully at the ads. Mary asks her students to count and categorize the ads (How many ads for upscale home furnishings? How many for discount stores?) to find out characteristics of the magazine's audience. Advertisers research an audience before paying big bucks to buy an ad—and writers can use this information to craft stories targeted to those groups.

Read trade publications about writing and marketing your writing. *Writer's Digest* and *The Writer* are particularly helpful, offering advice on writing techniques and selling to markets.

Take a look at *Advertising Age*, a trade publication for advertisers, which often runs ads placed by magazines trying to define their readers. An ad for *Redbook*, for example, called "Mothers & Shakers," read: "There's no such thing as 'virtual motherhood.' If you're in it, you're on it, 24 hours a day, 7 days a week—at least in your heart. If ever I think I'm losing my balance between the me and the we, there's *Redbook* like a good friend on the other end of my see saw."

Another *Advertising Age* advertisement read: "At *Essence*, we reach deeper—into the very soul of the African-American woman. We're more than just fashion, we're families. We're more than just beauty, we're brains. We are, quite simply, the bible for today's affluent African-American Woman. A woman who is clearly in charge, in control and ready to spend. The only question is, Are you reaching her?" A question a *writer* for the magazine might also ask.

3. Find the right theme. When you market your idea, you're matching it to the target audience of a particular magazine, much like trying to find common ground for conversation with a guest at a dinner party. This usually means finding the right theme. Michael Bugeja, in his *Guide to Writing Magazine Nonfiction* (Allyn and Bacon, 1998), explains that magazine editors usually buy themes, not topics, and if you change a theme, you change the market for your work. For example, a story on divorce would focus on the theme of obsession for *Cosmopolitan*, on healing for *Parents*, and on commitment for *Guideposts*.

Linda Vaccariello, senior editor of *Cincinnati Magazine*, notes that story ideas in this regional publication, as in many other regional publications, must be closely tied to the area—an obvious notion, perhaps, but one that many people miss. For example, a California writer once convinced Vaccariello he could write a story about stained glass for the magazine. It turned out to be a generic article about stained glass, with a few local quotes dropped in for local color. It was written from a place where people have new homes and where stained glass is trendy. But Cincinnati is full of Victorian homes loaded with the original antiques. *Cincinnati Magazine* readers are sophisticated about the topic, Vaccariello said, and the gee-whiz approach the writer took just did not work.

4. Get the guidelines. Now that you're really reading magazines, hold off on writing your query. First, get the magazine's writer's guidelines by writing to the magazine, checking the magazine's Web site or visiting www.writersdigest.com, which offers more than eleven hundred magazines' writer's guidelines. These guidelines often tell you critical information, such as what topics the magazine covers

The Contract

Congratulations. You've written a query that has earned you an assignment to write for a magazine. Before you start dialing for your first interview, do one final bit of preparation: Read the contract before you sign it. Not all magazines use contracts, and those that do may not give many breaks to the writer.

Good contracts delineate the story idea, the rights you're selling to the publisher, the pay, the kill fee (if any) and the due date. We've included in this chapter the National Writers Union model contract (see page 149).

While you can sign away many rights, it's important to know what they mean before doing so. "The more schooled the writer is about his rights, the more likely the writer is to get a better contract," says NWU contract advisor and freelancer Sarah Bewley.

However, without a written contract stating which rights are being sold, the law states that freelancers grant permission for publication only once. That means they can later resell the same material to other publications.

One item not mentioned at all in this model contract is a kill fee. A publication may pay a writer this fee, often 25 to 33 percent of the agreed-upon price, if it doesn't publish a piece after it's written. The union believes that kill fees allow editors to assign stories capriciously. Kill fees, however, remain common, and some writers appreciate being paid something if the story isn't published.

The NWU contract also asks publications to pay writers for the right to use each work each time they publish it, whether that's on paper or in electronic form. Many publications try to buy all rights to a work for one fee. Bewley says she has never signed an all-rights contract. Once, she lost a monthly gig with a magazine that suddenly wanted her to sign over not only the first right to publish her work, but all rights. She refused and sent a flurry of queries to other publications. "I ended up getting work with a bigger magazine," she said.

Electronic rights can mean publication online, in databases, on CD-ROMs or in other interactive media. The NWU suggests you try to get some payment for each use of your work in any of these media. Some contracts limit the time the publisher may use the work online and in databases, after which the rights revert to the writer. Some writers have negotiated nonexclusive rights to electronic publications, meaning the writers can sell the works elsewhere. Some publishers offer a split of the royalties.

It may be such a heady feeling for some beginning writers to sell their work to magazines that they are happy for even minimal payment for all rights. But the union believes that writers, even beginners, should be able to negotiate for fair and timely compensation and for separate payments for separate rights. Besides, says Bewley, "If you say things like this, they won't think you *are* a beginner."

Stringing for Newspapers

Newspapers rarely have enough reporters to cover the stories in their areas, and many, particularly smaller papers, welcome freelancers. In the newspaper business, freelancers are called "stringers."

Stringers often begin at a newspaper by reporting on official meetings—of school boards, town commissions and the like. Some papers publish special sections written by stringers, and some use feature stories from freelancers. If you want to string for a paper, it helps to have taken at least one journalism course to understand how to report accurately and write fast. A journalism degree helps even more.

Weekly community newspapers are often the easiest places to begin. But larger metropolitan daily papers also are traditionally understaffed and do hire stringers. To find such a job, write a simple business letter to the managing editor of a larger paper or the editor of a smaller one asking if it needs stringers. You may not have to come up with story ideas yourself, but include one or two if you know the paper hasn't covered them. Mention any writing experience you have, include clips and a resume and state that you'll call to follow up.

Then call. First ask if it is a good time to call, since deadline pressure precludes phone conversations at certain times. If they need help, the editors will be willing to talk with you or direct you to the editor who handles stringers.

Some newspapers (again, especially smaller ones) allow stringers to write columns. If you have an idea for a column, prove in your letter to the paper that you have expertise in the subject, be it taxes, parenting or stamp collecting. Include three or four columns you've already written to show you can write. Be prepared to give a list of future ideas and to churn them out regularly and on time.

While it may be easier to win a newspaper assignment than one from a magazine, the financial rewards are usually far less. The range is from about $25 per story for small papers to $150 or more at larger ones. But you get more than money by working for a paper. You get published, and your clips can help you land bigger jobs. If you're lucky, you'll also get a good editor who will work with you and your copy. You'll learn to be a writer.

and who reads it. They may explain its mission, its recommended story lengths, its departments open to freelancers and its pay rates.

Some guidelines are more useful than others. For example, *Wired* magazine's start off: "Amaze us. We know a lot about digital computers and we are bored with them. Tell us something about them we've never heard before, in a way we've never seen before."

Other guidelines offer more concrete advice. *Working Woman* magazine, for example, notes: "The best sections through which to break into our magazine are Fast Forward and Workshop. Fast Forward pieces are usually 200 to 500 words. They are trend-oriented stories featuring new technology, business strategies, people or products and demographic data that are changing the face of their respective markets. The voice of this section is insider, edgy and irreverent. Although the articles are short, they are heavily reported and must be tightly focused."

Parenting magazine's guidelines point out that the publication "addresses readers who are considering pregnancy or expecting a child, as well as parents of children from birth through age twelve. The magazine covers both the psychological and practical aspects of parenting. . . . For writers new to *Parenting*, the best opportunities are the departments, which are comprised of pieces that range from 100 to 800 words."

Such information is invaluable. Use it to mold your proposal to a particular market or to find a market suited to your idea.

Finally, Craft a Query Letter

Reading the magazine and studying the writer's guidelines are the two biggest favors you can do for yourself before trying to write a story for any magazine. Once you've done these, you're ready to craft a query letter.

Queries are one or two pages—editors are notoriously overworked and sensitive to demands on their time. Queries are brief yet comprehensive—try to give the editor an idea of the breadth of your story, the sources and the angle. Above all, queries should be interesting. "Hook me. I'm going to take whatever idea you've got and twist it anyway," says *Backpacker's* Gorman. "I don't mean to be arrogant about that. But there are few writers who aren't longtime professionals or who haven't sat in an editor's seat themselves, but who can insinuate themselves into the mindset of the magazine and lock onto and figure out what we're looking for."

The Online Writing Revolution

Although the terminology makes some of us cringe, content is necessary for all Internet publications, which is good news for writers.

To help writers plug into the electronic world of words, Debbie Ridpath Ohi started her Web site Inkspot (www.inkspot.com) in 1995 as a hobby. "There is such a mass of information available online now, it's easy to get lost. Inkspot acts as an information filter," says Ohi, who is a musician and composer and has published short stories, articles and poems and a book, *The Writer's Online Marketplace* (Writer's Digest Books, 2001).

Inkspot offers plenty of help for writers, including information about the craft of writing, markets here and abroad, chats (and transcripts of chats) with experts, links to writing-related sites, and an electronic newsletter about writing, called *Inklings*.

"There are many good market resources available through the Web," Ohi notes. "Some are searchable databases of submission guidelines, others are market newsletters available by E-mail. Because of the nature of the Web, writers can often find market information that is more up-to-date than available through print publications."

The Internet can offer a community to writers who don't have a local writers group, through online discussion groups, chats and writing-related news groups. And it can help with promotion, research, education and more.

While the pay traditionally has been low, or even nonexistent, for writing for online publications, the Internet as a publishing medium is still too young to have many traditions at all. Ohi says that before advertisers came to her site, she couldn't afford to pay contributors, but now she does.

"Writers should weigh the pros and cons before submitting material to a nonpaying market," Ohi says. "If the publication gets a fair amount of traffic, then the exposure of having an article published may help a new writer get established. Several of my writers have written to me after their articles appeared in *Inklings*, saying that they had gotten paying assignments as a result or enough feedback from readers to inspire other articles."

Put yourself in the editors' place. It's hard for them to take a chance on an unknown writer, particularly following reports of journalists making up sources or entire stories. Even if a magazine has a fact-checking department that finds a few errors, it's not easy to know at what point to doubt someone's entire story, noted *Cincinnati Magazine*'s Vaccariello. And even if a story is accurate, sometimes editors have to work hard to salvage a weak story, creating instead a mediocre story—and missing a chance to get a great story.

Remember that editors were, or still are, writers themselves. Vaccariello, a freelancer herself, says she hates rejecting writers. "But most of all," she says, "I hate explaining why." It's not easy telling someone, "Your writing just isn't good enough." Maybe that's why some editors never respond to freelancers at all.

To try to prevent rejection, or ceaseless silence, study a book on writing query letters before sending out your query. But certainly consider the following tips.

Narrow Your Idea

Think long and think hard about your idea. Perhaps because they lack experience in knowing how many words it takes to tell stories, some beginning writers have trouble narrowing an idea into a workable notion.

Sometimes writers propose articles "about enormous theological topics, which no one can cover in a magazine article—such as one that's going to solve the mystery of creation," says Heim of *The Christian Century*. "They can be that general, and there's nothing in the letter to suggest they're going to narrow this in a helpful way."

Focus is key. Dana Points, executive editor at *American Health* magazine, notes that unfocused queries say such things as, " 'I'd like to write a story on arthritis.' So my response is, 'What about arthritis? Why should I buy a story on arthritis *now*? What's new, what's special about the subject, and how is that piece going to be specifically tailored to my magazine?' "

Points adds, "So then I still get a lot of queries that say, 'I'm going to do a story about women and arthritis,' and my question is, 'Well what *about* women and arthritis?' "

When devising your ideas, slice and dice a topic. Focus on an angle, one person in the news, one aspect of a larger debate. Points advises writers to think of a headline that will make the editor sit up and take notice. Headlines help you focus your idea.

Show That You've Done Some Homework

No one expects freelancers to research an entire feature before asking an editor if she would be interested in buying it. But you have to know enough to convince an editor you've got a story. Read what your target magazine and similar publications have printed on your topic before querying; look for a fresh angle. You might also name your sources or give their occupations: "I plan to talk to school psychologists and teachers, as well as parents of children with this rare disease."

Be Meticulous

Pay attention to spelling, grammar and punctuation. Several editors say they would make exceptions for Sally Anybody, who makes no pretensions about being a writer but who proposes an intriguing personal-experience story. But all disapproved of a would-be writer misusing the tools of the trade. While a comma out of place probably won't sink your query, attention to detail is the hallmark of a good writer.

"If something is dated March 21 and I received it March 17—which is something that happened yesterday—it makes me think that perhaps the person is not very good about detail and probably won't be a good writer for *Writer's Digest*," says Melanie Rigney, editor. "But the *idea* is more important to me."

Write to the Right Person

Writer's Market (Writer's Digest Books) lists the names of editors to query at thousands of publications, but people change jobs frequently. Call to check who should get your query. Simply ask the secretary, "Who should receive a query for a piece in your [whatever] Department?" Also ask how to spell the editor's name.

Even if an editor doesn't care if you addressed your query to the wrong person, sending it to the right person makes querying more efficient—the letter is less likely to spend days bouncing from desk to desk.

Be careful if you're sending the same query to several magazines. Points notes that some writers who do so remember to change the address to Ms. Dana Points at *American Health*, but they leave the greeting as "Dear Ms. Smith." These, she says, become "instant trash."

Show Your Style

The query letter must convince the editor that you know how to write for the publication. Pitch the story with grace and verve. If a magazine adopts a particular tone of voice with its readers—a he-man voice for outdoor adventure magazines, for example—use that voice in your query. If the magazine allows different voices in its pages, let your own personality show through. If you've got a great anecdote or a quote, include it. Other writers could probably write the piece, but they might not be able to dig up the golden nuggets you have found.

Sound Confident

If you've done your homework and you know your stuff, you will sound sure of yourself. Sounding confident and professional is a far better way to garner a sale than sounding like a beginner pleading for a break. Tell the editor, "I'll write (not "I hope to write") about five ways mothers can help their daughters make friends and keep them."

If you have any nonwriting qualifications to write a particular story, note them. For a profile on a bookstore owner, for example, mention that you worked your way through college at Barnes and Noble.

Include Clips

Some editors recommend sending only clips that are similar to the article you're proposing. Thus, you should send clips from a children's publication if you want to write for another children's publication. But others want to see what you've written, anywhere. "I really look to the clips for a nice flair in the writing, one that's consistent from clip to clip and from publication to publication," Points says, "because there are a lot of nice clips out there that are the result of a lot of talented and hardworking *editors*."

Send two or three of your best clips with your query. But if you don't have any clips, don't highlight your inexperience; don't even mention it.

Include a self-addressed, stamped envelope so the editor can return the clips if she rejects your idea. Then send the query, tweaked to suit another audience, to a different editor, not to another editor at the same magazine. *Writer's Digest*, for example, records the idea and the writer's name of all rejected queries. "So don't bother submitting them again in a month or two and think we're not going to recognize them," Rigney says, "because we will."

While the Internet is a marvelous tool, don't tell a busy editor to spend time visiting your Web site to see your writing. "Give me a break," says Gorman of *Backpacker.* "No thank you."

In the beginning, aim for small victories. "Magazines have a terribly hard time getting people to do department stories and particularly briefs," Gorman says. "But I'd say 99 percent of people who query me are pitching features." Long feature stories more often go to writers with an established working relationship with the publication, simply because a magazine is reluctant to risk three thousand dollars on an unknown.

So examine the shorter pieces in the magazines that you enjoy reading, and think about what you can offer. The pay will be smaller, the glory is less splendiferous, but it may be the easiest way to break in. Besides, you may be able to complete smaller pieces more quickly and do more of them than longer articles.

Now all that's left is to write and send your queries. Writing great query letters will get your ideas accepted and your stories published, but they also can lead to having editors contacting *you* every month with assignments.

- the government or employee benefit programs on which they were relying to pay for necessary health care services may or may not be capable of processing their claims after January 1, 2000.

I thought that *American Health* readers would be interested in an article explaining the potential risks Y2K poses for health care consumers. I propose to look at what the affected industries—hospitals, insurance companies, pharmaceutical companies, medical device manufacturers, and health care software manufacturers—are doing to alleviate those risks. I will examine the steps that the federal government is taking to encourage those efforts, as well as the efforts the government itself is taking to ensure that federal benefit programs continue to function. Finally, I will recommend steps that consumers can take on their own to make sure that this potenital computer glitch does not adversely impact them or their families.

I am an attorney by training. I practiced for a decade as a lawyer/lobbyist at Akin, Gump, Strauss, Hauer & Feld in Washington, D.C. where I specialized in health care and food and drug issues. I moved to New Jersey last year, and began a second career as a freelance writer. I have written articles for legal publications in the past, but I am enclosing two briefer and more recent clips for your review.

I look forward to hearing from you soon.

Sincerely,

Jennifer Smith

Organized presentation of ideas.

Credentials as writer.

Clips enclosed.

NATIONAL WRITERS UNION STANDARD JOURNALISM CONTRACT

Comments from Sarah Bewley, full-time freelancer and NWU contract advisor

Contract between (Writer) _____ and (Publisher) _____

1. The Writer agrees to prepare an Article of _____ words on the subject of _____: for delivery on or before _____ (date). The Writer also agrees to provide one revision of the Article.

2. The Publisher agrees to pay the Writer a fee of $_____ within thirty (30) days of initial receipt of the Article as assigned above. (In other words, an original and coherent manuscript of approximately the above word count on the subject assigned, and for which appropriate research was completed.)

You don't want to be paid on publication. Some magazines hold pieces for a year. You want payment tied to the initial deadline or as close to that date as possible.

3. The Publisher agrees that the above fee purchases one-time North American hard-copy print publication rights only. All other rights, including the electronic reproduction, transmission, display, performance or distribution of the Article, are fully reserved by the Writer.

Try to retain the copyright of your material so you can sell it again. Negotiate for additional payment if your material is republished.

4. The Publisher agrees to reimburse the Writer for all previously agreed-upon and documented expenses within fifteen (15) days of submission of receipts.

You'll have bills coming in. For many writers, it's critical to be reimbursed quickly.

5. The Publisher agrees to make every reasonable effort to make available to the Writer the final, edited version of the Article while there is still time to make changes. In the event of a disagreement over the final form of the Article, the Writer reserves the right to withdraw his/her name from the Article without prejudicing the agreed-upon fee.

You really want this! You can make sure your story is accurate before it's published.

6. The Writer guarantees that the Article will not contain material that is consciously libelous or defamatory. In return, the Publisher agrees to provide and pay for counsel to defend the Writer in any litigation arising as a result of the Article.

Very important! Writers do not always have lawyers who are on retainer. Magazines do. They traditionally have stood by writers to defend against libel suits.

7. In the event of a dispute between the Writer and the Publisher that cannot be resolved through the National Writers Union (NWU) grievance process, the Writer will have the option of seeking to resolve the matter by arbitration, or in court. If arbitration is chosen, the Writer may be represented by the NWU in any procedures before the arbitrator. The arbitrator's fees shall be shared fifty percent (50%) by the Publisher and fifty percent (50%) by the Writer. Any decision reached by the arbitrator may be appealed pursuant to applicable law.

Many magazines don't expect you to question them. If you do, you have a procedure for handling disputes written in your contract.

Writer or Writer's Representative: _____ Date: _____

Publisher's Representative: _____ Date: _____

SAMPLE QUERY

Comments from Michael Embry, executive editor, Kentucky Monthly

August 15, 2000

Mr. Michael Embry
Executive Editor
Kentucky Monthly
P.O. Box 559
Frankfort, KY 40602-0559

Dear Mr. Embry,

Catchy lead. It got my attention to read with interest.

Phantoms Don't Drive Sports Cars. Zombies Don't Play Soccer. Frankenstein Doesn't Slam Hockey Pucks. It's a safe bet that most third-grade kids in the country would know that these are some titles in a popular children's book series, The Adventures of the Bailey School Kids. Yet even some of her students and fellow teachers in Lexington don't recognize the name of Marcia Thornton Jones as the author of the popular series.

Good background information about the authors.

Jones and fellow teacher and former Lexingtonian Debbie Dadey created The Bailey School Kids after a frustrating day in the classroom. Jones told Dadey that to make her students pay attention, she'd have to grow 10 feet tall, sprout horns and blow smoke out her nose. The two liked the idea so much, they wrote the first Bailey School Kids' book, *Vampires Don't Wear Polka Dots*, during their lunch breaks. It quickly sold 250,000 copies. Still, they had to work hard to persuade Scholastic Inc., its publisher, that another Bailey School Kids book could be successful. Forty more books have followed.

Writer is specific about proposal—a profile.

The story I propose is a profile about the ebullient Jones, who is a consultant for gifted and talented students in Lexington, but who still writes a book a month with Dadey, using E-mail. The authors also write two other series for Scholastic, and Jones travels the region as a teacher and speaker about writing.

Writer provides pertinent information about her writing experience.

Could you please let me know if you are interested in this article? I'm including a SASE and some clips. A former medical reporter, I have written articles for a wide variety of other magazines, including *American Health for Women*, *Health Management Technology* and *Curriculum Administrator*. I am currently cowriting a book for Writer's Digest Books, *The Writer's Market Companion*. I also teach journalism at Northern Kentucky University.

Thank you for your consideration.

Sincerely,

Mary Carmen Cupito

SAMPLE QUERY

Comments from Dana Points, executive editor, American Health

3 March 1999

Julie Editor
American Health
204 Broadway
New York, NY 10010

Dear Ms. Editor:

I am writing to propose an article for *American Health* on the impact of the Y2K problem on health care.

Timely topic.

With the exception of some serious computer geeks, few of us expect the Y2K problem to pose any long-term disruption to our lives next year. Most women will probably take what we assume to be reasonable precautions: we won't be flying on January 1, 2000; we'll have some cash on hand, in case the ATMs aren't working; we'll make sure to keep track of our bank statements and records of our mortgage payments.

Thought-provoking questions.

But what if your baby's due in February or March next year? Or your husband's doctor is recommending that he consider some elective surgery next year? Or your son is diagnosed with juvenile diabetes at the end of this year? As women, we're responsible for most of the family health care decisions—but how many of us have considered whether Y2K will affect our health, or the health of our families? It's not the first thought that leaps to mind. But maybe it should be according to a recent report from the United States Senate Special Committee on the Year 2000 Technology Problem. The Senate report says that the health care industry "is one of the worst-prepared for Y2K, and carries a significant potential for harm."

Health care consumers might not realize, for example, that:

Good facts/reasons to do story.

- the machines that would monitor their blood pressure and heart during an operation could contain date-sensitive computer chips that may, or may not, be functioning properly after January 1, 2000; or
- their patient records are being transmitted from their primary care doctor's office to their surgeon or hospital via a healthcare information network that, again, may or may not have been appropriately reprogrammed to deal with the Y2K problem; or
- they may require drugs which, because of manufacturing or distribution problems related to the Y2K issue, may or may not be available;

SAMPLE QUERY

Comments from Dana Points, executive editor, *American Health*

February 5, 2000

Meg Leder
U.S. Health
200 Heart Lane
Healthy, NY 10500

Dear Ms. Leder:

Personal angle/first-person anecdote is good.

As new parents, my husband, Jim, and I decided it was finally time to apply for some life insurance. The shock of having Jim denied coverage was followed by the even greater shock that he had tested positive for Hepatitis C Virus, a disease that was completely unknown to us. In that regard, we were not alone.

Good—facts about subject. News hook.

Although an estimated 4.8 million Americans have Hep C, less that 5 percent of them know it. Many of those at high risk are average people, including middle-aged housewives who had a cesarean delivery and Vietnam veterans. Since Hep C can be present for decades without causing any symptoms, denial of life insurance coverage is one leading way that Americans discover they have the disease. Those who are less fortunate may not discover they have the virus until their liver is severely damaged or destroyed. Nearly one-third of all liver transplants in the US are needed because the recipient has Hep c.

Shows knowledge of magazine and its columns.

I propose a 2,000-word article, which could be ready within 30 days, for your Medical Diary section. The article would detail how Jim and I learned about his disease, how we are coping with his treatment, and my return to work to help support our family. It would also include current information about Hep C, including how it is transmitted (the only high risk activites Jim ever engaged in were getting a tattoo of Yosemite Sam on his forearm twenty years ago and being inoculated in the Navy), prognosis, (without treatment, Hep C can destory the liver), and new treatments (Rebetron, the drug Jim is currently taking, Alferon N, and Maxamine are the three most promising drugs under study).

Credentials as writer.

A columnist for the *Pickerington Times-Sun* and *Daily Floridian* before moving to Denver, I have studied this subject in depth since Jim's diagnosis. My sources would include Dr. C. Everett Koop, former Surgeon-General of the United States and leading advocate in the fight against Hep C, the Digestive Disease Center at Baylor Hospital in Dallas, the American Liver Foundation, and the Centers for Disease Control and Prevention, Hepatitis Branch.

Hep C is called "the silent epidemic" because so many Americans have it (four times as many as have HIV), yet so few are aware that they do. I would greatly appreciate the opportunity to write this article for *U.S. Health*.

Sincerely,

Wendy Jones

CHAPTER NINE

Selling Your Nonfiction Book

John H. White Jr. was already an expert on railroad history, the curator of transportation at the Smithsonian Institution and an author of several books about trains—including *The American Railroad Passenger Car* (Johns Hopkins University Press, 1985), nominated for a National Book Award—when he first met with a New York literary agent. White tried to interest the agent in an idea for a new book about trains, but the agent said there wasn't much of a market for that type of book. He asked about White's other interests. When White mentioned that he enjoyed making furniture, the agent grew enthusiastic. That, he said, was worth writing a book about, because how-to books on woodworking keep selling and selling.

After thinking about this conversation, White came up with an idea for a book about how anyone could make replicas of antique furniture without investing in expensive woodworking tools. It might have been a terrific book. But then White realized that the only reason he would be writing it would be for the money, and, although the idea interested him, he was comfortable financially and transportation interested him more. He returned to writing books on the history of railroads and trains, happily publishing them with university and independent presses, without an agent.

The adage among writers is that you do your best work writing what you love. It remains as true today as ever. But there is another truth about writing books today: If you want to find a publisher for your manuscript, you have to understand what will sell and how to sell it. Simply having an idea that you love is the first step among many that must be taken before your wonderful notion is transformed into a book. This chapter will help you understand the steps to take to bring about that transformation.

The Publishers

The book-publishing world appears to be increasingly devolving toward monopoly. "With Bertelsmann's purchase of Random House, and other companies being bought and sold like baseball cards, power is now concentrated in the hands of four behemoth publishers: Random House/Bantam Doubleday Dell, Simon & Schuster, Penguin Putnam and HarperCollins," note Marilyn and Tom Ross, in their book *Jump Start Your Book Sales* (Communication Creativity, 1999). *Publishers Weekly* reports that small publishers have joined the consolidation craze, as small publishers buy smaller publishers or are absorbed by larger ones.

What this means for beginning writers is not clear. One view is that mega-publishers and chain bookstores are interested in only big books to market to millions, narrowing the entryway for beginners. But others disagree. Michael Larsen, literary agent and author of *How to Write a Book Proposal* (Writer's Digest Books, 1997), says that now is still a good time to be a writer because the major conglomerates are more competitive than ever. "The challenge is," he says, "that the bar keeps rising."

> I nearly always write the first chapter before trying to write a formal outline. While writing the chapter, I keep a large legal-sized notepad on the desk next to my typewriter stand. Almost every paragraph of chapter one, in the instant of being written, gives rise to at least one thought later in the book—along with thoughts about where this piece of material should appear in relation to other pieces. I jot these thoughts down on the notepad as they arise, and in the process I try to arrive at a rough and preliminary chapter-by-chapter structure for my book.
>
> —Max Gunther, *Writing and Selling a Nonfiction Book* (Writer, 1973)

Arnold Dolin, who left his job as senior vice-president/associate publisher with Dutton/Plume to become a freelance editor, says there's no hard evidence that it's harder for newcomers to break into print today. While larger publishers have been trimming their midlist authors, whose works aren't best-sellers, the bottom line remains that "publishers are always looking for something good," says Dolin, who has spent forty years in publishing.

Yet Andre Schiffrin, who left his job as managing director and editor in chief of Pantheon Books to become editor in chief of the not-for-profit publisher The New Press, criticizes the large houses for concentrating increasingly on light entertainment and commercial tie-ins. Schiffrin examined the catalogs of Random House, HarperCollins and Simon & Schuster. They included novels, memoirs and books on current affairs, he noted, but none offered a single title about serious history, scientific theory, philosophy, theology, literary criticism or art history, "all fields that were at one time or another represented, even if sparsely, in all of these catalogs," he wrote in March 1999. "The lesson we have drawn is that, although many types of books undeniably become harder to publish with every passing year, the audiences for many topics remain untapped, simply because no one has tried to reach them."

Independent and small presses, however, may try to do just that. And the number of small publishers is growing, despite the industry's consolidation. R.R. Bowker's *Books in Print* database indicates that the number of publishers with active titles has increased steadily from 49,040 in 1996 to 62,740 in 1998. While large publishers may pay larger advances and their imprints carry more cachet, smaller publishers possess other advantages for writers. They may give authors more personal attention, and they may find for books an audience that may not be massive, but abiding.

In 1998, the Book Industry Study Group surveyed 53,479 small publishers,

> **The decision to acquire a book is drawn from such intangible values as taste, instinct and passion. Yet these qualities may stand squarely in opposition to many relentless business realities. The tension between these values is as ancient as art itself and will never be satisfactorily resolved.**
>
> —Richard Curtis, *This Business of Publishing: An Insider's View of Current Trends and Tactics* (Allworth Press, 1998)

Average Manuscript Length
- Short-short story: 250–1,500 words
- Short story: 1,500–10,000 words
- Novella/novelette: 30,000–50,000 words
- Hardcover novel: 60,000 words and up
- Paperback original: 60,000–80,000 words
- Children's picture book: 150–1,500 words
- Juvenile book: 15,000–60,000 words
- Nonfiction book: 20,000–200,000 words
- Query letter: one full page, single-spaced words

Note: The average double-spaced full typewritten page contains 250 words of pica type.

Excerpted from *The Writer's Encyclopedia* (Writer's Digest Books, 1996).

which accounted for 77 percent of the titles listed in *Books in Print* and had sales of up to ten million dollars annually. It found that these publishers tend to print modest numbers of each book, with first printings of 2,500, 3,000 and 5,000—a fraction of that of large houses. But they also tended to keep their books in print longer. Small publishers that had been in business for six to fifteen years were still selling more than three-fourths of all the titles they had *ever* published.

Selling a book to any publisher, always a challenge for new writers, will continue to be so, but there are plenty of opportunities for writers to find houses that support them and their work.

Finding a Publisher

Because there are so many publishers, it's essential for writers to research the publishing house before sending in proposals. Many smaller publishers specialize in certain topics; many possess deeply held philosophies of what they will publish, and you, as a potential author, are expected to know those before you submit to them.

This is true even for university presses, which, in the face of shrinking budgets and declining library dollars for books, have become more sensitive to bottom-line issues and marketing. "For writers, it means that they need to study their publishers and know what kind of a book they have," says Henry Y.K. Tom, executive editor, social sciences, at Johns Hopkins University Press. "They need to do their homework and be familiar with the lists of different publishers so that they can identify a short list of possible publishers which are actively publishing the author's subject area."

Other editors echoed this notion. "If somebody sends me a proposal or manuscript for a business book or parenting book, I know they haven't looked at my catalog," says Tracy Carns, publishing director of the Overlook Press, which publishes about seventy-five fiction and nonfiction titles a year. "It just automatically goes back."

"Every time I get a fiction proposal, I don't bother to open it," says Kirsty Melville, publisher of the Ten Speed Press. Her company publishes only nonfiction, and often "offbeat and quirky" nonfiction at that (some of its titles are *White Trash Cooking* [1986], *Why Cats Paint* [1994] and *What Color Is Your Parachute?* [1999]). Writers improve their chances by being familiar with the types of books her house publishes and stating (in their book proposals) why their book would fit happily on the shelves beside them, Melville says.

While there is no secret list of hot topics that publishers will buy, at any given time certain topics are undeniably in vogue. You can scour *Publishers Weekly* looking for such trends. In mid-1999, for example, the publication noted that Wicca, along with other earth religions and nature-based belief systems like shamanism and Native American spirituality, represented one of the hottest trends in New Age publishing. But unless you've got a manuscript already prepared on Wicca (or an interest in banging one out quickly), such information probably doesn't do you much good. It's difficult for beginners to try to judge what topics will be hot two years from now, which is about how long it takes to get a book into print.

Nevertheless, popular authors choose popular topics. They may enjoy reading about cooking in medieval France, but they write about the great restaurants of

---

What editors really want is something they can't describe because it doesn't exist yet—the untold story, the fresh perspective, the new idea.

—Judith Appelbaum, *How to Get Happily Published* (HarperPerennial, 1998)

Paris, knowing that such books sell. So you have to decide whether you want to be a professional, full-time writer, with all the marketing savvy that requires, or if you will be happy simply writing about a topic that interests you, and finding a publisher of that type of book.

Frankly, it's not the topic that shoots down most book proposals. "My experience has been, with 99 percent of the submissions that come in, you don't have to read very far to say this is not worth it," Dolin says. "Most of them are not well written, and that's the first requirement."

Agents and editors advise beginners to think the book through, from conception to promotion, and to write and rewrite chapters. Then take them to a writing group and have others read and critique your work. At good writers groups, other writers will not only give you their opinions, but they'll also offer consolation, support and encouragement. If you can find no group near you, look for writers groups on the Internet or take a journalism or other writing course at a college. You'll probably meet at least one published writer—the teacher—who might be willing to help you. When you're confident you're writing your best, you're ready to start selling.

Make Your Book Competitive

"The first thing a writer should do if he has an idea for a nonfiction book is to check out the potential competition," says agent Michael Larsen. You'll have to know what other books already have been written on your topic to know how yours will fit in the mix. You might need some of the information in those books as background in your book. And you'll have to know what these books don't cover. Eventually, you'll include all this information in a book proposal to an agent or editor.

It's easy to visit an online bookstore, type in the title of a competitive book and then sit back and watch the computer pull up similar books. But it's also useful to head to the library and bookstore to scout the competition. Browsing in the real world gives you a look at covers, illustrations and heft of the books, and helps you visualize how you'd like your book to fit on the shelves. And you can chat with the bookstore owner about how the books are selling or with the librarian about how often people check out similar titles.

If your topic is weighted down by a whole shelf full of books, don't despair. That may well be a good thing—it proves that many editors believe many people are interested in reading about that topic.

When Janice Papolos was preparing her book proposal—reprinted in this chapter—for *The Virgin Homeowner* (W.W. Norton and Company, 1997), she went to *Books in Print*. She found that other books for new homeowners were massive, doorstop books that advised readers how to haul out expensive tools to fix everything from the basement floor to the roof. Each had been reprinted multiple times. That, she believes, proved there was a strong market, an ever-renewing reading populace.

She also knew her book would be different from other books on the market because it wasn't designed to show people how to fix things. After all, she points out, we're not all born with the Bob Vila gene. It instead would be a fun, and funny, book about her experiences learning about tending her house after living in apartments, her discovery of the meaning of such peculiar terminology as "flashing" and "phlange" and her realization of why it's important to know such things. "I like to say there are 3,000 components to a house and I was clueless about 2,999 of them," she says. "I thought my boiler had a higher IQ than I did." But she learned important things about owning a house, and she worked this notion into a theme of her book that would appeal to readers—what you don't know can hurt you.

The Query Letter

Seldom will an editor read an entire unsolicited manuscript. Many won't accept unsolicited material of any kind. Even if a publisher does, often an editorial assistant or an intern wades into the "slush pile" to read it. Agents can help smooth the way for writers by contacting editors they have worked with and whose tastes they understand, transforming the material from unsolicited to solicited.

It's your decision whether to approach an editor or an agent first, or both simultaneously (see page 164 for more about agents). But thankfully, both are looking for

The Nonfiction Book Proposal

Most proposals range from thirty-five to seventy-five pages. Your proposal will have three parts in a logical sequence. Each part has a goal. You must impress agents and editors enough with each part to convince them to go on to the next.

1. The Introduction

THE OVERVIEW

1. The subject hook: the most exciting, compelling thing that you can say that justifies the existence of your book: a quote, event, anecdote, statistic, idea or joke.

   The book hook includes 2, 3 and 4:

2. The title: it must tell and sell.
3. The book's selling handle: a sentence that begins, "[The title] will be the first book to . . ."
4. The length of the book (and number of illustrations) arrived at by estimating the back matter and outlining the book.
5. The book's special features: tone, humor, structure, anecdotes, checklists, exercises, sidebars and anything you will do to give the text visual appeal.
6. The name of a well-known authority who will give your book credibility and salability in fifty states who has agreed to write an introduction.
7. What you have done to answer technical or legal questions. If your book covers a specialized subject, name the expert who has reviewed it. If your book may present legal problems, name the literary attorney who has reviewed it.
8. Back matter: using comparable books as a guide.
9. Markets for the book, starting with the largest one.
10. Subsidiary rights possibilities, starting with the most commercial one.
11. Spin-offs: If your book can be a series or lends itself to sequels, mention the other books.
12. Your promotion plan: In descending order of importance, a list of what you will do to promote your book during its one-month launch window and forever after. For most books aimed at a wide audience, this list is eight times more important than the content of the book.
13. A list of books that will compete with and complement yours.

RESOURCES NEEDED TO COMPLETE THE BOOK

List out-of-pocket expenses for five hundred dollars or more, such as travel, illustrations, permissions or an introduction, and a round figure for how much they will cost.

continued

ABOUT THE AUTHOR
Include everything you want editors to know about you in descending order of relevance and importance.

2. The Outline
Write a paragraph to a page of prose outlining every chapter to prove that there's a book's worth of material in your idea and you have devised the best structure to organize it. Aim for one line of outline for every page of text you guesstimate, for example, nineteen lines of outline for a nineteen-page chapter.

3. Sample Chapters
Enclose one to three sample chapters (depending on length and the publisher's guidelines).

Excerpted from *How to Write a Book Proposal* by Michael Larsen (Writer's Digest Books, revised edition, 1997).

the same thing: a fresh idea, evidence that you know your material and an indication that you are the right person to write this book.

The first approach to either agent or editor is often a query letter. Queries are brief letters selling your idea and yourself. Aim for one page that piques the editor's interest. Mention the title of your book and explain what it is about, who its audience would be and why they'd be interested reading a book on this topic. If you've drafted your first chapter, its lead might work as the first paragraph in your query. Also include a paragraph of your writing credentials and your expertise.

A word about voice: Allow your voice in the letter to display the same enthusiasm as it does when you're talking with friends about your book. Agents and editors like writers who believe their books are wonderful, but they dislike being told, "This will be a best-seller." Impart your ardor for your work more subtly. Another comment about voice, from Kimberley Cameron, an agent with the Reece Halsey North Literary Agency: "I always say send the first couple of pages of the book, because the voice in the letter is not always the voice of the writer."

If you decide to query an editor, try to find out who would be the right one for your book by reading the acknowledgments in similar books. There, authors often thank their editors. If they don't, call the publisher's publicity department to find out who edits books on your topic. Scan *Writer's Market* (Writer's Digest Books) for publishers that publish the type of book you want to write. Read publications such as *Writer's Digest* and *The Writer* for stories that mention editors. An entertaining way of learning about the business and the people who work in it is reading publishing memoirs, inside stories mentioning editors—some of whom may appeal to you.

Make a list of possibilities, and then call each publisher. Check to see if the editor is still there. Ask for a catalog of the company's books (which often includes names of editors and agents for books) and for submission guidelines that tell you what to send. Many publishers have similar information online.

To contact an agent, try the *Guide to Literary Agents* (Writer's Digest Books) or online sites, such as the Association of Authors' Representatives site (see page 170). Finding an agent may be difficult, so persistence is key.

Remember that editors and agents are individuals. What strikes one as tired and derivative may strike another as a perfect entrant for a hot market. So if your query is rejected and you believe in it, send it to someone else on your list.

It should go without saying that the query letter should be typed, free of errors, unrumpled and polite—but editors and agents agree that this, nevertheless, must be said. (One agent even pointed out how unpleasant it is to open an envelope that reeks of cigarette smoke.) So check, double-check, proofread and have your spouse or best friend proofread to make the letter perfect before you lick the envelope.

End your query by asking the agent or editor if he would be interested in seeing more. Always include a self-addressed, stamped envelope for reply. But don't print out your query letter and mail it just yet. The agent or editor could give you a happy answer: "We love it. Send in the proposal," and writing one of those requires a lot more work.

The Book Proposal

Book proposals can take months to write. Some beginners might find it easier to write the book first, then use it to prepare a proposal—which editors say is not a

To Agent or Not to Agent?

While some publishers listed in *Writer's Market* note that they accept material from writers who don't have agents, many editors prefer to work with agents who understand their houses' needs and their own tastes.

"I think there's always a way for a talented writer to get published," says Tracy Carns, publishing director of the Overlook Press. But she advises beginning writers first to find an agent. "This is a business of relationships," she points out, "and agents have a relationship with the editor and publisher. They know what we like."

She is far more likely to read first a proposal sent by a trusted agent than a cold submission. "I'll obviously look at everything, but not all submissions are created equal," she says. "Selling a manuscript is a specialized skill. That's what agents do. Why should a writer be expected to do that? If you're a writer, you should write."

For each of the thirty books she acquires each year, Carns says she would rather deal with an agent. "If I'm going to deal on a business point, a financial point, it's good to have that professional intermediary," she says.

You can find lists of agents in many books and on the Internet (see the resource list on page 169-170). If you're worried about unscrupulous agents, check the *Guide to Literary Agents*, which requires agents to submit letters of recommendation before they can be listed. Web sites are also good sources for checking on the reputation of a particular agent.

The Association of Authors' Representatives sets high criteria for those who may join its ranks, requiring them, among other things, to agree annually to abide by a Canon of Ethics. Its Web site (www.bookwire.com/AAR) also lists questions to ask any agent interested in representing you.

You can also meet agents (and editors) at writers conferences, where you can size them up to determine whether you'd make good partners. Mystery writer C.J. Songer notes that she attended a number of writing conferences and local writers group meetings as she was writing her first book, listening to speakers and agents and analyzing what she wanted in someone who would be representing her work. She read how-to articles to help her not only find an agent "correctly," but also to determine which tactics might be overused. "That way, when I started sending out 'Agent Hook Packages,' I was as sure as I could be that I was representing myself to potential agents as someone who was professional enough to know what was required, and yet creative or quirky enough to be interesting and worth a thorough look," she says. It worked. She found an agent with whom she is quite comfortable, and Scribner has published the first two of her books in the Meg Gillis Crime Novel series, *Bait* (1998) and *Hook* (1999).

bad notion, since they want to be assured an unknown writer can produce an entire book before committing their house to the manuscript.

There isn't one right way of writing a nonfiction book proposal, just as there is no one right way to write a book. That said, here are some guidelines:

A **proposal** is about thirty pages or more. It contains an overview, an author's biographical sketch, a detailed outline of what will be in each chapter and two or three sample chapters. It should be concise and written in active voice, generally in third person.

The **overview** includes a strong title, a detailed description of what you plan to write, why it's important, who would want to read it, how it differs from other books on the market, how you'll research it, an estimated length, how long you'll take to write it (usually a year or less) and a description of illustrations, appendices and other back matter.

Spend time thinking of a good title for your book. It should intrigue and inform. Consider carefully who your readers will be, and research them. Whether your book is for new parents or dog owners, find out how many of these people there are, because the more there are, the better your chances of selling your book.

But not always. Robert Post, a historian who wanted to write a book about drag racing, noted in his book proposal that several popular periodicals, some with circulations of 275,000, 400,000 and 1 million, served racing enthusiasts. Even his agent was excited by those numbers, and put the book up for auction. But no New York publishing house was interested, believing that most racing fans don't read books.

(A footnote: Post's book *High Performance* was later published by Johns Hopkins University Press. Post says he had thought that only a small community of scholars of the history of technology would be the audience, and he had imagined finding "some hotshot professor" to write a blurb. "Hopkins thought that auto racing fans did read books, and that's who they were going to market it to," Post says. The publisher got blurbs from race drivers. It sold about 12,000 copies in about six years. "By academic press standards, that's a wild best-seller," Post laughingly says.)

You don't have to mention every competing book in your book proposal, of course, but choose a handful of successful books that will compete with or complement yours. Describe them in a sentence or two (try reading dustjackets to see how thousands of words can be boiled down to a few). Papolos gives another bit of advice here: Don't speak poorly of the competition. It scores no points with editors, and it may backfire. If you tell an editor that competing books are dreadful, that might indicate nobody cares enough to read them.

The **table of contents** should be a detailed outline of the book. Some experts advise condensing each chapter to a page or so. Larsen recommends a line of outline for every page of text in each chapter, so a twenty-page chapter would get twenty lines of summation. Note, however, that the chapter outline for *The Virgin Homeowner* provides sketchy, but catchy, lists for each chapter. In this proposal, the preface (which Janice Papolos submitted with the proposal) supplies more information about what the book will contain and how readers can use it.

The **biographical sketch** usually is written in the third person. It should highlight your experience and training and explain why you're writing this book.

Finally, **sample chapters** should prove that you know how to research and write. These are critically important; don't send rough drafts, and do choose chapters that are representative of the content and style of the whole book. Editors and agents will look for good writing, evidence of research and your ability to keep readers interested.

Larsen, who has developed a list of items for proposals for nonfiction books, believes a proposal that sells to large publishing houses also must include the author's plan for promoting the book. "I can usually tell from two things—a title and promotional plan—whether I can help a writer approach a major house," Larsen says. To make a nonfiction book for a wide national audience succeed, he says, the content of the book is only about 10 percent of the challenge, the right editor and right house are another 10 percent, but the promotional plan is 80 percent. "This is not necessarily true for serious biographies, works of science or reference books," he says, "but for most nonfiction books that have a wide national audience, the promotion of which has to be author-driven, that is the case."

He emphasizes that he represents books he believes he can sell to major houses and that New York publishers want nonfiction books to have first-year sales of at least fifteen thousand copies. If you want to try smaller, independent publishers, the promotional plan may not be such an important part of the proposal.

All proposals, however, must be professional, well written and comprehensive. "Proposals need to be much more complete and less speculative than they ever were," says agent Donna Downing of Pam Bernstein & Associates. Sample chapters didn't used to be part of the proposal, but now they're an important component, she notes. The editor or agent also must know in detail how the book is going to read, what topics it will cover, who would read it and why.

Downing adds, "One of the basic things we need to come across in a nonfiction proposal is the author's platform—how are you equipped to be the expert on this topic and how will you contribute to sales? The more you do, the better off you are. It can only improve sales, which in turn improves the next advance for your next book."

Yet, smaller publishers also appreciate promotional efforts by authors. "The content is what we're interested in first," says Kirsty Melville, "but then how the book might be sold is important. Long after we've published a book, it's the author's promotion of it and willingness to keep talking about it that helps to keep the sales going." However, she notes that many of Ten Speed Press's books fit niche markets and tend to be promoted regionally—so a proposal for a nationwide book tour probably would not make her editors' hearts sing. (See chapter fourteen for tips on promotion.)

Before you send in your proposal—with a self-addressed, stamped envelope so that it can be returned—keep in mind that agents and editors read all day. Anything you can do to make your letters and manuscripts easier on the eyes makes them more appealing.

- Don't type on both sides of the page.
- Don't use peculiar fonts just because you can.
- Do use wide margins of about 1¼–1½ inches (3.2–3.8 cm).
- Do use 12-point type.
- Do number the pages.
- Don't bind anything in your proposal.
- Double-space the chapters, but single-space the other parts of the proposal.
- Triple-check the spelling of the editor's or agent's name one last time before you drop the proposal in the mailbox.

Publishing Digitally

Publishing e-books may be the greatest thing to happen to the written word since Gutenberg. Or not. While publishing books electronically will certainly change the world of publishing, its benefits, and its drawbacks, to writers are not yet clear.

E-publishers may offer authors 20 to 50 percent of book sales, compared to about 8 to 15 percent royalties for traditional books. Digital books can be printed in small press runs and can stay "in print" much longer, as customers order copies and download them to their computers or other reading devices.

But the numbers of e-books sold has been far fewer than the numbers of paper books. Many people, including many reviewers, still regard digital books as a high-tech form of vanity press.

Some e-publishers accept all manuscript submissions, charging authors several hundred dollars or more for several months' listing and promotion at their Web sites. Other e-publishers say they accept fewer than 10 percent of the manuscripts e-mailed to them, and charge authors little or nothing.

Writers also have the option of publishing their books using on-demand printing, the cousin to e-book publishing. With on-demand printing, an author usually pays a fee to have his or her book digitized, and a special machine prints and binds copies on paper as customers request them.

For more information on e-books and print on demand, check out these sites:
- Association of Electronic Publishers (http://members.tripod.com/~BestBooks Com/AEP)
- Dark Star Publications (www.darkstarpublications.com)
- DiskUs Publishing (www.diskuspublishing.com)
- 1st Books (www.1stbooks.com)
- iUniverse (http://www.iuniverse.com/publish/)
- Starlight Writers Publications (www.starpublications.com)
- Peanut Press (www.peanutpress.com)

Remember one last cliché about the publishing business: Even brilliant writers were rejected by publishers, some of them several times. Some writers learn to appreciate rejection. "I get the greatest rejection letters I've ever seen," Papolos says. Editors may not agree to buy her books, but they tell her they are impressed with her proposals' professionalism and comprehensiveness, and that is some consolation.

If an editor tells you why she rejects your book proposal, don't let it crush you; let it teach you how to improve it. Then send it out to the next person on your list. Remember as you mail it off that as much as you hope to find a publisher for your beloved book, publishers are hoping to find a book they would love to publish.

Resources

BOOKS

Annual Directory of the Association of American University Presses, 584 Broadway, Suite 410, New York, NY 10012.

Guide to Literary Agents (Writer's Digest Books).

How to Get Happily Published by Judith Appelbaum (HarperCollins, 1998).

How to Write Attention-Grabbing Query and Cover Letters by John Wood (Writer's Digest Books, 1996).

How to Write Irresistible Query Letters by Lisa Collier Cool (Writer's Digest Books, 1990).

International Directory of Little Magazines and Small Presses (Dustbooks).

The Literary Agent's Guide to Getting Published by Bill Adler Jr. (Claren Books, 1999).

Literary Agents: The Essential Guide for Writers, Debby Mayer (Viking Penguin, 1998).

Literary Agents: What They Do, How They Do It, and How to Find and Work With the Right One for You by Michael Larsen (John Wiley and Sons, 1996).

Nonfiction Book Proposals Anybody Can Write: How to Get a Contract and an Advance Before Writing Your Book by Elizabeth Lyon (Blue Heron Publishing, 2000).

The Writer's Handbook, 1999 edition, edited by Sylvia Burack (Writer, Inc., 1998).

Writer's International Guide to Book Editors, Publishers, and Literary Agents by Jeff Herman (Prima Publishing, 1999).

Writer's Market (Writer's Digest Books).

WEB SITES

Association of Authors' Representatives, Inc. (www.bookwire.com/AAR). A listing of members of this organization of professional agents. Includes its code of ethics and questions to discuss with potential agents.

Association of Electronic Publishers (members.tripod.com/~BestBooks Com/AEP). Learn more about e-book companies.

Bookwire (www.bookwire.com). A terrific, comprehensive site about book publishing with good links to other useful sites.

Directory of Literary Agents (www.writers.net/agents_body.html). An online directory of literary agents who do not charge reading fees.

Publishers' Catalogues Home Page (www.lights.com/publisher/). Lists catalogs of publishers everywhere.

Writer's Federation of Nova Scotia (www.chebucto.ns.ca/Culture/WFNS /booknfic.html). Advice on writing a nonfiction book proposal.

NONFICTION BOOK PROPOSAL: TITLE PAGE

Comments from Donna Downing, Pam Bernstein & Associates

The Virgin Homeowner

The Essential Guide to Owning, Maintaining
and Surviving Your First Home

BY JANICE PAPOLOS

Proposal Table of Contents

- Concept, Style and Marketing Outline
- *The Virgin Homeowner* Table of Contents
- Annotated Table of Contents
- Preface to *The Virgin Homeowner*
- Sample Chapter 1: The Sorcerer's Apprentice: Or, Water, Water Everywhere
- Sample Chapter 2: Creosote Is a Dirty Word

Great proposal!

At least two sample chapters are a *must*. (Papolos submitted sample chapters with her original proposal, however they are not reprinted here.)

The Virgin Homeowner: Overview

THE CONCEPT

It is still the American dream to own a home, and according to the National Association of Realtors, home sales are surging to a fourteen-year high. Last year, some 4.2 million currently existing houses were sold in this country, and some 1,285,000 new houses were built.

> Proves that the market is growing. It's essential to prove how large the potential market is—and why this book is needed.

For the first-time homeowner, however, understanding how a house works to keep you warm, supply your shower with hot water, and funnel all the unmentionables to leaching fields can be downright mystifying. Maintaining a house is a whole other problem. Once everyone's shaken your hand at the closing, who clues you in on everything that needs to be done? Years ago families lived within close distance of each other, and a parent or older sibling could come over and educate the novice homeowner. Today, we live in a very mobile society, and often the only resources lie between the pages of books.

THE STYLE

All of the books [on this subject] currently on the market are written by men— men who are engineers or who could claim Bob Vila as kin. The books are useful as references, but are dry and impersonal, written in a sort of medical-text style. None of them deal with the welter of feelings and insecurities that are aroused as you go through the first year or two with a new home.

> Key difference with this book vs. the competition. Good explanation of why this author is the perfect "expert" on the topic.

The Virgin Homeowner differs from anything on the market because it will be written with humor, insight and depth by a woman who actually is (or recently was) a virgin homeowner.

I haven't forgotten how frightening and confusing it is to make that transition from apartment renter to mistress of a house, and also how short your attention span is as you deal with the excitement and anxiety of this very major purchase, the move and the change in lifestyle. Therefore, my goal would be to make the book lively and engaging, anecdotal and sympathetic. Just as Dr. Spock sits on the nursery shelf offering knowledge and comfort to fledgling parents, I expect *The Virgin Homeowner* will sit within easy reach of a new homeowner and educate with a light and memorable touch.

> All these words appeal to women.

> This author gives an exact picture of what the finished book will look like—very impressive—she's done her homework.

THE FORMAT

The book will be approximately 250 pages and chock-full of facts and rich stories of life on the new-home front. It will be fully indexed and include a number of elegant line drawings and humorous cartoons. Sidebar and boxed material will be included for easy-reference, at-a-glance information.

In order to broaden the scope of the book and to add other voices and perspectives, I am scheduling focus groups with other new homeowners in this area. I am a member of New Neighbors of Westport, so my organization would help identify other "virgins" who could share their experiences. I also intend to interview men and women in California, Arizona, North Carolina, Wisconsin and Vermont so that the book reflects regional specifics and concerns.

Among the accomplished craftsmen I intend to interview are Americo Renzulli (the plumber featured in Martha Stewart's *This New Old House*); Jim Locke, author of *The Well-Built House* and owner of Apple Corps Construction; Don Fredriksson, author of *The Complete House Inspection Book*; and Duane Johnson, columnist for *The Family Handyman* magazine. A few of these preliminary interviews confirmed that anxiety and hysteria are pandemic among the first-time homeowner population and that there's a real need for this book.

THE COMPETITION

The books currently on the market are encyclopedic in their approach. Two of the best and most popular are *The New York Times Season-by-Season Guide to Home Maintenance* by John Warde and *Better Homes and Gardens Complete Guide to Home Repair, Maintenance & Improvement*. Both of these books run about 500 pages in length and teach the homeowner how to insulate his or her attic entrance as well as how to repoint crumbling brickwork, repair the roofing and change toilets in the bathrooms. New homeowners, and particularly a majority of women, cannot—at this point—quite picture themselves in those scenarios. The Better Homes and Gardens book was originally published in 1980 and is currently in its fifteenth printing.

Consumer Reports Books publishes *Year-Round House Care* by Graham Blackburn. It was originally published under another title in 1981 and revised in 1991. In April of 1992 it had a second printing. This book is straightforward and helpful. I ordered it from Consumer Reports after reading its title in *Books in Print*. I have never seen it in a bookstore.

Two books with a different focus bear mentioning. They are Sunset Publishing Corporation's *Home Repair Handbook* and Henry Holt's *How Things Work in Your*

Important to include a cross section of homeowners.

It's important to say how your book is better than the competition without being condescending to those other books— well done here.

Papolos/HOMEOWNER PROPOSAL   2

Home. The Sunset book is 185 pages long and now in its ninth printing. Unfortunately, some very clearly written information is tucked amid many projects that are quite beyond the scope of many homeowners, especially first timers. *How Things Work in Your Home* is beautifully written and illustrated. It covers the systems of a house, but its major emphasis is on the appliances used in a home—from vacuums to coffeemakers to chain saws. This is a Time-Life revised edition that had five printings in hardcover and is currently in its fourth printing in trade paperback.

MARKETS

> This is the place for your marketing ideas and/or contacts. You are offering ideas and suggestions to the publisher's marketing department, which is becoming more of a powerful decision-making force in acquisitions.

While every bookstore has a "Home" section, and *The Virgin Homeowner* would fit easily within this niche, the book would also make a natural gift. There are many catalogs that target the homeowner, and a picture and description in the pages of *Paragon*, *Lillian Vernon*, *The Safety Zone*, *Seasons*, etc., would reach millions of people—first timers and the people who know them.

Another excellent market would be the several hundred Home Depots and eight hundred Sears stores across the nation. The first thing my husband and I did after our closing was to drive to Home Depot, and this store or a Sears is an excellent place to come face-to-face with *The Virgin Homeowner*.

Surely one of the best markets for this book is the realty business. Professional realtors are the very people who can identify first-time homeowners and who almost always buy them gifts after the closings. Therefore, it seems a custom fit for a large national franchise corporation such as Century 21 to purchase this book in quantity and distribute it to its more than 5,000 offices across the country.

The National Association of Realtors (NAR) has over 800,000 members, and the organization publishes two magazines: *Home Guide* and *Real Estate Review*. An ad in their pages would reach an impressive number of realtors quite handily.

Another possible outlet would be a flyer distributed through Welcome Wagon of America. Typically, new homeowners call this organization and a representative comes to the home with all kinds of pamphlets and gifts to help them get settled in their home and community (I found my chimney sweep and handyman through Welcome Wagon).

TIME FRAME

> Should be no more than one year.

I am currently researching and writing the book, and it should take about ten months to complete the manuscript.

**NONFICTION BOOK PROPOSAL:
TABLE OF CONTENTS**

TABLE OF CONTENTS

Preface

Acknowledgments

"But First, a Word About Money . . ."

She's clearly thought this project through completely. There is little left to speculation.

1. Ground Zero: What I Should Have Learned From the Home Inspection
2. The Inner Mysteries: Heating, Electrical and Plumbing Systems
3. To Rid-X or Not to Rid-X: You and Your Septic System
4. Creosote Is a Dirty Word
5. The Sorcerer's Apprentice: Or, Water, Water Everywhere
6. Where Has All the Gravel Gone? Driveways, Pathways and Parking Areas
7. The Uninvited Guest, Part I: Ants, Termites and Other Creepy Crawlies
8. The Uninvited Guest, Part II: Security Systems and Burglar Alarms

Catchy phrases and chapter titles prove this will not be a dry reference manual. We get a good sense of her intelligent humor!

9. The Healthy House
10. Ventilation Is the Name of the Game
11. The Age of Innocence: Childproofing Inside and Out
12. Finally Home

Appendices

- The "On-Track" Calendar
- House Doctors Directory
- Paint Palette Page (or How Can We Touch Up That Room If We Can't Remember What We Used?)
- Notes of a New Homeowner
- Bibliography
- Indices

**NONFICTION BOOK PROPOSAL:
ANNOTATED TABLE OF CONTENTS**

ANNOTATED TABLE OF CONTENTS

You don't need too much detail in the annotated table of contents. Again, the challenge here is to keep this material interesting to the reader—give us ideas we can relate to.

1. Ground Zero: What I Should Have Learned From the Home Inspection. The future was in front of me, and I took lunch orders instead; what does the inspection accomplish? How do you find a reputable inspector? The inspector as teacher; your role as student, checklist of prepared questions, how to read and understand the report, follow-up on the recommendations; an "Inspection Follow-Up Page" that lets the reader extrapolate the recommendations, notate them in this book, and check them off when attended to; the radon report.

2. The Inner Mysteries: Heating, Electrical and Plumbing Systems. Thank God I got a service contract! Anatomy of a heating system, ducted or gravity: gas- or oil-fired furnaces, hot water/forced hot air, radiant heat, heat pumps, solar, electric, the pluses and minuses of each one; servicing each system before the heating season, how to reset a furnace, how I overcame my fear of bleeding radiators, budget plans, Move Over Sharon Stone! How I Failed to Flag My Fuel Line, Let the Snow Plower Bury It Beneath a Mountain of Ice, and How I Had to Attack It All Morning With Ice Picks Because We'd Run Out of Oil. Discussion of flagging methods. Anatomy of the water supply system, how to locate the main shutoff valve, hot water heaters, understanding a well, drips and running toilets and other things that drive you crazy, when to turn the garden water supply off so the pipes don't freeze.

3. To Rid-X or Not to Rid-X: You and Your Septic System. The World Beneath Our Feet: Anatomy of a septic system and leaching fields, the fascinating work of bacteria and the filtration of viruses, pump-out maintenance, the argument over a monthly treatment with Rid-X.

4. Creosote Is a Dirty Word. What is creosote and why is everyone saying such terrible things about it? The anatomy of a fireplace, how do you find a chimney sweep and what does he or she do? How my friend Marshall does the job himself. How to build a fire that would make a boy scout weep.

5. **The Sorcerer's Apprentice: Or, Water, Water Everywhere.** Anatomy of a roof, the impregnation of shingles, how the roof might let you down and leak, "Is There a Problem with Your Flashing?" Guttertalk, Damn Those Ice Dams, locating the leak and getting it fixed, water in the basement: sump pumps, cracks in the foundation, regrading around the foundation.

6. **Where Has All the Gravel Gone? Driveways, Pathways and Parking Areas.** Reviving gravel after the winter, repairing cracks and holes in black-top, driveway sealers, costs.

7. **The Uninvited Guest, Part I: Ants, Termites and Other Creepy Crawlies.** How to tell who's visiting (diagnosing diagrams), the best defense systems, how to find professionals to deal with the problem, discussion of yearly service contracts.

8. **The Uninvited Guest, Part II: Security Systems and Burglary Alarms.** The "False Step" and other early warning systems, your options other than a full-scale moat, how long do they take to install? How much do they cost? Safety Tips if You Go Away.

9. **The Healthy House.** Environmental concerns: radon, asbestos, lead, water quality; discussion of toxic materials and outgassing, carbon monoxide and alarms that detect its presence.

10. **Ventilation Is the Name of the Game.** Why do I keep hearing about this concept and what are those holes in the side and roof of my house? How proper ventilation protects your house and performs the important functions of comfort control and moisture control, passive ventilation: gable ridge roof, soffit vents and turbine vents, electric attic fans, opening and closing vents in the crawl space, cleaning vents.

11. **The Age of Innocence: Childproofing Inside and Out.** Modifying the environment, gates, cords, wires, electrical shields, hazardous household products and plants, the 1⅜" diameter test, the high toll of untempered glass, Are Glass Coffee Tables in the Picture? Safety Tips in the Kitchen and Bathroom, A Safer Out-of-Doors, Check Chart.

12. **Finally Home.** A psychological look at the moving and the new home-owner experience; interviews with other "virgins," what concerned them, what parts of the process they found overwhelming, how they got comfortable with their new role in life and how they put down roots in their new communities.

NONFICTION BOOK PROPOSAL: PREFACE

PREFACE

Gives us a good sense of how the book will read—her voice comes through, and it's warm and reassuring. Informational *and* funny.

In 1993, after the birth of our second child, and after living in New York City apartments for over twenty years, my husband and I joined the grown-up world and bought a house. While every now and then funny and disastrous scenes from *The Money Pit*, *Mr. Blandings Builds His Dream House* and *Baby Boom* would surface to conscious levels, we tamped them down with assurances to ourselves that these were merely Hollywood's comedic exaggerations. We were so busy figuring out how to finance the house and negotiate this major move—physically and emotionally— we had little energy left to figure out the mysterious workings of a house and what our part would be in maintaining it. As I look back now, I am stunned that I didn't know what a new homeowner was supposed to do, not only to keep the house comfortable and running economically, but to keep disaster from coming in from every crack and crevice! I think I thought it would all sort itself out gradually while we found our sea legs and got more comfortable in our new surroundings.

Not likely! There is no honeymoon with a house. There are things we should have been learning and doing right from the time of the inspection that would have resulted in less mishap and panic-filled moments.

Part of the problem was that I had this mystified awe of the house. I swear, there were times (thankfully rare) when I viewed it as more intelligent and more powerful than we were. And while I'm in a confessional mode: There was a time or two in which I felt the house was being downright vindictive. (If you own your own home, you may understand this paranoid fantasy.)

Little by little, though, we began to learn from the plumber, the electrician and the oil burner servicemen. And our friends. I kept bumping up against new vocabulary and concepts like "flashing," "creosote" and "ventilation." Since I thought flashing had something to do with elderly gentlemen in raincoats, and

I'm still a little unsure as to why my furnace is not breathing enough oxygen, I'm afraid we were rather amusing to our house "doctors."

One day, while sitting in front of the fireplace I had fortunately found out I was supposed to have cleaned (see Chapter 5, "Creosote Is a Dirty Word"), I sighed and said to my husband, Demitri, "Somebody should write a book for the virgin homeowner." He laughed and pointed a finger my way.

All right, I thought. Let me look into it. Gingerly, I broached the subject with friends and family. They were amused and enthusiastic and proceeded immediately to tell me all the funny and perilous situations they had encountered—and survived—as first-time homeowners. It turns out that none of us are very enlightened. And we're all so very anxious.

So that's what these pages are all about: helping new homeowners level the playing field, so to speak, and become knowledgeable about and comfortable with their new habitat. Even if you haven't been lucky enough to have inherited the "Bob Vila" gene for home repair, my objective in this book is to prove to you that taking care of a house does indeed fall under the category of "totally doable." (After all, this is all coming from a woman whose greatest victory on the mechanical front prior to owning a home was the successful changing of a halogen lightbulb!)

HOW TO USE THIS BOOK

In the best of all possible worlds, readers would come across this book just before they begin house hunting. Starting with "Ground Zero," they could read it straight through and tour all potential homes with an informed and educated eye. Then, when the right house appears, they could choose the right home inspector and do a bang-up job at the home inspection. Weeks later, and after the moving van departs, they would be comfortable with the systems of a house and clued in to its maintenance routines.

But life doesn't work like that. Many of you will pick this book up in the hectic days just before the move, or some months into your adventures on the domestic frontier. The ungodly time crunch of this settling-in period may not afford your reading every word from beginning to end, in one or two sittings. So let me highlight some of the important safety issues you need to take care of first.

Before you spend a night (or another night) in your new home, make sure you have working smoke detectors in all the right places and an emergency plan for escape in the event of a fire and install two carbon monoxide detectors.

If your chimney doesn't have a chimney cap, call a chimney sweep and have one made for it without delay (see page 23 of "Creosote Is a Dirty Word"). Have the chimney checked and cleaned at the same time. Then make sure all heating equipment is tuned up and checked before the start of the heating season.

If you have municipal water and didn't have your water tested for lead during the home inspection, run a test according to the directions in Chapter 9, "The Healthy House," and while you're open to that section, scan the elements of a healthy, nontoxic home so that you make informed decisions when choosing paints and any new furnishings. And by all means, if you've got a toddler or two, read "The Age of Innocence" and secure windows and stairways, check the automatic garage doors and order any other safety paraphernalia before you even think of letting your little roadrunners loose in their new and unfamiliar environment. (And while you're checking doors and windows, make sure that they're providing the appropriate level of physical security as discussed in the first half of Chapter 8, "The Uninvited Guest, Part II.")

Once you're all relatively safe and sound, familiarize yourself with the major systems of your house by reading Chapters 2, 3 and 4. This way, if the circuit breaker trips or a fuse blows and/or a leak develops there'll be no cause for panic. You'll also understand what a delicate flower your septic system is and how best to keep it healthy.

And if—when all the chaos subsides—you get hit with a bit of "Post-Parting Depression" and keenly miss your friends and former lifestyle, I hope that the last chapter, "Finally Home," is heartening as well as helpful as you go through the emotional experience of turning a house into a home and carving out a niche for yourself in a new community.

So sit down on your packing boxes, or in a corner of your probably under-furnished new home, and delve into this volume. Then get ready to appreciate what a marvelous facility a house is. Think of it. Physics and chemistry and electricity combine to give you and your loved ones shelter, warmth, comfort and convenience. . . . A house is a goodly thing. You keep the house; the house will keep you.

BUT FIRST A WORD ABOUT MONEY . . .

Before we begin, let me say a few words about the eye-popping estimates for home repairs you're going to see scattered throughout this text. They may be a bit on the high side because many of them are quotes from a metropolitan area, but house repairs are not cheap, not in Arizona, not in Alabama. As my friend David Wright from the tiny town of Edenton, North Carolina, likes to say, "My house accepts contributions only in denominations of one hundred dollar bills."

So, accepting that home repairs are expensive and that they're a fact of life, we need to ask ourselves two questions: How much money do we need to have in reserve to pay for annual repairs and maintenance, and—here's the biggie— where is all this money coming from?

Much depends of course on how old and needy the house is when you move in. If you know the roof is going to have to be replaced in five years and the quote was $6,000 for the job, you've got some serious saving to do. If the old oil tank has to be excavated and a new one installed in your basement, start scanning the horizon for that $3,000 now. Beyond the imminent projects you already know about are the miscellaneous repairs that crop up all the time. They may always be different, but you can count on them to occur. As my mother is fond of saying, "Once you own a house, you'll never have to wonder where your next nickel is going."

I spoke with Elizabeth Lewin, author of *Your Personal Financial Fitness Program* (Facts on File), and she told me that, depending on the age and location of the house a homeowner should budget between one and two percent of the value of the house for major annual home repairs (a new roof, a driveway re-paving, the curing of a leaky basement, the outdoor paint job, falling trees that don't hit the insured roof and so the homeowner pays for their removal, and other major repairs). Ouch! This easily translates to a couple of thousand dollars a year, and with mortgages, monthly bills, 401(k) contributions, college savings plans and crooked little teeth to straighten, what is a homeowner to do (besides pray avidly)?

Elizabeth suggests a more rational approach. She advises that a homeowner set up a savings account marked "House Reserve" and make a fairly frequent, routinized deposit into it. For example, when you pay your mortgage, make a deposit in the house account. A money market account or short-term mutual bond fund (money could be automatically withdrawn from your checking account monthly for this) are other ways to save. Eventually you'll build up a nice little nest egg for your nest egg.

Elizabeth Lewin made a point to say that very new homeowners (she laughed and called them "extra virgin" homeowners) will probably not establish this savings account in the first months or year of homeownership. There are just too many setup costs to allow much savings to take place.

Somehow we all manage, and you won't be the exception, but there's definitely a period of adjustment while you figure out where to spend less money in some areas because you have a big, new, superhungry category called "The House." Try to strike a balance where you don't deprive yourself, but you don't get caught by a total lack of planning.

You know, sometimes the house serves as a goad or a motivator, even, and you just might find more economic opportunities coming your way because you are more focused and you simply have to create them in order to feed your house.

Once you adjust your thinking and begin to enjoy your home, the pride of ownership will make taking care of it more of a tonic and less of a bitter pill. This is your corner of the world now. Tend it well. And remember, the house and its maintenance and repairs and improvement are just a transferring of assets. What you give out will come back to you.

Bring it all together.

CHAPTER TEN

Selling Your Fiction

When he was thirty-four and unpublished, Charles Turner decided to get serious about writing short fiction. He sat down with four issues of his wife's *Good House-keeping* magazine and read, really read, the fiction, "feeling the fabric."

Turner discovered some common denominators in each of the stories: They were all warm and affirmative. They were written in a friendly tone. Their heroines were familiar characters to most women. The endings often indicated a strengthening of relationships. Then, using those characteristics as guides, Turner wrote a short story, based on an idea he had discarded long before.

Good Housekeeping's editors liked it, but suggested some changes to his main character. He understood their concerns, made the changes and sold the story to the magazine and later to eight foreign magazines. "I don't think that's a bad accounting for a piece written with one special market in mind," he wrote in the *Handbook of Short Story Writing* (Writer's Digest Books, 1981).

The lesson is as fresh today: While you must find your own voice and your own truth in your writing, you must also find a market for that writing. Doing so requires reading the magazines that publish fiction to determine what types of stories they print. Writing only for yourself may stroke the ego, but you probably also want to write for other readers, which can help feed the body. In fact, you can do both without compromising your professional or personal integrity.

Rather than viewing the similarities in the fiction as restrictions against creativity, Turner saw them more as the parameters of publication. The story he wrote was good enough for the magazine he targeted, and he then found other markets that appreciated similar fiction.

Short Fiction

The competition for publishing short fiction, always fierce, is getting fiercer. Many magazines that once published short stories do so no longer. Yet, magazines that publish fiction are always hungry for new voices. (Fiction writers might benefit from chapter eight, "Selling Your Articles and Other Short Nonfiction," because many of the same principles apply: Each publication has its own personality, and a writer who doesn't respect that will soon see his fiction again—in his self-addressed, stamped envelope.)

Short fiction currently published in magazines often has strong plots, with characters who grow or change in the course of the story. The introspective, minimalist fiction of the 1980s has all but disappeared. Unusual, even bizarre stories—about bearded ladies and mourners who build paper furniture for the dead—offer diversion for readers. Short short stories of fewer than 1,500 words are ever more popular. Mysteries and romances remain in vogue. But these are general trends; publications exist for every style of writing.

The key to selling to magazines and reviews is reading them first. In addition, most will tell you the type of fiction they want; look in their writer's guidelines,

---

I know my book *The Artist's Way* has sold probably a million and a half copies by now. When I sent it to my agent at William Morris, my agent said, "Julia, there's no market for this." So I self-published the book, and of course discovered there was quite a market for it. The thing that I would over and over again tell writers is that, "If you want to be writers, simply write. Trust that what you care about will be cared about by others."

—Julia Cameron, interview in *Writer's Digest*, July 1999

---

many of which can be accessed online (www.writersdigest.com offers more than a thousand). *Good Housekeeping*'s guidelines, for example, state: "We welcome short fiction submissions (1,000 to 3,000 words). We look for stories with strong emotional interest—stories revolving around, for example, courtship, romance, marriage, family, friendships, personal growth, coming-of-age. The best way to gauge whether your story might be appropriate for us is to read the fiction in several of our recent issues."

Editors agree. "The best advice I can give," says Jill Adams, editor of *The Barcelona Review*, "is to read the guidelines carefully and take them seriously." Adams says she is frustrated when writers ignore her electronic literary review's maximum word length of 4,000 words and send 10,000-word manuscripts, saying that they couldn't possibly cut the piece and retain its integrity. "Maybe not," Adams says, "but then it's not the story for our review, and my time—and the writer's—has been wasted."

To improve your chances of having a story accepted, read widely to discover those markets that suit your style. Editors like to think writers choose to submit to their publications because they read and enjoy them, not because they copied the address from some list.

Before approaching any magazine, make sure your writing is as good as it can be. Editors say they see far too much work that simply isn't nearly polished enough for publication. Several agents and editors suggested taking your work to writers groups for honest feedback and suggestions.

Submitting

When the story is ready and when you've targeted a publication, include a brief cover letter with your short story and send it to a specific editor. (Call to find out the appropriate person.) Because reading a flat page is simpler than one that's been folded in thirds and squashed into a business envelope, send submissions in a 9″ × 12″ envelope, with a self-addressed, stamped return envelope. If the publication accepts E-mail submissions, follow the instructions carefully; sending an unreadable file is, obviously, self-defeating.

A cover letter is polite business correspondence, acting as an introduction to your story. It should include the name of the story, a sentence or two on what it's about, its word count, a mention of why you're sending it to a particular magazine and a paragraph about who you are. The cover letter won't make the sale—that depends on your story—but a sloppy or typo-ridden one can easily kill the sale.

Adams notes that she does not welcome plot summaries in cover letters, because "a short story should speak for itself." In fact, four editors interviewed for the 1999 *Novel and Short Story Writer's Market* (Writer's Digest Books) agreed that cover letters should be simple and brief (one suggested no more than a paragraph). They also said cover letters simply aren't worth sweating over (another called them "so insignificant"). Save the sweat for your stories. "I think writers worry so much about cover letters and other things because they feel like it's us versus them," Greg Michalson, managing editor of *The Missouri Review*, notes in *Writer's Market* (Writer's Digest Books). "I understand the feeling, but I don't think it's true. Every editor I've known who's worth two dead flies is excited to come across a good manuscript."

As with all written correspondence, the cover letter should be typed, checked for typos and sent with a self-addressed, stamped envelope, unless the magazine says it cannot return submissions or you mention that it's a disposable manuscript. Always keep a copy for yourself and a record of where and when you sent it.

Be prepared to be persistent, because magazines, online and on paper, report being inundated with submissions for fiction. At *Barcelona*, which *Writer's Digest* noted in 1999 was "publishing some of today's best fiction—online or anywhere," only about one of the 150 submissions received each month is accepted, and sometimes not that many. If your short story is sent back, send it out again.

While some publishers of short fiction pay little or nothing, publication in a solid review or magazine may improve your chances of selling longer works and novels.

In writing a query letter, remember you are engaged in business correspondence, so be brief. The person receiving it is pressed for time. When you remember that the person you write may get thousands of queries each year—most of them unprofessional or illiterate and very few even truly worth a reply—you can see why your letter must be outstanding.

—Oscar Collier, with Frances Spatz Leighton, *How to Write and Sell Your First Novel* (Writer's Digest Books, 1997)

Selling Your Novel

Frustrated in her job as a junior administrator at a university, Jeanne M. Dams took up writing because "I had some silly idea there was an easier way to make a living than what I was doing." She had so little time to devote to writing that it took five years to finish her first novel, about an American woman and her cat who solve a murder mystery. Eventually, she quit her job and devoted herself to finishing and then selling the book. "Everybody tells you not to do that, and everybody's right," Dams now says. "There were times I really wasn't sure how we were going to pay the electric bill."

It would be two years before she found a publisher for the novel, *The Body in the Transept* (Walker and Company, 1995), a "cozy" mystery, so named because it's an Agatha Christie type of book, one to cuddle up with in an armchair on a rainy day with a cup of tea. "I obeyed the rules and sent it to one publisher at a time," she says. "Then I got sick and tired of the time lag." So she began sending queries, synopses and/or sample chapters to several publishers and several agents at once.

Dams attended writers conferences to learn her craft and to make contacts. She submitted the manuscript for critiques. Eventually, she attended a Mystery Writers of America conference, called "Of Dark and Stormy Nights," noting that she went the first time because she liked the name, but also because her work could be critiqued by an agent or an editor rather than other writers. Her manuscript landed in the hands of Michael Seidman, an editor of mysteries at Walker and Company.

Knowing that Seidman had a reputation for disliking cozies, Dams determined that she would simply have to steel herself and learn from the experience. "I was extremely upset," she recalls. She was flabbergasted when Seidman simply looked at her and asked, "Why hasn't this already been published?" It soon was. Armed with Seidman's comments, she found an agent. *The Body in the Transept* was the first of what became the Dorothy Martin mystery series, edited by Seidman and published by Walker. It won the Agatha Award at Malice Domestic's annual convention saluting "mysteries of manners" books.

Finding a publisher for a novel is a matter of persistence, talent and luck. It involves first writing well, then researching publishers and agents, then sending and resending material until it reaches someone who appreciates it as much as you do.

Selling a novel to an agent or publisher depends on a happy coincidence of taste. Kimberley Cameron, an agent with the Reece Halsey North Literary Agency, says it's not unusual for one editor to tell her how marvelous a manuscript is and another to call it a real waste of time. "It's the same book," she notes, "so this is a subjective business."

Selling your novel usually does not mean trying to figure out what type of fiction is hot and writing to meet the demand. "I thought I would knock off a quick and easy formula mystery to see if I could do it," says C.J. Songer, who writes mystery/suspense novels. "I discovered the hard way I can't. It seems to come down to the creative will being stronger than the immediate financial desire. . . . Gosh, I hate having values!" Despite her values, or probably because of them, her books, *Bait* (1998) and *Hook* (1999), later found a publisher (Scribner).

As Cameron puts it, "Write with your heart, write what you love, because that's the best writing there is."

Submitting

Some book publishers want to see only a query first, but many want a letter with sample chapters, an outline or, rarely, even the complete manuscript. The query letter is the introduction of writer to editor or agent, but it is also a sales pitch. It tells enough about the book to intrigue the reader, mentions the title, offers the author's credentials and expertise, and asks for a chance to send in more of the manuscript.

Editors and agents say they look to the query not only for the idea but also for a sense of how a writer uses words, and they say they usually can tell people *cannot* write simply by reading their letters. When writers send an interesting query, says Judith Shepard, editor in chief of the Permanent Press, she often asks them to send the first twenty pages of the manuscript. "So if someone wants to send me a query with the first twenty pages, that's more practical," she says. "What I prefer not to have, but what I often get, are entire full manuscripts."

Cameron says she always listens for the author's voice in the query or in the first

The Book Proposal

There is no agreed-upon formula for what to include in a book proposal for fiction. Proposals generally include a cover letter with any or all of the following: an author's bio; one or two sample chapters; an outline that tells what happens in the book, chapter by chapter; a synopsis that briefly describes what happens in the story, from start to end; a list of publications. (The terms *outline* and *synopsis* are used interchangeably, so be sure which the publisher prefers before mailing your proposal, along with a self-addressed, stamped envelope.) Read the publishers' submissions guidelines for information about how each prefers to be approached.

Sometimes a writer attaches a query letter for his novel onto a synopsis and sends them together to a publisher. In this case, the query does double duty, also acting as a cover letter, introducing the author and the novel and asking the editor to read the enclosed material. But it should also hook the reader to the story, making her want to read more.

Outlines and synopses summarize the plot, subplots and main characters; they are stories in concentrate. Synopses generally run to three pages. Outlines are longer summaries of up to thirty pages, divided by chapter. (Remember, the terms are used interchangeably, so check guidelines carefully to determine which a publisher prefers.)

In your book, you'll have time for fine-tuning characterization, explaining motivation and weaving description, narration and exposition into a fascinating tale. In the synopsis or outline, you try to tell the story in as few words as possible. It should, however, engage the reader. (See an example of a short and a long synopsis at the end of this chapter.)

To write a synopsis or outline, imagine yourself sitting at the kitchen table drinking coffee with an old friend you haven't seen in years. Imagine that your friend must leave in ten minutes but wants to know what your book is about first. You would tell him about the main characters in the opening paragraph in a sentence or phrase. Describe their situations. Mention major plot turns and changes in relationships as the story progresses. Finally, tell how the conflict is resolved and how the book ends. Your goal is to prove you know how to map out a story. If it's done right, the reader will want to see more of your writing in your sample chapters.

An author's bio is written in third person. It should touch on the highlights of your writing life and your experience, particularly as they pertain to your book. Don't make the bio a resume; make it a story about yourself. If you have published elsewhere, cite your most relevant or impressive publications first.

couple pages of the book. "I look for a voice that communicates and touches me in some way and really gets my attention," she says.

Before mailing anything, put yourself in the place of an editor. The Permanent Press, which publishes about twelve books a year, receives about seven thousand submissions annually. "We get so many submissions I almost hate to see the postman come," Shepard says. "But if someone is completely unknown, it's the letter that gets me. I'm very taken by the words that people use . . . how people express themselves. I'm not as interested in the story. There simply aren't that many new stories."

Shepard says she does not appreciate writers telling her in their letters that their books will make a lot of money. "That's just being naïve," she says. And she prefers synopses to outlines, because synopses are shorter. "In a synopsis you see how the person's mind is working, what they're trying to show, their perspective," she says. "You see the kinds of issues they're looking at."

"The first thing we look for in fiction is the quality of the writing," says Donna Downing, an agent with Pam Bernstein & Associates. That means *all* the writing, including the query letter. If it's good there, the sample chapters will be the showcase for the author's style.

Seidman notes that most people send the cover letter along with a synopsis and a couple of chapters. "I can look at the chapters and know within three paragraphs whether I'm going to bother reading it. But I can know from the query letter, too. I never read the synopsis until after I've read the sample chapters. I've never bought anything from a synopsis alone, not from a writer I don't know, anyway."

To find a particular editor to query, the standard advice has been to find books that are like the ones you want to write, call the publisher to find out who edited them and submit a query to those editors. That's logical, but problematic as well. Editors on the receiving end grow weary of reading queries about books that all begin to sound alike.

Seidman recalls sharing a speaker's panel with an agent who told the two hundred or so writers present what types of books were selling and advised them to write accordingly. But Seidman says he needs no more novels about little old ladies with cats that solve mysteries. "Why don't you write something different," he told the audience, "and *create* the bandwagon?" The agent responded that no editor would read something unless it's like everything else that's currently hot. "At which point I just laughed hysterically," Seidman says. "I do not believe in that. I do not accept it. I think it's destructive. That's not writing. Writing is *creating* something." Even in mysteries, which have a certain form—or formula, even—there is room for creativity.

Juris Jurjevics, president and publisher of the Soho Press, notes that his company receives about seven thousand submissions a year and publishes twenty-five to thirty-five books, about 40 percent from authors without agents. "Some years it is a desperate hunt to find those few who can do it, who have it," he says. Pressed to define what "it" is, Jurjevics laughs, saying, "Simultaneity."

Some authors, he says, have a voice that's appealing, a sort of a literary personality. And readers will follow that voice just about anywhere. It's equivalent to an opera singer singing the telephone book, Jurjevics says. Some people wouldn't mind what she sings, just as long as they can listen to that voice. Other authors may not have such a writer's voice, but are terrific storytellers.

Jurjevics adds that Soho isn't interested in story lines "involving drugs or green-eyed characters." Plots about drugs are overdone, and yes, he means that comment about green-eyed characters literally. Green eyes in the gene pool are extraordinarily rare, he notes, but characters with green eyes show up in novels with ridiculous frequency.

Writers should *not* work out long rationales about the marketing of the book, he says. Some publishers of fiction ask potential authors where and how their book could be marketed. Others don't care, so if you include marketing information, be brief. "They are really a bore," Jurjevics says. "They make you tired."

So what if you've written a book about golfers and there are 17 billion golfers in the world? Seidman asks. They're probably playing golf, not reading novels.

The author's ability to promote a book may be more important in selling a nonfiction manuscript than a novel to a publisher, but promotional ideas can come in useful after a house has agreed to publish the novel. "It really doesn't have any influence on me [in a proposal]," says Shepard of the Permanent Press. "However, if we accept the book, the possibilities for promotion that the author can generate along with us are very useful. In fact, more and more authors are trying to promote their own books. There just isn't a tremendous chance otherwise." (See chapter fourteen, "Promoting Your Business and Yourself.")

A Final Word

Publishing is peopled by folks who love the written word. Editors and agents say they are stunned by submissions that show the writer doesn't care much about words or isn't even a reader. They advise beginners to spend most of their time learning the craft before trying to get anything published. People who want to be writers need to take a good, long, hard look at their work, evaluate its weaknesses and rewrite until it's as good as it can be, says Tracy Carns, publishing director of the Overlook Press. "If it's good," she says, "somebody will want to agent it, somebody will want to publish it."

Resources

BOOKS

Book Editors Talk to Writers by Judy Mandell (John Wiley and Sons, 1995).

The Elements of Fiction Writing series (Writer's Digest Books).

Fiction: The Art and Craft of Writing and Getting Published by Michael Seidman (Pomegranate Press, 1999).

Formatting and Submitting Your Manuscript by Jack and Glenda Neff, Don Prues and the editors of *Writer's Market* (Writer's Digest Books, 2000).

Guide to Literary Agents edited by Donya Dickerson (Writer's Digest Books).

How to Get Happily Published by Judith Appelbaum (HarperPerennials, 1998).

How to Write and Sell Your First Novel by Oscar Collier, with Frances Spatz Leighton (Writer's Digest Books, 1997).

Novel and Short Story Writer's Market edited by Anne Bowling (Writer's Digest Books).

The Sell-Your-Novel Toolkit: Everything You Need to Know About Queries, Synopses, Marketing and Breaking In by Elizabeth Lyon (Blue Heron Publishing, 1997).

Writer's Digest Handbook of Novel Writing by the editors of *Writer's Digest* (Writer's Digest Books, 1992).

Writer's International Guide to Book Editors, Publishers, and Literary Agents by Jeff Herman (Prima Publishing, 1999).

Writing and Selling Your Novel by Jack M. Bickham (Writer's Digest Books, 1996).

PERIODICALS

Fiction Writer, F&W Publications, 1507 Dana Ave., Cincinnati, OH 45207. Monthly, tips on writing and selling to fiction markets.

Fiction Writer's Guideline, P.O. Box 4065, Deerfield Beach, FL 33442. Newsletter on writing and selling fiction and more.

Gila Queen's Guide to Markets, P.O. Box 97, Newton, NJ 07860-0097. Monthly, includes guidelines for a variety of fiction.

New Writer's Magazine, P.O. Box 5976, Sarasota, FL 34277. Bimonthly, news, how-tos, markets and more.

Writer's Digest, F&W Publications, 1507 Dana Ave., Cincinnati, OH 45207. Monthly, tips on writing and selling in all markets.

WEB SITES

The Association of Literary Scholars and Critics (www.socialist.com/ALSC). Links for writers to the Internet.

Authorlink (www.authorlink.com). An excellent site for news about publishing and articles about writing.

Booktalk (www.booktalk.com). Connections to publishers and bulletin boards; some news about the industry.

Bookzone (www.bookzone.com). A terrific starting point for information about the publishing industry.

Eclectics.com (www.eclectics.com). For fiction writers, offers discussion board, advice on writing, and information on many genres.

Inkspot (www.inkspot.com). Links to many types of writing, including e-publishing and genre writing.

Poets & Writers (www.pw.org). *Poets & Writers* online site, with links to workshops, services and publications of interest to writers.

Pure Fiction (www.purefiction.co.uk). Offers news about publishing, links to writing-related sites.

Society of Children's Book Writers and Illustrators (www.scbwi.org). Offers articles from the group's newsletter, advice, events.

Sisters in Crime Internet Chapter (www.sinc-ic.org). Comprehensive site for mystery writers, male and female.

SAMPLE QUERY

September 28, 1994

Jane Agent
500 Madison Ave.
New York, NY 10020

Dear Ms. Agent:

I've written a mystery novel, the first of a projected series, that I'd like to submit for your consideration. The enclosed synopsis will outline the basics; let me say here why I believe *Sounding Brass** could succeed in today's market:

(1) The book is in the classic "cozy" tradition, involving pleasant people in an attractive English setting. (2) The protagonist is a sixtyish American woman with whom many mystery readers will be able to identify. (3) The bright, upbeat tone is refreshing for a genre that is growing ever more grim and gritty. (4) The cat is an appealing creature who helps solve the mystery without ever behaving like anything but a cat.

There are no gimmicks, no nonsense, just careful, literate writing and a strongly individual voice.

Although this is my first book, I've published in national (*Guideposts*, *Woman's World*, *Military History*) and local markets. I was a feature writer for over a year for a local newspaper. In addition to the second and third novels of the series, I'm working at present on a small guidebook to London's little museums.

I hope you will agree to read the manuscript of *Sounding Brass*. (Although I am querying several agents at once, I will of course send the MS to only one at a time. I realize that no one—including me—has time to waste.)

I look forward to hearing from you.

Sincerely,

Jeanne M. Dams

*title was later changed to *The Body in the Transept*

SAMPLE BOOK QUERY COVER LETTER

This was written following favorable comments at a writers conference and uses those comments to sell the novel.

October 15, 1994

Jack Agent
850 Broadway
New York, NY 10005

Dear Mr. Agent:

The enclosed sample of my mystery novel *Sounding Brass* comes with Michael Seidman's recommendation. He critiqued the first chapter for this year's "Of Dark and Stormy Nights" conference in Chicago and was enthusiastic about it. (I enclose his comments.) I asked him about agents; he named you "one of the few agents I trust."

Sounding Brass is a traditional mystery (which is why I was surprised as well as pleased when Seidman liked it so much). It is my first novel, although I've published shorter work. I am at work on the second and third books of the series and planning another series set in the Midwest. I have, also at Seidman's suggestion, sent the full MS of *Sounding Brass* to Amy Sattos at St. Martin's, but I doubt that the slush pile is her first concern. No one else is reading the book.

As a beginner in this peculiar business I am aware that I badly need a literary agent, and hope very much that you will consider representing me and my work. I look forward to your reply.

Cordially,

Jeanne M. Dams

TO: Jeanne Dams
FROM: Michael Seidman

I enjoyed reading this very much. . . . I don't think I made a mark on a page. Your voice, your story, your characters . . . everything just comes together.

I guess the only question is why it hasn't been published yet. I'd recommend starting the novel on its rounds immediately . . . and if nothing happens by February, get in touch with me, because that's when I expect to be looking for more manuscripts.

My first shot would be St. Martin's Malice Domestic contest; this seems far better than anything I've read from it so far.

SAMPLE ONE-PAGE SYNOPSIS

NOTE: For detailed information about submitting a synopsis, See *Formatting and Submitting Your Manuscript* by Jack Neff, Glenda Neff, Don Prues and the editors of *Writer's Market* (Writer's Digest Books, 2000).

ınding Brass

ANNE M. DAMS

Mountain View Office
415-390-3900

ctyish, recently widowed and living in the small
own of Sherebury. On Christmas Eve, after at-
edral, she literally stumbles over a body in one

of CANON BILLINGS, the cathedral's librarian, a
liked by almost everyone who knew him. He was
olar (he was a lecturer at Sherebury University as
the list of suspects is nearly limitless, because of
se of the thousands of people in the cathedral that
s likely. One of these is a university student, NIGEL
EVANS, to whom Dorothy's neighbor JANE has taken a liking. Jane, an old maid with a way with kids, is sure Nigel is innocent, although he worked for the canon and hated him more than most. Dorothy begins nosing around partly to help clear Nigel, but also because the loneliness and depression of her widowed and expatriate state is too much to bear without something to occupy her time.

She makes a new friend, ALAN NESBITT, the Chief Constable of the county. Alan, though unenthusiastic about Dorothy's meddling, is strongly attracted to her (he is a widower) and somewhat grudgingly cooperates. She learns, through gossip and her own observation, that there are at least three excellent suspects besides Nigel: a verger at the cathedral, the cathedral's organist/choirmaster, and an ambitious businessman. The canon represented a threat of one kind or another to all three. Dorothy's favorite is the verger until he also turns up dead, burnt nearly beyond recognition in an arson-caused fire at the late canon's house.

After a conversation with a friend at the British Museum, Dorothy becomes curious about the canon's last research project; he seems to have been closemouthed about its topic. Dorothy asks everyone; Nigel doesn't know, the Dean of the cathedral thinks it had to do with St. Paul, and GEORGE CHAMBERS, Billings's colleague at the university and an old friend of Dorothy and her late husband, says it was about Nero.

Dorothy is distressed after she visits George and catches him in a compromising situation with a coed, because she thinks he might have had reason to kill the censorious canon. When her beloved cat, ESMERELDA, is poisoned in a way that points to George, Dorothy is sure he is the murderer. Esmerelda recovers, though, and the Chief Constable proves that George's motive is a washout.

When Dorothy finally figures out what the canon was working on, she realizes that George is the villain after all, for academic motives: Billings's research would have ruined George's reputation and chances for advancement. In a slow-motion chase through the shadowy reaches of the medieval cathedral, Dorothy is nearly killed, a priceless ancient document is destroyed, and George dies in a fall to the cathedral floor.*

*In its original 8½" × 11" format, this synopsis ran one page.

SAMPLE FIVE-PAGE SYNOPSIS

Sounding Brass

BY JEANNE M. DAMS

DOROTHY MARTIN, a sixtyish American, recently widowed, has rented a house in the small English cathedral and university town of Sherebury, as she and her husband had long planned to do. At Christmastime, a rainy, blustery Christmas entirely unlike Dorothy's idea of the way the holiday should be, she is beginning to regret her move. She feels isolated among people who, though friendly, are essentially strangers and "don't speak her language," in more ways than one. Perhaps she was foolish to leave the familiar in her search for a new life.

On Christmas Eve, at midnight mass in the cathedral, she makes the acquaintance of ALAN NESBITT, a pleasant man who happens to be Chief Constable for the county. When the service ends well after midnight Nesbitt offers to see Dorothy home, but as they are making their way through a darkened passage she stumbles over a body.

The deceased turns out to be one JONATHAN BILLINGS, Canon and Librarian of the cathedral. Billings, a distinguished scholar, was also a cold, judgmental man heartily disliked by almost everyone. Although the death appears to be accidental, the police must still investigate, and since Nesbitt is on the spot and a good friend, the Dean of the cathedral asks him to take charge of matters. By Christmas afternoon the police have established the fact that Billings did not die where he was found, and that the severe wound to his head was caused neither by his fall nor by the heavy altar candlestick found near the body. Verdict: murder.

The TV report of the findings does nothing to cheer Dorothy's Christmas, nor does her tea the next day with GEORGE and ALICE CHAMBERS, old friends from the days when Dorothy's late husband spent a sabbatical year at Shere-bury University. George, under the guise of comforting Dorothy, really wants to gossip about possible murderers, especially young NIGEL EVANS, whom Dorothy has seen in the cathedral with her best friend and next-door neighbor, JANE LANGLAND. Dorothy, retorting that, given Billings's character, almost anyone might have done him in, changes the subject to George's book on an obscure biblical topic, now nearing completion and, according to Alice, des-tined for great academic distinction.

On the way home from George's, Dorothy, depressed and wet through from the penetrating fog, calls on Jane, a redoubtable spinster. There she receives comfort and a warming glass of whiskey, but also learns that Nigel worked for Billings in the cathedral library, had a terrible fight with him and was fired, and has a minor criminal record. Jane, who makes a habit of adopt-ing stray dogs and students, is strongly partisan in his favor and convinced of his innocence, but realizes the police will consider him a prime suspect. Dorothy is distressed, while privately thinking that Nigel does, in fact, sound like a possible murderer.

She is not at all reassured by a conversation with Alan Nesbitt, who shows up at her door exuding charm underlaid by faint menace. A little skillful con-versation extracts her suspicions of Nigel, her interest in the classic English mystery, and her half-formed intent to do some poking around on her own. His warning that murder investigation is a dangerous business, best left to professionals, serves if anything to strengthen her desire to become further involved.

Two important things transpire at church the next day. Dorothy learns from JEREMY SAYERS, the quirky, acid-tongued cathedral organist, that there are two other excellent suspects: a verger who has been stealing from the collection (although no one has been able to prove it) and Sayers himself! Apparently, Billings was about to get the goods on the verger, ROBERT WALL-INGFORD, and Wallingford might have killed to protect himself. And Sayers, who quarreled bitterly with Billings about cathedral music, was in danger of being fired. Dorothy, eager to talk over new developments with Jane, has the wind taken out of her sails when Jane already knows all about cathedral gossip and scandal and doesn't much care, because Nigel has been arrested.

Nigel is freed on Monday for lack of solid evidence, and Dorothy, exasperated with the whole situation, keeps a date with friends for shopping, sightseeing, and tea in London. Even in the metropolis, though, she can't get away from the murder. A chance-met acquaintance in the British Museum knew Billings, and hints that there was something mysterious about the piece of research engaging the scholarly cleric at the time of his death.

The continued rain, mist, and general dreariness make Dorothy long, for the tenth time, for some proper Dickensian snow. Even the cat ESMERALDA is irritable. On Tuesday Billings's memorial service provides further gloom. Stopping at Jane's before the funeral to cheer herself up, Dorothy meets Nigel for the first time and is charmed, but even more apprehensive. Nigel's temper seems quite hot enough for murder, and he's not talking much about his activities Christmas Eve. After the service Dorothy is captured by Alan (Nesbitt—they're on first-name terms by this time) and taken to tea. She's jollied into a better mood, but can't get Alan to talk about police progress into the investigation. Dinner that night at an inn owned by Dorothy's old friends, the Endicotts, makes matters much worse. Although the Endicotts mention an ambitious developer who is delighted Billings is dead, it turns out that the whole Endicott family had good reason to wish the clergyman ill. Not only was he, in his capacity as town councilman, obstructing vital plans for expansion of the inn, but young INGA ENDICOTT is all-but-engaged to Nigel Evans and mightily resented Billings's treatment of him.

A strained conversation with Nigel reveals that he was actually at the cathedral on Christmas Eve, some hours before midnight mass. He's sure Billings's body wasn't in the side chapel then, but he did see Inga, apparently coming out of Billings's house in the cathedral close. If the two have each been suspecting the other, both are innocent, but are they both telling the truth? Dorothy goes to the cathedral for some answers and learns that Wallingford, the verger, was missing for much of Christmas Eve when he should have been working, and that Sayers, the organist, was at the organ practicing most of the early evening. Good—Dorothy likes Sayers much better than Wallingford, and the case against the verger is getting better and better. She also learns that the Dean's wife placidly accepts the presence of the ghost monk Dorothy thinks she's seen once or twice in the cathedral.

The next day is New Year's Eve. Before going to a party at Jane's, Dorothy learns from the Dean of the cathedral that Billings's research may have involved the writings of St. Paul, but the canon was very secretive about his work. Her curiosity grows. Could his work have something to do with his murder? At the party an increasingly attentive Alan gives Dorothy the interesting information that George Chambers is a skirt chaser, but before she can digest what that might mean, the party is interrupted by a fire in the cathedral close just down the street. Canon Billings's house is burning! The investigators find that the fire was set; they also find the body of Wallingford, the verger, in the burned house. He was not the culprit, however, since he was dead before the fire started. There goes Dorothy's favorite suspect. And the rest were, at the time of the fire, either at Jane's party or, in the case of the Endicotts, working in plain view of several dozen people. Dorothy becomes even more eager to know about Billings's research project.

The next day Dorothy drags herself, after very little sleep, to see George. If anyone knows about Billings's work, it will be his colleague at the University. She finds him heading—on New Year's Day—for his office, and with him a very pretty female student. Not just with him, either, but obviously together. Suddenly Dorothy sees a motive for George. What if Billings had threatened to tell Alice, who has the money in the family? She tries to calm down and ask George about the canon's work, but George isn't sure—thinks it had to do with Nero. Billings had just returned from a trip to Corinth, which flourished during Nero's reign. She can make nothing of that, and after a little awkward conversation about the dead plant in the dented pot, she escapes.

A call from her London friends is most welcome. She is invited to join them for dinner at a charming country pub and is able to relax more than she has since the murder. On her return home, however, she finds that someone has tried to murder her beloved cat, Esmeralda, by giving her antifreeze to drink. By the time, hours later, she's sure the cat is going to be all right, she's worked out that it must have been George who did the poisoning. George, who knows little about cars, wouldn't know that there would be no antifreeze in the garage of a Volkswagen Beetle, and would think the poisoning might be taken for an accident. He also knows how devoted Dorothy and Emmy are; Emmy's death would keep Dorothy out of the way for a while. He must have decided she was getting too near the truth when she saw him with the girl. He has to be the murderer!

When she tells Alan and he investigates, however, she is once more out of suspects. It's true enough that George is carrying on with the girl and makes a habit of it, but Alice has known for years and puts up with it. There was nothing for Billings to reveal. Dorothy, grimly determined to avenge Emmy, thinks the whole thing through from the beginning, and finally comes up with the truth.

Going to the cathedral to verify her conclusions in the library, she finds George there. George, dressed up like a monk. George, the "ghost" who has been haunting the cathedral lately. He has in his hands the ancient manuscript Billings was working on when he died, a priceless "lost" letter from St. Paul. Its very existence makes George's book—and his academic future—worthless. It is for this that George has killed twice. In a slow-motion chase through the shadowy reaches of the medieval cathedral, Dorothy is nearly made a third victim to George's ambition, the ancient scroll is destroyed, and George dies in a fall to the cathedral floor.

When it's all over and the police have finished with her, Dorothy leaves, alone. She thinks she sees a monkish figure, but is too numb and exhausted to notice anything for sure except that the snow she has longed for is finally falling, pure and cleansing.

CHAPTER ELEVEN

Selling Your Scripts

Somebody should make a movie: *Hollywood: Planet of the Paradox*.

The television and movie industry that defines Hollywood is located in one of the most sprawling metropolises on Earth, but its social system operates like nothing so much as a small town.

It represents an industry where aspiring writers are told to write what they know best and love most, no matter how noncommercial, while studios and networks produce only scripts that they hope make millions.

It is a place where nothing—no film, no movie of the week, no hour-long drama, no half-hour sitcom—could begin without the written word. But it's also a place where writers' words are rewritten routinely by other writers, directors, producers, executives, even actors.

Yet, writing for TV and the movies remains the dream of millions. Type in *screenwriter* in any search engine on the Web, and you'll find screen after screen of sites feeding the desires of multitudes. Books devoted to writing and selling scripts fill bookshelves. How-to articles abound.

But selling your first script remains one of the most elusive dreams—virtually the stuff of drama. That's in part because the road to Hollywood is actually many roads. "There's no track," says sitcom writer David Chambers. "Everybody has to find their own way. There's a premium on hustling and selling. You're always selling yourself. It's a constant matter of being in sales."

As Jared Rappaport, a writer-director for film and television who got his start after studying directing at the American Film Institute, puts it, "Everybody absolutely manufactures his own way in."

Write Your Own Calling Card

The good news is that there are plenty of markets for scripts. In television, soap operas, situation comedies, hour-long dramas, movies of the week and animated features all need writers. First-run syndication series and made-for-cable series—which often hire small staffs, but more freelancers—helped boost television employment almost 7 percent between 1996 and 1997, according to the Writers Guild of America, West. The number of writers for the big screen has held steady for several years. But all told, about ten thousand people were members of the two Writers Guilds by the end of the 1990s.

No matter which genre you choose, before trying to sell your script, you should work prodigiously on the writing. Your script should not simply be as good as anything you see on the big or small screen; it should be better.

Hollywood is awash in scripts sent in on speculation by would-be writers and from professional writers who are looking for work after their shows have been canceled. A highly rated television show, for example, may receive two thousand to four thousand such scripts—called spec scripts—a year, excluding those from agents.

So your spec script must stand out from the rest. It must be polished until each line of dialogue sparkles. The one thing people in Hollywood agree on is that a good script will find its way in.

"There's almost no shortage of people who will be happy to do something with a good script. As soon as they smell something really good, they'll be all over it," Rappaport says. "But there are so few good scripts." He recalled working at Warner Brothers in an office beside that of a reader—the first person to read spec scripts, write descriptions of them and decide if they are worth another look by someone higher in the organization.

"These scripts are by and large submitted by agents, and most of them are good agents," Rappaport says. "And most of them are really crappy scripts." Each year, tens of thousands of scripts floated in, he said, while only a couple dozen were made into movies.

His point, one made again and again by professionals: The script must be sterling. Come up with a good story. Learn how to write scripts, either from books or in university courses or workshops. After you write it, rewrite it. Make it shine.

This script is your calling card.

The calling card proves to a producer or an agent that you know how to tell a story through dialogue, how to format properly, how to write for existing characters or invent entertaining ones of your own, how to make 'em laugh or cry, how to craft an intriguing plot—in short, how to write a script.

"You want to be able to write a *great* spec script," says Richard Allen, a soap opera writer who also teaches at Texas Christian University. Your spec script must earn universal praise. If you show it to ten people, and eight love it but two say it's OK, it's just not good enough, Allen says. Your best bet is to find a mentor who will look at your script as you rewrite it again and again, someone you respect, someone who has some industry experience, someone who will be honest with you, someone who will encourage you to write your best.

Once you do that, you're ready to try to find someone to read it. But know that, paradoxically, even if a producer or director loves your script, it may never be made into a movie or television show. Because the calling card is usually only that: your introduction to the business. The producer or director might like your script enough to ask you to help rewrite someone else's (it happens all the time) or work on another project with him. Or the script may be your introduction to an agent.

In television, few shows accept unsolicited manuscripts anymore. But if producers like your spec script, they may ask you to write another.

For film, too, it's highly unlikely your spec script will actually be made into a movie. "But—and this is a major 'but'—many of the better scripts written by beginning writers do actually get into the production pipeline and live a life on the path to actually being made into a film," says Ronald Tobias, who wrote and rewrote scripts for network television for eleven years and now teaches and makes documentaries for television. "They don't make it to the screen (the odds are still stacked against the writer), but there is income and a reputation to be made."

For example, Rappaport, who has worked in Hollywood for more than a decade and who teaches at California State University at Northridge, noted that his first screenplay launched his career without ever being produced. A comedy about a boy who canceled his bar mitzvah because he didn't know what it was to be a man, the script was liked by everyone who read it. But it was thought to be too narrow in its appeal. Nonetheless, Rappaport earned many studio writing assignments as a result of this script. "It was a very uncommercial thing, and I knew it, but I had this idea and I wanted to write it," he says. "I think you should always write what you can write best. Period. There is no other rule."

Find an Agent

Once you've made your script as good as it can be, finding someone working in the business to read it is the next, difficult step. Fortunately, there are salespeople whose job it is to help get your scripts into the right hands; they're called agents. Unfortunately, it's often said that getting an agent to represent you is harder than getting your first film produced.

But it's essential, believes Richard Walter, professor and chairman of the UCLA Film and Television Writing Program. He explains: Good scriptwriters imagine themselves living the lives of another character. "If you're writing *Babe*, you get to be a pig. If you're writing *The Lion King*, you get to be a lion cub," Walter says. So, too, should a scriptwriter imagine himself as a Hollywood producer who receives dozens of offers of scripts a day. "Anybody who receives a script direct from an author has got to wonder, Why isn't this submitted by an agent?" he says. "If you want to be a professional, you must treat yourself like a professional—and professionals have professional representation."

Agents need to read what you've written to decide if they'll represent you. And

From Stand-Up Comedy to Film: John Riggi

Comedy writer John Riggi took his place at the long conference table, ready to pitch an idea to Steven Spielberg and Jeffrey Katzenberg. Before the meeting began, an assistant asked if anyone would like coffee.

"Sure," Riggi said, gesturing toward the end of the table, where a huge model of the mother ship from *E.T.* loomed. "Does this cappuccino machine down here work?"

Riggi has always had the gift of making people laugh. But, oddly, he doesn't see himself as somebody who can set up a punchline. "When I was doing stand-up, I never told jokes," Riggi says. "Everything I talked about was like a scene. It was more visually oriented—it was like a picture story. For me, my best time on stage was when I could look at the audience and think, 'They can see exactly what I'm describing now.' "

This scene-setting ability helped him switch from being a stand-up comedian to writing comedy for television and film in 1991. Riggi never had written down his stand-up routines, and he learned to write scripts from books. "I bought the Syd Field books. I read them. I certainly attempted to follow the rules," Riggi says. "But I also think some people are really good at telling a story, and some people aren't. There are tools you can locate, resources that can help you augment your ability to do it. But I think it's something you know you can do, or you can't."

Like many people, Riggi got his first job in Hollywood in part because he knew somebody. Comedian Dennis Miller, then a late-night talk show host on WGN, saw Riggi's act at The Improv in Chicago and asked him to move to Los Angeles to write for his show.

When Miller's show was canceled, Riggi wrote a spec script for Gary Shandling's *The Larry Sanders Show* on HBO. Shandling had worked alongside Riggi as a comic and hired him as a staff writer; Riggi later became executive producer. "Networking is the word you don't want to say, but it's the truth," Riggi says. "Honestly, it's a small town."

For people who don't know anyone working in television, Riggi believes the best way to get your script noticed is to find an agent. "Most shows won't accept unsolicited scripts," Riggi says. "If they do accept unsolicited scripts, they will not from a freelance writer who doesn't have an agent."

But getting a good agent probably won't be easy—it wasn't for him. "I was with a really bad agency," he recalls. "They were like a federal witness protection program for comics. If you wanted obscurity, this was the place you wanted to be."

Eventually, he found an agent with International Creative Management, one of the

continued

most powerful agencies in Hollywood. His advice to beginners is to find smaller, "boutique" agencies, with a few agents with good connections. They may get your script to a person "who may be three levels below the guy who makes a difference," but if someone reads it and hands it off to someone else, things can start to happen. "It's about making somebody aware that this property is coming into their offices," he says.

More often, word of mouth provides an entryway. "I get phone calls all the time from people saying, 'Would you mind giving this to your agent,' or, 'Could you get my script to your executive at Fox?' " Riggi says.

While Riggi is now working for Fox to develop new television comedy series, he is also pursuing another career—writing for films. Although a successful television writer, he is nonetheless viewed as unproven in the world of film. So far, he has completed two screenplay rewrites, one for a film called *Save Me* and one for a film for DreamWorks SKG called *Beached*.

"My next goal is to write an original screenplay and sell it," Riggi says. "I don't think people realize how much time writing TV comedy is going to take, and how life altering it is. You can forget about your social life when you're in production. Writing for film is so much easier on your time."

even though agents are always looking for the next hot property, many say they won't read scripts sent in cold.

They might, however, read a query letter. Think of a query letter as "a seduction, a tease, a preview of coming attractions," Walter says. It is usually one page and has a brief description of your idea, a brief summation of your accomplishments and a brief request for the agent to read the script. Don't go into detail about your script in your query, he advises, because it simply makes a "bigger target to shoot at."

In his book *Screenwriting: The Art, Craft, and Business of Film and Television Writing* (New American Library Trade, 1992), Walter recounts the success of a four-sentence query letter by a former student. The entire description of his screenplay was: "I have written a screenplay, SHADOWCLAN, an action/adventure story set in contemporary New York City and ninth-century Scotland." Every agent who read the letter wanted to read the script, Walter said. An agent later sold it for $300,000 to a major studio, which spent $20 million producing it, as the film *Highlander*.

Yet, query letters flood Hollywood, too. Ed Silver, who owns The ES Agency in San Francisco, says he receives fifty to seventy-five query letters a week. "I can read maybe two or three at the outside," he says. "You can put yourself in the place of somebody receiving all those queries. Why would they take yours?"

Vincent Panettiere started as a writer in Hollywood, sold a couple scripts that never got produced and later opened his own agency, Panettiere & Co. Talent Agency in Los Angeles. Feeling an affinity to writers, he at first read every script sent to him. Then he realized, "I was wasting my time. My job is to make money for the clients I have." So he would read forty-five pages, then thirty pages, then twenty pages. Now, he says, he can tell if it's a worthwhile script after five pages.

Often, the writing is dull, he says. People haven't taken the time to know that scripts should be on three-holed paper held together with brads. They don't format scripts properly (see pages 220-221). They don't send self-addressed, stamped envelopes. They don't know *their* and *there* are different words. "I know that's picky, but my entire life has been as a writer and reporter," Panettiere says. "Spelling matters. Grammar matters." One writer gave him a film script only sixty pages long, instead of the usual minimum of about one hundred, saying, "The director will fill in the rest," Panettiere says. "It's that kind of ignorance that ticks me off."

Panettiere opened two query letters and read them aloud. One, written by someone who works in a nursing home, addressed him as "Spence" and pitched a script about a con man who inherits a nursing home. Despite the wrong name, Panettiere liked the idea and said he might well ask to see the script. Another was from a woman who'd written a comedy about an overbearing mother. Not interested, he said immediately immediately, because it smacked of autobiography. Sure, you should write what you know, Panettiere says. "But that doesn't mean it's going to be interesting. It's *theatrical* writing."

Frankly, getting an agent interested in your idea depends on the agent's interests, too. Panettiere had just finished reading a book on polygamy when a writer queried him about a script involving a boy who falls in love with a girl from a polygamous family. "It rang very true," he says. "I think a lot of it, or at least some of it, has to do with luck."

Kimberley Cameron of the Reece Halsey North Literary Agency in Tiburon,

---

Writing Online

The Web is a burgeoning new medium for scriptwriters. As Hollywood studios, television networks and video game developers moved online, a Writers Guild committee study of writing opportunities on the Web concluded in 1999 that the best opportunities for Web writers were in entertainment, online games, children's materials and news and information.

Opportunities for writers will only increase, since new media companies have begun to use the Web as a place to test news shows and concepts, and mainstream entertainment shows, such as *Sesame Street*, have begun to explore the multimedia capabilities of the Web. For more information on writing for Web sites, try visiting a Webzine called *Contentious* (www.contentious.com). This site is for Web writers and editors, and it features an E-mail discussion list. A copy of the WGA's full report is at wga.org/tools/Internet.

California, now focuses solely on representing book authors, but had worked for years representing scriptwriters in Hollywood. She advises writers to include in their queries a few details about themselves—their training, where they went to school, if they have written or produced anything else. "You never know if somebody's going to be interesting to you—maybe you went to the same school," she says. The letters must also be polite and, of course, well written. "I can't tell you how many times I knew the writer couldn't write by reading his query letter," she says.

Agents do things differently, she notes. While many people advise against sending the whole script to an agent, she believes "it doesn't hurt to send the first three pages." And make sure you send it to a person, not the agency. Dorris Halsey, founder of the Reese Halsey agency, still gets letters addressed to "Mr. Halsey," Cameron says, "and Reese Halsey unfortunately, died more than ten years ago."

You can get a list of agents' addresses and telephone numbers from the Writers Guild of America (WGA). The list, which notes which agencies will consider new writers, is also published on the WGA West Web site (www.wga.org) (see page 218-220). This list gives you a bit of protection from unscrupulous people, because every agency on the list has agreed to the guild's minimum terms and conditions.

It's still a good idea to check out the agencies, asking agents how many clients they represent, how many scripts they've sold and had produced, how long they have been in business. An agent will take at least 10 percent of everything you earn, but a good agent will open doors that remain firmly closed to many beginners.

Network

In the small town that is Hollywood, knowing somebody—or knowing somebody who knows somebody—also is a key to being allowed in.

Justin Adler's story is as typical as anything ever is in Hollywood. Adler wanted to write scripts, moved to the West Coast right after college and got a job as a production assistant, an entry-level job, on *The Larry Sanders Show*. "I got it through family connections, which seems to be the way everything works out here," Adler says. "My uncle's second wife—her first husband's sister's husband was a line producer of *The Larry Sanders Show*." It was his first step toward writing for television.

Between getting coffee for his bosses and answering the phones, Adler learned to write by watching staff writers write and rewrite scripts. And he kept writing himself. "I feel afraid to fail. I feel compelled to succeed. I feel you have to keep writing in order to have anything," he says. "I ended up making great contacts and also learned a lot about the writing process."

Eventually, he wrote a spec script and showed it to writers he had met on the job. A couple liked it enough to show it to their own agents. From those contacts, he got calls to meet with agents—and learned that one good script isn't enough. All asked if he had another. "I lied and said I was writing one," he said. "So I frantically went and wrote an *Everybody Loves Raymond* show, a show I had never seen."

After watching tapes of the show again and again, he banged out a script in four days. It was enough to get him an agent with the powerful William Morris Company. And the agent helped him find a job as a writer on the animated television show *Futurama*. That job ended after eleven weeks. "So, now I'm with no job again," he says, sounding sure that it won't last long. "In the meantime, I'm getting my agent the first draft of a movie I have written."

The lesson: Use contacts and networks, but keep writing. Even if your first script is a pearl, you'll be expected to write more.

Many people think that if you want to write for Hollywood, you must move to Hollywood. That's because one of the best ways of getting someone to look at your script is to have someone else, already working in the business, recommend it to a friend. Even if that friend has few connections to the person actually making the decision about buying it, he may recommend it to others, or he may remember your script when he moves up in the business.

If you don't live in Hollywood, find a connection to someone who does. Ask your friends if they know anyone in the business. Ask your neighbors. Take a course at a local college from someone who has worked in television or film. Every successful person in Hollywood was a beginner once, and many remember how it feels.

Market the Script on Your Own

If you don't have an agent and have few to no contacts in the business, you can still market your script on your own. Before you try, however, take one preparatory step: Register your script with the Writers Guild. Registration provides a dated record of the writer's claim to authorship and can be used as evidence in legal disputes. Note the number the guild assigns you on the title page.

Then, try to get someone to read it. There are, of course, many ways to do that.

If you want to break into television, it's generally not a good idea to write scripts for a series of your own invention. Full-time, experienced, professional writers earn monumental salaries doing just that; why compete with them? Instead, tape several shows of an existing series. Watch them repeatedly. Learn who the characters are, how they would behave in any situation. One writer even advised typing up the script as you watch to help you understand the flow of the dialogue. Then, write a spec script for that show's characters.

Also watch the credits of a show you enjoy, noting the names of the producers. You can write to them, asking them to read your script. "I've never met a producer who wouldn't kill to get a great script out of the blue sky one morning," J. Michael

Straczynski wrote in his *The Complete Book of Scriptwriting* (Writer's Digest Books, 1996). After targeting a show, Straczynski advises writing polite query letters to producers or story editors (usually these are people who help rewrite scripts and deal with freelancers), explaining your fondness for and familiarity with the show and your desire to send in a spec script.

At any given time, certain shows are hot markets for spec scripts. If you have a friend who knows anyone working in television, you can try to find out which shows "everybody" is writing spec scripts for. But Richard Allen, the soap opera writer and teacher, believes it's better to pick a show that you enjoy, that is climbing in the ratings, but that isn't a hit. After all, there are only so many *Everybody Loves Raymond* scripts any one person can stand to read.

Once you write a script, remember another Hollywood paradox: Rarely is a spec script for a show ever bought and produced by that particular show. In fact, many writers advise against even trying to show it to anyone involved with the show. Why? Because the writers of that show know their characters better than anyone else, and rarely can an outsider create a script better than they. One writer suggested that it's rarer still for a producer to admit someone outside his show even could.

Yet, even if your script is rejected, it may be a good enough calling card to get you invited to pitch other ideas to the producers (see "Making the Pitch," page 215).

To sell a film script, you need to match your script with the appropriate market. The best bet for a beginning screenwriter is a "little" movie, not a big-budget, special effects–laden extravaganza, says Ronald Tobias, the television and documentary writer and author of *The Insider's Guide to Writing for Screen and Television* (Writer's Digest Books, 1997). This means you can indulge in little of the sweeping action of a *Saving Private Ryan*, for example, but you can develop an original story line and compelling characters. "A friend of mine just sold a script to Bill Pullman's production company [Big Town Productions/Castle Rock] in which Pullman is slated to star," Tobias says. "Its budget is under $10 million. There's no question that the film wouldn't have made it as far as it has if it had been written as a $30 million to $50 million picture."

Whatever type of movies you enjoy writing, remember to study film credits. Note what types of movies a producer, director or actor typically makes, because you can pitch your script to any of them.

Making the Pitch

Even if a producer rejects your script, she still may like your writing style and invite you to pitch more ideas—in person. It may seem paradoxical that someone who is good at writing would be asked to explain his ideas orally, but that's how it works.

Like most difficult things, pitching gets easier with practice. Practice pitching orally—in front of a mirror, to your friends, to your dog. Just tell your story as if you're talking to a best friend who has to leave in five minutes. Be enthusiastic. Remember how much you love your story. Recount the big picture, but expect to be asked questions about details. Above all else, be brief.

Remember to relax. As Heidi Wall, founder of the Flash Forward Institute, a coaching center for the entertainment industry, once told a WGA writer: "Everyone already knows how to pitch. We do it all the time. Whenever you try to convince someone to go to a movie with you, you're pitching."

Go to a pitch meeting armed with several ideas. If the first one doesn't fly, you'll have something to say if an executive eyes you and asks, "So what else are you working on?"

Straczynski advises listing production companies that might be interested in a script similar to yours, then calling the story department to get the name of the story editor. Write this person a one-page query letter (see *Formatting and Submitting Your Manuscript* [Writer's Digest Books, 2000] for a sample query letter to a production company) and hope it will grab her attention. *The Hollywood Creative Directory* (Hollywood Creative Directory) lists the staff, with job titles, for hundreds of production companies.

Many producers will not look at a script unless it is sent by an agent, but some of them will. Even if you have an agent, Tobias believes, simply waiting for him to sell your script may waste time. Competition is so keen that writers today must be innovative in finding ways to get people to read their scripts. "I once gave a studio head a script by having his endodontist (a friend and co-conspirator) drop it in his lap while he was in the chair," Tobias says. "He thought the approach so novel, he laughed and took it home and read it. Creativity is the key. Find ways around the barricades."

Sending scripts to actors' agents is the worst thing to do, he said, because they are "trained to turn people and material away." But you can directly ask actors, directors and producers to read your script. In his hometown of Bozeman, Montana, for example, Tobias says he can contact at least fifty well-known actors, producers and directors who pass through. Except for the biggest names, most of these people are approachable—particularly if you are friendly, ask politely for help and defer to their judgment.

Check your local phone book for a film commission, an agency that encourages moviemakers to come to town. Find local actors, who may be listed in the phone book. They might be kind enough to read your script, have contacts in the business and send it on to be read by their friends. Ask.

Another way in is to write. Tobias once had a student who wrote the producer of the television show *Matt Houston*, criticizing the direction the characters had been taking in the program. The result: The show's producer called her, talked with her for two hours, and asked if she would move to Los Angeles to work with him on a new series.

The book *Opening the Doors to Hollywood* (Random House, 1997) recounts how David Permut, who later produced such movies as *Dragnet* and *Blind Date*, started his career by sending hundreds of letters around Hollywood, asking for "any advice you might have that might further my career." He received hundreds of form letter responses, but also some personal ones. One from writer Sidney Sheldon said, "I can think of nothing that would offer you as much future security, with the possible exception of going over Niagara Falls in a leaky raft. But if you are really interested in pursuing this endeavor, please call me."

UCLA film school chairman Walter says beginners might also try writing flattering letters to other writers or to producers. The letters may help you make a friend of someone who remembers how hard it is to break in, and who, eventually, might agree to help you.

While many experts caution against sending your full script to anyone unasked, doing so has, paradoxically, worked. When Cynthia Whitcomb, a columnist for *Writer's Digest*, was starting out, her first spec scripts accumulated 120 consecutive rejections. Then, she read a *Los Angeles Times* article about producer Tony Bill, who produced *The Sting*, starting a new production company. She got his address from the Producers Guild and dropped off her script—a period piece similar to *The*

Sting—cold. He called. He told her, among other things, her film would be too expensive to produce. But he asked her to work with him on another project. That began a career that has since included the production of more than twenty feature-length scripts.

One final paradox to keep in mind: Even if someone in Hollywood adores your script and buys it, chances are it will be rewritten—if not by you, then by others. Film and television are collaborative media, and writers must learn to expect changes to their scripts. It's been estimated that a film is rewritten an average of three to five times, but some are rewritten far more. Screenwriter Jim Burnstein told a reporter once that only the title and lead character's first name remained from his first draft of the movie *Renaissance Man*.

Keep in mind, however, that the words are the foundation for all movies and every television comedy or drama ever made. Hollywood will recognize a good script, and the writer who created it will be rewarded.

Understanding the Business Helps Writers Sell Their Work

Reading industry publications helps beginning writers procure some marketing savvy: You will learn who makes what types of films—and you won't make the mistake of sending an idea for a musical comedy, for example, to Oliver Stone. Once you learn how much things cost to produce (the average movie costs about $53 million to make and market, or roughly $530,000 per page of script), you might cast your film as a smaller-budget movie. You will learn whether a film studio already is working on a movie that you thought was your very own idea.

Learning about the business of television and film, therefore, can help you sell your scripts. Read some or all of these publications to increase your chances of selling your script.

- Major newspapers, such as *The New York Times* and the *Los Angeles Times*, offer useful information about film and television production. Trade publications, such as *Variety* or *The Hollywood Reporter*, available in many libraries and also online, not only report what types of deals are being made, but also list movies and shows in production, along with contact information of some key players.
- By far the most readable of the trade publications, however, is *Written By*, the

magazine of the Writers Guild of America, West. This magazine includes interviews with writers about writing, stories about how writers broke in to the business and a section listing television shows, with the names and phone numbers for writers to contact.

- Many publications offer addresses and phone numbers of people who may be interested in your script. You can find the address for a writer or his agent from the Writers Guild, (323) 951-4000, for an actor's agent or production company from the Screen Actors Guild, (323) 954-1600, for directors through the Directors Guild of America, (310) 289-2000, and for producers from the Producers Guild of America, (310) 557-0807. The Directors Guild and Writers Guild also publish directories of their members.

- The *Hollywood Creative Directory*, published online and three times a year in paper form, includes detailed staff lists for studios and production companies.

- Books also can help you target the right market for selling scripts and finding agents. *Opening the Doors to Hollywood*, for example, includes lists of producers of television movies of the week and lists of film producers by genre—comedies, thrillers, action movies—in addition to advice on how to write and market scripts. The *Guide to Literary Agents* (Writer's Digest Books) lists agencies according to their interests in handling ten categories of movies and television programs, from animation to variety shows, and also according to subject matter, from action/adventure to westerns/frontier. (See the resource list starting on page 221 for further information.)

The Writers Guild of America (WGA)

The Writers Guild of America is a union that you must join once you are employed as a scriptwriter, but it's also useful to beginners who have never sold a word.

Actually, there are two Writers Guilds, one on the East Coast (WGAE), one on the West Coast (WGAW). They split because in 1954, live television was based primarily in New York and filmed television and films were in Hollywood. Although the guilds' contracts became national by 1981, their governance remained split.

Talks to merge the two unions failed in 1998, and the West is by far the larger organization.

The WGAW publishes a monthly magazine, *Written By*, that covers topics of interest to writers, as well as a list of television shows in production, along with contact names and phone numbers.

The WGAW's Web site is full of information. It includes sections on tools of the trade, interviews with writers about how they got their first breaks and questions from beginning writers to WGA "mentors." It includes links to sites and experts who can help writers research stories. It lists agents who have agreed to abide by the WGA's standards for representing writers, including those who will accept new writers.

The Writers Guilds on both coasts offer another service to nonmembers: They register written works for radio, theater, television, motion pictures, videocassettes or video discs, and interactive media. You can register scripts, treatments, synopses, outlines and written ideas. Registration can be used as evidence in legal disputes about who wrote what when. At the Writers Guild, West, the service costs twenty dollars for nonmembers.

You can put the words "Registered WGAW No. [fill in the number]" on your title sheet as proof that you have registered your work. The guild records the time and date it receives the material and keeps it in a sealed envelope for five years. You can renew the registration for another five years after that. If it's not renewed, the WGA will destroy the material.

To register, send a copy of your material and a cover sheet with its title and the writer's full legal name, Social Security numbers, return address and phone number of one of the writers to the WGA, West Registration Department, 7000 W. Third St., Los Angeles, CA 90048. The phone number is (213) 782-4500.

The Writers Guild, East's registration process is similar. However, its registration remains valid for ten years, and the cost varies according to the length, the packaging of material and whether a writer is a student. See its Web site (www.wgaeast.org/reg/index.htm) for details. Or contact the organization at the Writers Guild of America, East, Inc., 555 W. Fifty-seventh St., New York, NY 10019, (212) 767-7800.

Please note that registration with the Writers Guild does *not* take the place of copyrighting your material. To obtain a copyright, call the U.S. Copyright Office at (800) 688-9889 or download forms from the U.S. Copyright Office's Web site (lcweb.loc.gov/copyright/forms).

Vital Statistics

NUMBER OF NEW MEMBERS ADMITTED TO WGAW EACH YEAR

1995: 492

1996: 599

1997: 607

1998: 586

NUMBER OF WGAW MEMBERS EMPLOYED

1995: 3,931 (50.6%)

1996: 4,126 (51.8%)

1997: 4,306 (52.1%)

1998: 4,490 (53.8%)

MEDIAN EARNINGS OF WGAW MEMBERSHIP

1995: $77,500

1996: $90,000

1997: $83,119

1998: $82,169

Source: 1999 Annual Report to Writers, Writers Guild of America, West

Form and Format

A mark of a serious writer is attention to detail. Paying attention to the way scripts should appear on the page marks you as serious about the craft of scriptwriting.

The sometimes esoteric formatting rules, which vary by genre, are explained in many scriptwriting textbooks. These are wise investments for beginning writers. But simply studying scripts—analyzing which lines are capitalized, how large the margins are and whether lines are single- or double-spaced—is also necessary.

Margins are set in pica type; word processing manuals can help you set them up. You can invest in a software program that automatically formats your script according to the appropriate genre.

Many good resources are available for scriptwriters looking for formatting tips (see resources list below). The Writers Guild of America has published an online review by Robert M. Goodman of many scriptwriting software programs (www.wga.org/tools/ScriptSoftware/) with a chart comparing cost, formatting ability, platform and much more. Other online aids are also available such as Screenplay Template Maker (gladstone.uoregon.edu/~milholer/template.html).

Resources

BOOKS

Adventures in the Screen Trade: A Personal View of Hollywood and Screenwriting by William Goldman (Warner Books, 1983).

All You Need to Know About the Movie and T.V. Business by Gail Resnik and Scott Trost (Simon & Schuster, 1996).

Breaking and Entering: Land Your First Job in Film Production by April Fitzsimmons (Lone Eagle Publishing, 1997).

The Complete Book of Scriptwriting by J. Michael Straczynski (Writer's Digest Books, 1996).

The Complete Guide to Standard Script Formats by Hillis R. Cole and Judith H. Haag (CMC Publishing, 1988).

Elements of Style for Screen Writers by Paul Argentini (Lone Eagle Publishing, 1998).

Formatting and Submitting Your Manuscript by Jack and Glenda Neff, Don Prues, and the editors of *Writer's Market* (Writer's Digest Books, 2000).

Four Screenplays: Studies in the American Screenplay by Syd Field (Dell Publishing, 1994).

From Script to Screen: The Collaborative Art of Filmmaking by Linda Seger and Edward J. Whetmore (Holt, 1994).

Guide to Literary Agents (Writer's Digest Books).

The Hollywood Job-Hunter's Survival Guide by Hugh Taylor (Lone Eagle Publishing, 1993).

How to Sell Your Screenplay: The Real Rules of Film and Television by Carl Sautter (New Chapter Press, 1988).

How to Write a Selling Screenplay by Christopher Keane (Broadway Books, 1998).

The Insider's Guide to Writing for Screen and Television by Ronald Tobias (Writer's Digest Books, 1997).

Making a Good Script Great by Linda Seger (Samuel French Trade, 1994).

The New Screenwriter Looks at the New Screenwriter by William Froug (Silman-James Press, 1992).

Opening the Doors to Hollywood by Carlos De Abreu and Howard J. Smith (Random House, 1997).

Screenplay: The Foundations of Screenwriting by Syd Field (Fine Communications, 1998).

The Screenwriter's Bible: A Complete Guide to Writing, Formatting, and Selling Your Script by David Trottier (Silman-James Press, 1998).

Screenwriters on Screenwriting: The Best in the Business Discuss Their Craft by Joel Engel (Hyperion, 1995).

The Screenwriter's Problem Solver: How to Recognize, Identify, and Define Screenwriting Problems by Syd Field (Dell Publishing, 1998).

The Screenwriter's Workbook by Syd Field (Dell Publishing, 1984).

Screenwriting: The Art, Craft, and Business of Film and Television Writing by Richard Walter (New American Library Trade, 1992).

Screenwriting Tricks of the Trade by William Froug (Silman-James Press, 1993).

The Script Is Finished, Now What Do I Do? by K. Callan (Sweden Press, 1993).

Successful Scriptwriting by Jurgen Wolff and Kerry Cox (Writer's Digest Books, 1991).

Successful Sitcom Writing by Jurgen Wolff, with L.P. Ferrante (St. Martin's Press, 1996).

TV Scriptwriter's Handbook: Dramatic Writing for Television and Film by Alfred Brenner (Silman-James Press, 1992).

Writing Screenplays That Sell by Michael Hauge (HarperPerennial, 1991).

BOOKSTORES

These stores can help you find copies of books on screenwriting, on Hollywood and scripts themselves. Ask for catalogues.

Book City, Dept. 101, 308 N. San Fernando Blvd., Burbank, CA 91502, (818) 848-4417, and 6627-31 Hollywood Blvd., Hollywood, CA 90028, (800) 4-CINEMA.

Samuel French Theatre & Film Bookshops, 7623 Sunset Blvd., Hollywood, CA 90046, (213) 876-0570.

Script City, 8033 Sunset Blvd., Suite 1500, Hollywood, CA 90046, (800) 676-2522.

MAGAZINES/DIRECTORIES

Entertainment Weekly, 1675 Broadway, New York, NY 10016, (212) 522-5600.

Guide to Literary Agents. (Writer's Digest Books).

Hollywood Creative Directory, 3000 Olympic Blvd., Suite 2413, Santa Monica, CA 90404, (310) 315-4815, (800) 815-0503 (outside California) (www.hcdonline.com). Directory of production executives, development executives, producers for motion pictures and TV.

The Hollywood Reporter, 5055 Wilshire Blvd., Los Angeles, CA 90036, (323) 525-2150 (www.hollywoodreporter.com). Daily information about what's going on in the businesses of filmmaking and television. A Tuesday Film Production section includes specifics about films starting or ending production.

Hollywood Scriptwriter, 1626 N. Wilcox, #385, Hollywood, CA 90028. (hollywoodscriptwriter.com).

New York Screenwriter, 548 Eighth Ave., Suite 401, New York, NY 10018.

Premiere, 1633 Broadway, New York, NY 10019, (212) 767-5400, (www
.premieremag.com).

Scenario: The Magazine of Screenwriting Art, 104 Fifth Ave., New York, NY
1011, (212) 463-0600. A quarterly magazine that publishes four complete
scripts in each issue.

Script Magazine, Forum, P.O. Box 7, Long Green Pike, Baldwin, MD 21013-
0007.

Spec Screenplay Sales Directory, compiled and edited by Howard Meibach, In
Good Company Products, 3250 Olympic Blvd., #79, Santa Monica, CA
90404, (310) 828-4946.

Variety (weekly and daily), 5700 Wilshire Blvd., Suite 120, Los Angeles, CA
90036, (800) 323-4345, (323) 857-6600 (www.variety.com). The
quintessential Hollywood newspaper covering film, television, music and
theater.

Writer's Digest, F&W Publications, Inc., 1507 Dana Ave., Cincinnati, OH
45207, (800) 333-0133, (513) 531-2000 (www.writersdigest.com).
Includes articles on scriptwriting and selling.

Written By, Journal of the Writers Guild of America, 7000 W. Third St., Los
Angeles, CA 90048, (323) 782-4542, (888) WRITNBY. Includes
interviews with writers, WGA news and a TV market list, with contact
information for shows in production.

WEB SITES
Daily Variety
(nt.excite.com/142/variety)
Done Deal
(www.scriptsales.com)
Drew's Scripts-O-Rama
(www.scriptorama.com/table.shtml or www.script-rama.com)
The Hollywood Network
(hollywoodnetwork.com)
The Hollywood Reporter

(www.hollywoodreporter.com)
In Hollywood
(www.inhollywood.com)
Screenwriters and Playwrights Home Page
(www.teleport.com/~cdeemer/screwriter.html)
Screenwriter's Heaven
(www.impactpc.demon.co.uk)
Screenwriters Online
(screenwriter.com/insider/news.html)
Writers Guild of America, East
(www.wgaeast.org)
Writers Guild of America, West
(www.wga.org/) To sign up for WGA's e-newsletter: join-wga@sparklist.com.

WEB SITES—AGENTS
Agent Research and Evaluation
(www.agentresearch.com)
WritersNet
(www.writers.net)
Writer's Guild of Amcrica List of Signatory Agents
(www.wga.org/agency.html)

ORGANIZATIONS

Directors Guild of America, 7920 Sunset Blvd., Los Angeles, CA 90046 (310) 389-2000 or (310) 289-2000; 110 W. Fifty-seventh St., New York, NY 10019, (212) 581-0370; 400 N. Michigan Ave., Suite 307, Chicago, IL 60611, (312) 664-5050; 330 N. Federal Highway, Hollywood, FL 33020, (954) 927-3338.

Producers Guild of America, 400 S. Beverly Dr., Suite 211, Beverly Hills, CA 90212, (310) 557-0807 (www.producersguild.com).

Screen Actors Guild, 5757 Wilshire Blvd., Los Angeles, CA 90036, (323)

954-1600 or 1515 Broadway, 44th Floor, New York, NY 10036, (212) 944-1030 (www.sag.com).

Writers Guild of America, East, 555 W. Fifty-seventh St., New York, NY 10019, (212) 767-7800.

Writers Guild of America, West, 7000 W. Third St., Los Angeles, CA 90048-4329, (323) 951-4000.

SEMINARS AND WORKSHOPS

Michael Hauge, Hilltop Productions, P.O. Box 55728, Sherman Oaks, CA 91413, (818) 995-8118; (800) 477-1947.

Robert McKee, Two Arts, Inc., 12021 Wilshire Blvd., Suite 868, Los Angeles, CA 90025, (310) 312-1002, (212) 463-7889 (www.mckeestory.com).

Linda Seger, 2038 Louella Ave., Venice, CA 90291, (310) 390-1951.

CHAPTER TWELVE

Selling to Corporations

The health care industry in America spends more than $1.3 billion a year on printed materials. The auto industry spends nearly as much. Retailers, beverage makers, computer companies and telecommunications firms spend billions more. In fact, the twenty-five leading industries in the U.S. spend more than $8 billion a year on printed material, be it brochures, newsletters, catalogs, signage, instruction manuals, press releases, speeches, new home descriptions or employee handbooks. Words are everywhere we look—and someone has to write them, which gives freelance writers an endless number of markets.

Even the magazine market extends far beyond the well-known titles you typically find at bookstores and newsstands. There are literally tens of thousands of specialty magazines published by corporations, trade groups and other organizations. The subject matter may be narrow in scope and sometimes technical in nature, but an article that is worth $300 to a consumer magazine could be worth ten times that much to the right corporate client.

The trick is to find the right buyer. Fortunately the opportunities have never been greater. Corporations of every type (including nonprofit) are finding that hiring freelancers cuts overhead costs. In addition, they can hire freelancers only when needed instead of hiring an employee who may be idle during slow work periods. The advent of fax machines, computers and E-mail enables freelance writers to interact with any company regardless of location.

Savvy freelancers keep tabs on the local business scene to find out about new businesses in town or changes in existing businesses that may indicate a need for freelance help, such as new ownership or expansion. As in any area of business, networking is important when looking for corporate assignments.

Call all writing-related professional organizations in your area and join the active ones. Women in Communications, the Public Relations Society of America, the International Association of Business Communicators, the Society for Technical Communications—these national organizations may have branches in your area. Most of them publish directories of their members, often listing each member's place of employment. This gives you an automatic contact—especially if you've involved yourself in the social networking system these organizations encourage.

Take a look at the business community in your area: Who are the ten or twenty biggest employers? Your local business newspaper can give you this information. Keep your eyes and ears open for listings of all kinds; search them out in business newspapers as well as those provided by the Chamber of Commerce or tourism bureau, and collect directories of every type. Brainstorm in your local library where there are directories published for a variety of fields, often indexed geographically, including the *Encyclopedia of Associations* (Gale Research) and *The Directory of Directories* (Information Enterprises).

To get an idea of just how far you can take this game of "who needs writers?" try this exercise: Consciously look around today at written copy wherever you are—a calendar that has photo captions, signs on the backs of benches or high up on billboards, even your own mail, especially direct mail (also called junk mail). These were all written by someone, somewhere, who presumably collected a nice paycheck for his trouble. Of course not all of these were written by freelancers, but it's safe to assume that any of them could have been. There is no communications area left (with the possible exception of top secret government agencies) that excludes work for hire as a possibility.

Once you've located which businesses might need your help, send a cover letter with a short bio and a few clips to someone in the communications, public relations or media relations department. Make sure you have a specific name and the correct spelling.

It's probably not practical to be a freelance generalist and hire yourself out for any kind of writing. As in most any profession, specialization is the key. When you do find work, be sure to get everything in writing. At the very least make sure the assignment, deadline and payment terms are clearly outlined in a letter of agreement. In the business world especially these kinds of agreements are a sign of professionalism and are appreciated on all sides.

Advertising and PR

One way to sell your writing is to target the kind of company that depends on writers and may frequently use freelance writers: advertising and public relations firms. These are the experts to whom many companies turn for help in developing their various communications-related projects. In fact, if you go to a company on your own to vie for a freelance assignment, you may compete against agencies. But for now, let's look at how to get an assignment from such a firm and what the advantages of selecting this route are.

The biggest advantage—once you've made the connection—is that the agency finds the clients; all you have to do is complete the work. This can be attractive if you tire of freelance hustling and especially if you can become a regular in an agency's stable of freelancers. You may assure yourself a steady source of income, and if it's a quality firm, you enhance your own reputation by association.

If you already have some experience with a specific kind of assignment (you designed and wrote brochures in your last job) or you're well grounded in a certain area of expertise (you're a volunteer or a past employee in an organization that caters to senior citizens), sell yourself as an expert in this area.

There are two main reasons public relations firms might hire freelance help. Sometimes expertise is needed, such as in writing about engineering, medicine or accounting. So it's good to have special knowledge or develop an expertise. Secondly, because they must produce a large volume of collateral material, firms sometimes find themselves in need of freelance help when the workload gets heavy. This collateral material can take the form of a postcard, a brochure or a direct-mail piece.

Sometimes a company will be looking for someone who can shepherd a project from conceptualization to production. Other times the firm may only need simple copywriting.

Some large—and not so large—organizations may have their own in-house creative departments that are in need of occasional—or not so occasional—assistance. The person to contact at a larger company may go by any number of titles. It may be a director of publications, corporate communications or public relations. If the company has a sophisticated operation, it may have borrowed the term *creative services director* from the advertising industry, particularly if it uses both print and audiovisual media. Sometimes the word *marketing* will be in the title; other times that word will lead you into the wrong department altogether. It depends on the kind of company. If in doubt—especially if you are cold calling—a phone call to the personnel or human resources department will probably get you the name of the appropriate department, staff person and title.

To identify new businesses, ask the chamber of commerce to send you material on small businesses. Scout local business newspapers or the business sections of daily newspapers to identify companies that have just applied for vendors' licenses. Then send them each a letter to generate interest in what you have to offer.

Hospitals are a case in point. Federal cutbacks and outside competition have forced hospitals to walk a financial tightrope—while producing more written copy. It's no coincidence that hospitals have increased their use of freelancers to supplement or replace in-house employees. Many arts organizations are facing a similar trend.

Practically every corporation that has senior executives has speechwriters. Executives don't hire speechwriters the way a politician might hire one. Someone from public relations is usually assigned to do the job on top of her normal duties. It may be something you can do a few times a year, along with numerous other assignments. So if you find you have a particular knack for it, serve it up as an area of expertise.

The usual methods of networking through colleagues as well as professional associations, combined with cold calling, will help you locate the jobs you seek. But whether you are approaching an agency, a company or an individual, it's always wise to parlay your previous experience into new opportunities.

Resources

PROFESSIONAL ORGANIZATIONS

American Marketing Association, 311 S. Wacker Dr., Suite 5800, Chicago, IL 60606, phone: (800) 262-1150, fax: (312) 542-9001, info@ama.org (www.ama.org).

Association for Women in Communications, 1244 Ritchie Highway, Suite 6, Arnold, MD 21012, phone: (410) 544-7442, fax: (410) 544-4640 (www .womcom.org)

Public Relations Society of America, 33 Irving Place, New York, NY 10003, (212) 995-2230, hq@aprsa.org (www.prsa.org)

OTHER RESOURCES

Direct Marketing magazine, Hoke Communications, 224 Seventh St., Garden City, NY 11530, (516) 746-6700 (www.hokecomm.com)

Standard Directory of Advertising Agencies, aka the "Red Book" (National Register Publishing). Lists fourteen thousand agencies worldwide along with their areas of specialization, annual billings, account rosters, key personnel and contact information.

Technical Writing

While the goal of creative writing is to entertain and that of advertising writing is to sell, the primary goal of technical writing is to relay information clearly and accurately. Technical writing, then, can be described as putting complicated information into plain language—in a format that is easy to understand. The tone is objective and favors content over style. (This does not mean, however, that you should present the subject in a formal, stunted style.) Above all, technical writing should be concise, complete, clear and consistent. The best way to achieve all these is to make sure your writing is well organized.

By far the biggest area for technical writers is in the computer industry, though there is a wide variety of possible assignments, including preparation of customer letters, utility bills, owner manuals, insurance benefit packages and even contracts (some states have "plain language" laws that require contracts and insurance policies to be written in simple English). In any technical field, writers who can bridge the gap between the engineers who design the things and the customers who buy and use them are in high demand.

Technical writers do not necessarily need formal training in the areas they cover. To the contrary, one of the greatest talents a technical writer brings to a project is the ability to take a step back from the technical details and see the subject from a different perspective than the engineers, scientists and experts. Thus, a technical writer becomes familiar with a subject by interviewing experts, reading journals and reports, reviewing drawings, studying specifications and examining product samples.

Technical writers themselves often shy away from the term *freelance writer*, preferring to be known instead as independent contractors or consultants. This probably has a lot to do with the fact that technical writers work mostly with corporations, where the term *independent contractor* sounds more impressive. It's very important to establish and maintain a high degree of credibility when working with firms.

The ways to enter the technical writing field are as varied as the people entering it. There are a number of ways to locate these jobs (besides word of mouth) as you build a reputation for good work. If you're cold calling large companies, contact the manager of technical communications or manager of documentation. There are also a number of contracting agencies that act as liaisons between the companies and people looking for work. They can be found in your local yellow pages under Engineering Consultants. They are also listed in several directory-like periodicals.

One way to find work is to register with placement agencies. If you lack experience, build a portfolio by volunteering to write material for a nonprofit organization, or offer to help your colleagues prepare reports and presentations. If you are interested in pursuing this type of work, it is probably a good idea to join the Society for Technical Communications (STC; see resource list). There you can network to gain contacts in the industry. Many businesses hire writers from the STC talent pool.

The National Technical Employment Service (see resource list) is another good source of work. Through its weekly newspaper, *Hot Flash*, it gives job listings for contract employees nationwide. The annual subscription rate also includes a quarterly directory of companies as well as a "shopper index" that publishes summaries of contractors seeking employment in this field.

Resources

BOOKS

The Art of Technical Documentation by Katherine Haramundanis (Digital Press, 1998).

The Complete Guide to Writing Readable User Manuals by Herman Holtz (Dow Jones-Irwin, 1988).

Designing and Writing Online Documentation, by William Horton (Wiley, 1994).

The Elements of Technical Writing by Gary Blake and Robert Bly (Macmillan Publishing, 1993).

Good Style: Writing for Science and Technology by John Kirkman (E&FN Spon, 1992).

How to Write a Manual by Elizabeth Slatkin (Ten Speed Press, 1991).

Science and Technical Writing: A Manual of Style edited by Phillip Rubens (Holt, 1992).

Successful Technical Writing: Documentation for Business and Industry by Bill Wesley Brown (Goodheart-Willcox, 1999).

Technical Writer's Freelancing Guide by Peter Kent (Sterling Publishing, 1992).

Writing Better Computer User Documentation: From Paper to Hypertext by R. John Brockmann (John Wiley and Sons, 1990).

PROFESSIONAL ORGANIZATIONS

American Medical Writers Association (AMWA), 9650 Rockville Pike, Bethesda, MD 20814, (301) 493-0003.

Aviation/Space Writers Association, 17 S. High St., Suite 1200, Columbus, OH 43215, (614) 681-1900.

Computer Press Association, 1260 Twenty-fifth Ave., San Francisco, CA 94122, (415) 681-5464.

Council of Biology Editors, 11 S. LaSalle, Suite 1400, Chicago, IL 60603-1210, phone: (312) 201-0101, fax: (312) 201-0214.

National Technical Employment Service, P.O. Box 217, Scottsboro, AL 35768, (205) 259-1828.

Society for Technical Communications, 901 N. Stuart St., Suite 904, Arlington, VA 22203-1854, phone: (703) 522-2075, stc@tmn.com (www.clark.net/publ/stc/www/home2.html).

Copyediting and Proofreading

The real heroes of the writing profession are the copyeditors and proofreaders who labor to make the rest of us look good. If you've ever known someone who excels at copyediting and proofreading, you know that both take real talent. For those who possess the unique ability, copyediting and proofreading can be a good source of additional income.

Copyediting

The writer's direct supervisor or editor usually edits stories for content and organization. The role of the copyeditor, then, is to look for additional spelling errors and typos. He may raise questions about conflicting statements and may be charged with smoothing awkward text transitions and ensuring uniform typestyle. In some cases a copyeditor may even rewrite portions of copy to improve the flow of text or to maintain a uniform tone. A copyeditor may also be expected to keep an eye out for libel. At newspapers and magazines, it is often the copyeditor's job to write headlines and photo captions. At some smaller and medium-sized newspapers, copyeditors are also called upon to design pages. This can include selecting and laying out pictures and graphics. (Before beginning any job, freelance editors should determine the level of work expected and base their fees accordingly.)

Proofreading

Proofreaders are charged with looking for typographical and mechanical errors after all other editing is complete. Proofreaders may check typeset copy word for word

Job Banks and Agencies

Writers have banded together in many places for mutual aid in finding work. National, regional and local groups offer help for writers seeking anything from freelance assignments to full-time jobs.

- The National Association, Inc. and its affiliated group, Associated Business Writers of America, offer information about freelance market opportunities through their monthly newsletter.
- The American Society of Journalists and Authors offers its members a listing in an annual directory that may be used by editors in search of writers. It also offers its Dial-a-Writer referral service, which refers editors to writers who meet those needs.
- Local organizations or local chapters of national groups also offer job banks. For instance, the Editorial Freelancers Association offers a database of its members for potential clients in the New York City area. The National Writers Union has job banks with listings of opportunities for writers in major cities.
- Many cities also have for-profit agencies that provide work for freelance writers and editors. The agencies generally screen freelance writers to determine their interests, credentials and fees. Such agencies can become your marketing department and your collection bureau. The disadvantage is that you might make less than if you market your work directly to the end user.
- Specialties handled by different agencies include copywriting, technical writing, advertising copywriting, book editing, newsletters, scriptwriting and press releases. In some instances writers become employees of the agency and receive insurance, retirement, disability and vacation benefits.
- Traditional employment agencies and temporary services firms can also provide work for freelancers. Though this is rare, it's easy enough to look them up and call. Nothing ventured, nothing gained.

against a manuscript and identify any deviations. They look for misspellings, missing copy, typos, misnumbering, mislabeling and incorrect cross-references. Proofreaders may also check copy for conformity to type specifications and ensure attractive typography by checking letter or word spacing, margins and repetitive word breaks.

The extent to which a copyeditor or proofreader must verify facts varies widely. Often this is the job of a separate fact checker. A fact checker does not make editorial changes, but simply verifies accuracy. One client may request that the fact checker verify all statements, while another client may request the verification of addresses and trademarks only.

Copyeditors and proofreaders are in high demand, so if you look hard enough and are willing to start small enough you are likely to find work. Smaller papers frequently need help. The pay may not be great, but jobs like that can build a resume and provide an extra source of income. Of course, publications are not the only places that rely on copyeditors and proofreaders. So don't overlook nonprofit organizations and big companies—any place that publishes anything.

To get any work you will almost certainly have to pass a test. To do this, study a style manual *The Associated Press Stylebook and Libel Manual* (Addison-Wesley Publishing) or *The Chicago Manual of Style* (University of Chicago Press) and a list of most commonly misspelled words. You'll fare better than most of the competition.

Resources

CORRESPONDENCE COURSES

Editcetera, 1600 Shattuck Ave., Suite 224, Berkeley, CA 94709, (510) 849-1110, editcetera@aol.com (www.editcetera.com).

The Graduate School, USDA, Correspondence Program, South Agriculture Building, Room 1112, Fourteenth St. and Independence Ave. SW, Washington, DC 20250, phone: (203) 314-3670 (888) 744-GRAD, fax: (202) 690-1516, Correspond@grad.usda.gov (grad.usda.gov).

University of California Extension, Center for Media and Independent Learning, 2000 Center St., Suite 400, Berkeley, CA 94704, phone: (510) 642-4124, fax: (510) 643-9271, askcmil@uclink4.berkeley.edu (www.cmil .unex.berkeley.edu).

University of Minnesota, 101 Wesbrook Hall, 77 Pleasant St. SE, Minneapolis, MN 55455, phone: (612) 625-3333, fax: (612) 625-1511, ceeadv@mail.cee.umn.edu (www.cee.umn.edu/dis/bulletin/active/index .ENGW.shtml).

University of Wisconsin Learning Innovations, Room 104, Extension Building, 432 N. Lake St., Madison, WI 53706, (800) 442-6460, ilearn @admin.uwex.edu (learn.wisconsin.edu).

ONLINE WORKSHOPS

American Press Institute, 11690 Sunrise Valley Dr., Reston, VA 20191, phone: (703) 620-3611, fax: (703) 620-5814, api@apireston.org (www .newspaper.org).

The New School for Social Research, 66 W. Twelveth St., New York, NY 10011, phone: (212) 229-5690, fax: (212) 229-5648, admissions@dialnsa .edu (www.dialnsa.edu).

University of California Extension, Center for Media and Independent Learning, 2000 Center St., Suite 400, Berkeley, CA 94704, phone: (510) 642-8245, fax: (510) 643-9271, askcmil@uclink4.berkeley.edu (learn.berke ley.edu).

University of California, Los Angeles, OnlineLearning.net, 924 Westwood Blvd., Suite 650, Los Angeles, CA 90024, phone: (800) 784-8436, fax: (310) 794-8424, info@onlinelearning.net (www.onlinelearning.net).

Indexing

The indexes in the back of most nonfiction books are another source of income for freelance wordsmiths. While the index is usually the responsibility of the book's author, few authors actually do it themselves. Usually the work is done by freelance indexers who are hired by the publisher. The indexer's fee is then subtracted from whatever payment the publisher owes the author.

To do the job, an indexer will typically receive a set of page proofs, which are exact images of how pages will appear in the book, complete with page numbers. The indexer reads these proofs and compiles a list of subject headings, subheads and the location of each key reference. Upon completing a rough draft of the index, the indexer then edits it, formats it and proofreads it.

Since indexing is one of the last steps in completing a book, indexers frequently work under intense pressure and time constraints. Indexing cannot be started until final page proofs are available. By that time the printer wants to get the job on the press because the publisher is demanding a finished product.

The indexing features of good word processing programs can help you handle the page numbering and sorting that is necessary for indexing. Special software is also available to help with editing, sorting and formatting. But the bulk of the work must still be done manually.

Publishers do not usually require specific degrees unless they are looking for someone with specific expertise in the subject of the book that needs indexing. What skilled indexers must possess is the ability to work well under pressure, good language skills, attention to detail, patience and an analytical mind.

Any college with an information science or library science program is likely to offer indexing courses. You can also enroll in indexing correspondence courses offered by the U.S. Department of Agriculture. But before you invest in any training, research the field thoroughly to make sure you have what it takes.

Probably the best way to break into the business is to send resumes with cover letters to publishers. You can find their addresses in *Literary Market Place*, (R.R. Bowker Co.), *Writer's Market* (Writer's Digest Books) and *Books in Print* (R.R. Bowker Co.). It is hard to get established in the business, but once you do get work—and do it well—it is easier to get jobs through word of mouth and a little networking.

Resources

PROFESSIONAL GROUPS

American Society of Indexers, P.O. Box 48267, Seattle, WA 98148-0267, phone: (206) 241-9196, fax: (206) 727-6430, asi@well.com (www.well .com/user/asi).

Indexing and Abstracting Society of Canada, P.O. Box 744 Station F, Toronto, Ontario M4Y 2N6 Canada, (514) 487-9204.

National Federation of Abstracting and Information Services, 1429 Walnut St., Philadelphia, PA 19102, phone: (215) 563-2406, fax: (215) 563-2848.

PUBLICATIONS

The Art of Indexing by Larry Bonura (John Wiley and Sons, 1994).

Indexing: A Basic Reading List compiled by Hans Wellisch (American Society of Indexers, 1994).

Indexing Books by Nancy Mulvany (University of Chicago Press, 1994).

Indexing From A to Z by Hans Wellisch (H.W. Wilson, 1995).

COURSES AND TRAINING

Editorial Experts, 66 Canal Center Plaza, Suite 200, Alexandria, VA 22314, phone: (703) 683-0683, fax: (703) 683-4915. Offers two-day indexing workshop.

The Graduate School, USDA, Correspondence Programs, AG Box 9911, South Agriculture Building, Room 1114, Fourteenth St. and Independence Ave. SW, Washington, DC 20250, (202) 720-7123. Offers indexing correspondence courses.

St. John's University, Division of Library and Information Science, Jamaica, NY 11439, phone: (718) 990-6200, fax: (718) 380-0353. Offers one-day principles and techniques seminar.

Ghostwriting

When a book is ghostwritten, the person whose name appears on the book as primary author has done little or none of the actually writing. She is merely a source of information—providing content, background information and, hopefully, credibility. Typically these people are celebrities or well respected in their fields of expertise. While they have the experience and the name recognition that can make for best-selling books, they lack professional writing credentials. As a result, the so-called authors rely on more experienced writers—ghostwriters—to put their ideas into book form.

The ghostwriter gathers information for the book by interviewing the author, and will often conduct her own research and interview several other sources as well for background material. While every collaboration is different, the author will usually review the manuscript and possibly even edit it for content. For their part, ghostwriters may be credited as coauthors or get no visible credit at all. (Their motivation is often a five- or six-figure check and the opportunity to get even more lucrative work either as authors or as ghostwriters.)

The arrangement that a ghostwriter walks into is inherently more complex than the typical relationship between a writer and publisher (which is complex enough). It's easy for misunderstandings to arise between the so-called author and the publisher, with the ghostwriter being caught in the middle. In one sense the ghostwriter is a translator— taking what the author has to offer and trying to deliver what the publisher expects. The best way to avoid such conflict is to clearly map out in writing what each party expects from the arrangement. When all is said and done there may still be misunderstandings, but at least the ghostwriter can justify what she has done.

There are a number of ways to break into ghostwriting. One is to seek out a rising star, either in sports, entertainment, business or politics. Publishers are often in search of new talent and new celebrities. Armed with a collaboration agreement and the right amount of talent, you can sell your services to such a publisher.

As you gain experience and become specialized in a certain subject area, you will find it easier to sell your talents to publishers who are looking for ghostwriters in that field of expertise. Along the way you can build your resume by collaborating on magazine articles with celebrities or experts in your chosen field of specialization. Magazines do not knowingly accept ghostwritten articles, but they would accept, for instance, an article on the modern history of baseball "as told to" John Doe.

Often successful executives or entrepreneurs are looking for writers who can help them self-publish books. The finished books are then distributed through their businesses to clients, co-workers and relatives. This is a great way to get work and hone your talents, and possibly even make a name for yourself.

CHAPTER THIRTEEN

Protecting Your Writing

History offers few greater mismatches than that of publisher and writer: on one side, one of the world's largest and most profitable industries with armies of lawyers at its disposal; on the other, one of the world's most competitive, low-paying and unprotected professions. Many writers trust editors and publishers they've never met, without the benefit of written contracts or anything else prudent souls would consider security.

Clearly the best security you can have as a writer is a written contract. For books, contracts are the norm. But understanding a contract's implications can be difficult. For articles, contracts are somewhat less common. Of course a contract is only as good as your ability to enforce it. If the language is vague, or the cost of a lawsuit far outweighs the potential benefits, the contract becomes fairly useless. And if drafted the wrong way, a contract can become more like a chain than a bond.

As a writer, you probably can't afford to level the playing field by having a lawyer on retainer. But you can learn your way around the legal terrain. The following sections describe contracts and the law as they apply to writers. While not comprehensive, this information offers most of what you need to know to bypass some of the common and more costly mistakes.

Your Rights

Understanding what rights you're selling to a publisher is important. The term *selling* may not even be a good word. In most cases it is more like you are "licensing" your work to a publisher. Here is an overview of the options you have when offering your work to a publisher.

- When you sell "all rights" the publisher is essentially buying ownership of your work. You are giving up the right to sell that particular piece of work again. This sounds bad, but many articles are so tailored to a specific publication, no one else would ever buy them. Even so, you should never sell all rights unless you absolutely have to, or the money is excellent.

- Offering someone "first rights" (sometimes called "first North American rights" or "first serial rights") allows the buyer to be the first to publish a particular piece of work. After that, all rights to the work belong to you. If the publisher wishes to reprint the article in another publication, it must negotiate additional payment with you.

- "One-time rights" are similar to first rights, except that you have the added advantage of being able to sell the same piece of work to two or more publishers at the same time. (As a professional courtesy, you should always alert a publisher to the fact that you are making simultaneous submissions.)

- "Second rights" (sometimes called "reprint rights") are contracted for when your article has already been published at least once before.

Rights are nearly always negotiable. If you feel uncomfortable with a publisher's proposal, ask if she would consider other terms. If you do sign away all rights to a piece of work, you are normally only selling the rights to a particular group of words set in a particular order. In many cases you can take the same information, rewrite it from a different angle and resell it.

In the absence of any written agreement, in most cases the copyright law assumes that an author is only giving a publisher one-time rights. The key exception is a work-for-hire arrangement. In this case the work becomes the property of the publisher. Generally something is considered a work for hire if it is produced by an employee, such as a staff writer. In some cases freelancers have also been subjected to work-for-hire arrangements. But in most instances freelancers and independent contractors own the rights to their creative work unless they stipulate otherwise in writing.

With the proliferation of books and magazines on the Internet and on CD-ROM, electronic rights have become a controversial issue. In one high-profile case the federal courts first sided with publishers in 1999, allowing them to reproduce articles in electronic form without owing the authors additional compensation. In that case involving *The New York Times, Newsday* and *The Atlantic Monthly*, among others (Plaintiffs vs. *The New York Times, Newsday, Time, The Atlantic Monthly*, Mead Data Central and University Microfilms Inc.), the court ruled that putting articles into electronic databases and onto CDs fell under the "collective works" provision of the Copyright Act. The case has since been overturned on appeal and will likely go all the way to the Supreme Court before it is finally settled.

Given the current state of technology, is putting an article in a database that much different than storing a magazine on microfiche? On the other hand, some publications are developing pages on the Internet that have the potential to become quite profitable. Tracking user "hits" on particular articles is relatively easy, and some writers want a share of those profits. As technology—and its use—continues to evolve, these issues are far from settled. Depending on the situation, writers of books and articles may want to make electronic rights a point of negotiation.

Magazine Contracts

Contracts and negotiations for periodicals are relatively simple. In some cases there will be no contract at all, just an editor giving you the go-ahead to write an article. Yet whenever possible you should try to get some kind of written agreement, even if it's just an informal assignment letter from the editor. If you get nothing in writing, try sending your own letter confirming the assignment. If nothing else it may clear up costly misunderstandings.

If you are presented with a contract or letter of agreement, it should cover the following key issues. In cases where there is no written agreement, you should at least talk through these key issues so you are clear on what the publication expects of you.

- What rights are you granting to the publisher? First rights (as defined earlier in this chapter) are a good starting point.
- How and when will you be paid? The best option is to be paid on acceptance, since publication will often occur months, sometimes many months, later.
- What kill fee will the publisher pay if the finished article is rejected? Under what circumstances is a kill fee normally paid?
- What expenses will the publisher cover?
- Is the publisher responsible for defending you in a libel suit? Few writers can afford such a defense on their own.
- Will you have the right to approve the final version of your work? Most publications retain the right to edit for space and style. This can mean almost anything. But generally if you write professionally and follow the style of the publication, you won't experience much revision. (Before most publications will seriously alter your work, they will kick it back to you for editing or a rewrite.)
- Are you expected to provide additional materials, such as sidebars, photographs or illustrations? If so, the agreement should spell out whether you will be paid separately for them.
- Will you receive complimentary copies of the publication in which your work appears? You should receive at least a couple copies of the publication.
- Don't forget one of the most important points: when the work is due. This should be spelled out clearly.

When you are presented with a contract, remember that many points can be negotiable. If you're new to the game you may have less of a chance to negotiate. But as you gain more publishing credits, along with a solid reputation, you will also gain more leverage.

Book Contracts

Regardless of your excitement about getting a book deal, take a long, hard look at how you're treated under the terms of the contract. Better yet, get a lawyer familiar with the publishing industry to do so. After all, you will have to live with the terms of the contract for years.

Book contracts fall within a fairly standard format, but you have every right to negotiate the individual terms. There are no "right" ways to handle the various issues in a book contract. You should simply hold out for the best overall deal. Some points are more important to the publisher than others, just as some points are more important to you. Try to hold firm on the issues of most importance to you, while "giving in" on other points that are more important to the publisher.

The following are some of the major contract issues that may come up:

- When is the advance to be paid? If payable in two or three stages (as is the norm) what are these stages? If some stages are delayed for reasons beyond your control, is there a time limit to prevent foot-dragging by the publisher?

- Are royalties based on a percentage of the list price or the publisher's net profit? In the latter case, getting a fair accounting becomes harder. Most writers organizations recommend royalties be based on list prices. Also, is there a provision for an audit of the publisher's records in accounting for royalties due you?

- Does the contract provide a time frame in which the manuscript is considered to be accepted even if the publisher does not expressly do so?

- Do you have the right to review the edited manuscript? If so, how long is the review period? Does the contract specify a time frame in which you must complete any revisions? If so, is it enough time?

- If an accepted manuscript is never published, does the contract become void, allowing you to sell it elsewhere? If so, do you retain the money paid in advance?

- Is there an arbitration clause that allows for peaceful resolution of disputes? If arbitration of contract disputes is called for, the arbitration should be in accordance with the American Arbitration Association's rules. Also, does the contract state the place for the arbitration? It should be a locale equally convenient to both parties.

- If the book is to be indexed, who is responsible for hiring and paying the indexer? Who is responsible for the cost of providing photographs and illustrations? If you are responsible for such costs, are they to be withheld from the advance or royalties? This is in the writer's best interest.

- Do you have veto power over the title of the book and the cover design?
- Does the contract provide for free copies to be furnished to you? Can you purchase additional copies at a discount?
- Does the contract specify a dollar amount for publisher's promotional expense? Does it obligate you to make promotional appearances without being paid for your time and expenses?
- Does the contract give the publisher any options on your future work? Unless the publisher wants to pay you for this option, you should probably reject it.
- Does the contract have a "noncompete" clause prohibiting you from writing, editing or publishing another competing book without written permission of the publisher? Some clauses are so vaguely worded that they seemingly would give the publisher control over virtually anything else you produce. If you must have such a clause, make sure it's narrowly worded.
- Do publication rights revert to you when the book goes out of print? Do you have the right of consent to any sales of subsidiary rights, such as motion picture, book club or anthology rights? Is there a provision for full subsidiary rights to revert to you should the publisher fail to exercise such rights in a specified time? Many writers mistakenly hand over potentially lucrative rights to publishers who have no interest or expertise in exercising such deals.
- Does the publisher promise to pay for legal expenses arising from any libel action in connection with the book? If so, do you have the right to choose your own lawyer? If you are partly responsible for any of the legal costs, does the publisher agree not to settle any claim without your consent? Finally, can the publisher freeze royalty payments after a suit is filed? If so, what are the provisions for the resumption of payments following a settlement?

Agents and Attorneys

Whenever you are faced with a lucrative contract or complex negotiations you should consider the services of a literary agent or attorney. This is the norm. Four of five books sold to publishers are sold through agents. Many book publishers and film producers will not even deal directly with writers when it comes to contract issues and negotiations.

Of course the money in question must be substantial for the services of an agent or attorney to be worthwhile. Most agents want 15 percent share of your proceeds. Attorneys charge $150 or more an hour, and most negotiations will consume at least several hours of expensive legal service. Accordingly it is not in your best interest (nor theirs) for agents or attorneys to get involved unless several thousand dollars are at stake.

In some cases agents and attorneys are well worth the cost, and can frequently increase your net income. Here's how.

1. Good agents and attorneys know more about contracts and negotiations than most writers can ever learn. And by keeping you out of the direct negotiations, they enable you to preserve your working relationship with publishers and editors. Any hard feelings following a difficult round of bargaining will not reflect directly on you.

2. Professional representation by an agent or attorney shows a publisher that someone with credibility thinks your work is worthwhile. It means more when someone else does your boasting for you—especially when it's an agent or attorney who understands the publishing world.

3. Most important of all, agents and attorneys relieve much of the work and stress involved in building a successful career. This allows you to be more productive as a writer.

While both agents and attorneys can be equally beneficial, there are major differences in what each can do for you. Attorneys only come into play once you have a contract to negotiate. Agents are often necessary long before to help you find a publisher. An agent's role can be that of salesman and business consultant. Some will even work with you to develop your talent.

One of the best ways to find an agent or literary attorney is to talk with satisfied customers—other writers. You can also get leads through the Association of Authors' Representatives (AAR), based in New York, or the Writers Guild of America, based in Los Angeles and New York. Agents are also listed in *Writer's Market* (Writer's

Digest Books) and the *Guide to Literary Agents* (Writer's Digest Books). The National Writers Union also maintains a list of reputable agents as a service to its members.

While an agent can be a great benefit in negotiating contracts on your behalf, consider carefully the terms of the agreement you sign with an agent. Agents customarily make at least nominal contact with all the appropriate publishers. How vigorously and competently they handle those contacts is another issue. If the writer, entirely through his own efforts, later lands a deal with one of those publishers, the agent could still be entitled to a cut, depending on how the relationship is structured.

Contracts with agents should spell out the agents' responsibilities clearly and prevent agents from claiming a share of income from projects they didn't procure. That's one reason to negotiate short-term agent contracts rather than long-term relationships.

Beware of an agent who charges a fee to review a manuscript. The fees don't obligate the agent to make any other effort on your behalf and can end up costing you several hundred dollars.

Copyright

The basic rules of copyright are easy to understand. All works created after 1977 are protected for the length of the author's life and another seventy years thereafter. After that the work falls into the public domain and anyone can use it without permission. (Any work created in 1977 or earlier can be copyrighted for up to seventy-five years from the time of its first publication or its registration with the copyright office.)

Obtaining a copyright for your work is truly effortless. The way the law is structured today, copyright is assumed the moment your words hit the paper or the computer screen. Technically, you need not even place a copyright notice on your work. There are, however, additional steps you can take to secure your rights.

- Adding a copyright notice allows you to defeat claims of "innocent infringement."

- You must register your work with the copyright office before you can file suit against someone who steals your work. If you wait to register your work until after the theft takes place, you may not be able to recover attorney fees and some damages from the defendant.

To register a copyright, request the proper form (usually form TX) from the Register of Copyrights, Library of Congress, Washington, DC 20559. You'll need to send the completed form and registration fee.

Of course, not even a registered copyright can protect your most valued assets—your ideas. In reality, most articles are written on the basis of idea proposals, or queries, which protect you from starting pieces without being paid. But since you can't copyright ideas, you must trust the editors who read your queries. Fortunately, the vast majority of editors are trustworthy. They have to be. An editor with a reputation for stealing other people's ideas won't last long in the business. (Sometimes what appears to be piracy is simply the result of a project being already in the works when your query arrives. An editor, however, should inform you of this when rejecting your query.)

The American Society of Journalists and Authors defines a story idea as a "subject combined with an approach." It says a writer shall have a proprietary right to an idea suggested to an editor and have first shot at developing it. Any editor with integrity will respect this ethical standard.

Fair Use

Aside from protecting their work, the copyright issue of most concern to writers is the doctrine of fair use. It is this principle that allows you to quote briefly from someone else's work without their express permission. It's important to note, however, that the rules of fair use have never been clearly defined by the courts, nor have they been spelled out in law. Fair use can only be judged in the context in which it occurs. If you are unsure of the limits, obtain permission before quoting from any copyrighted material.

To get permission to quote from copyrighted material, you must submit a request to the copyright owner, which usually means contacting the publisher. In a brief

letter explain exactly what you want to quote, and note when and where it was first published. Be sure to give information about how you will use the material and the name of the publication in which it will appear. In most cases you will be granted permission, on the condition that you credit the original source. In some cases you may have to pay a fee, which can range from a few dollars to a few hundred dollars. You must decide whether the material is worth the cost involved.

Libel

You are guilty of libel if you publish a false statement that is damaging to another living person's reputation. The false statement can be unintentional and still be ruled libelous in court, which is why the law requires writers to take every reasonable step to check for accuracy. While it is up to the plaintiff to prove falsehood, it is up to you to prove that you made every reasonable effort to be accurate.

Few writers would knowingly publish falsehoods. Yet the pitfalls for writers are numerous. You can accurately print what you have been told and still commit libel—if the person giving you the information was wrong in his facts. Many writers get in trouble simply by failing to check minor facts, which is why you must double-check and triple-check information—even when you believe it is correct.

Misspell someone's name while writing about a crime and you can implicate an innocent person in wrongdoing. That's libel. You can be held just as libelous if you falsely state someone has died. The "lucky living" have won such cases on claims of undue hardship and emotional distress. Errors in something as innocent as a high school sports story have even resulted in libel suits. While such instances are rare, the important point is that nearly any form of writing can put you at risk of libel.

The only way to be safe is to always be 100 percent certain of your facts. An *Associated Press Stylebook and Libel Manual* (Addison-Wesley Publishing) is an excellent source of information on libel and how to protect yourself.

Freelance writers have some special issues of concern with libel. First, keep in mind that you aren't necessarily going to be defended by the publisher if your work prompts a libel suit. If the publisher alone is sued and loses, it could come after you for damages.

To protect yourself from groundless suits, it's good to have tapes of your interviews. Bear in mind, however, that taping phone conversations is illegal in some states unless the other party is aware she is being taped.

Not all libel suits stem from anything the writer did. Bad editing can cause errors that result in a suit. The best protection is to see a proof of the edited version, including headlines and photo captions. For your own protection keep a hard copy of manuscripts you send to a publisher.

Resources

- Several writers groups offer legal advice and contract help for writers, including the National Writers Union, the Writers Guild of America and The Authors Guild. (For addresses and phone numbers see chapter two.)
- Volunteer Lawyers for the Arts (VLA), 1 E. Fifty-third St., New York, New York 10022, (212) 319-2787, has dozens of chapters throughout North America. The organization also sells a variety of handbooks on legal issues. VLA members can consult volunteer lawyers for free.

   Most VLA chapters have an income ceiling for members. If you don't meet the VLA guidelines, a VLA chapter may be able to refer you to an experienced lawyer. Your local bar association can also refer you to an attorney experienced in whatever legal issue you are facing. You may be able to arrange a consultation with a lawyer for a relatively small fee before committing yourself to further services.

CHAPTER FOURTEEN

Promoting Your Business and Yourself

When she was a newspaper columnist in 1978, Victoria Secunda was invited to speak to a singles group. She accepted, even though the thought of giving a speech made her so nervous her breath came in gasps and her knees trembled. "I have to learn to do this," she thought, "because someday I might get to go on the *Today Show*."

One speaking engagement led to another and Secunda left newspaper work to concentrate on writing books, eventually writing eight. And she did go on to do the *Today Show*, as well as many other national television and radio shows. Early on, she had learned a lesson: "Publishing is more than writing a book. It is also about doing all the things that can feed your book, and that includes public speaking, the thought of which make writers take to their beds."

She laughingly adds, "There's nothing to it. You just take tranquilizers."

Although she still may need antianxiety medicine before a speaking engagement, Secunda proudly says she is tireless in her efforts to promote her books, noting that she spends nearly as much time on promotion as on writing and research. You know your book better than anyone, Secunda says, and that means you can promote it better than anyone. Ideally, authors should work together with publicists to find promotional strategies that work.

Secunda's books focus on relationships and psychology, including *When You and Your Mother Can't Be Friends* (Delacorte Press, 1990), *When Madness Comes Home* (Hyperion, 1997) and *Women and Their Fathers* (Delacorte Press, 1992). Having been raised by dysfunctional parents and having a sister who was mentally ill, she says that the maxim about writing what you know is true for her. "I have found through my experience that my entire family was grist for my mill," she says. When she speaks to physicians groups, her first words are often "I am among the credentially impaired. But I know what madness looks like twenty-four hours a day." And they listen.

They listen not only because of her experience, but because she spends so much energy on research, Secunda says. It is "terribly important" to have a specialty, to develop an expertise, she says. This means she has to read everything published on her topic. It means she is never content with a magazine's or newspaper's report on a study, but reads the study itself. It means she also finds backups for primary sources, because even those sometimes have errors. "There is no substitute for back-breaking research," she says. "You don't want to be caught making sloppy mistakes."

Secunda's research extends to finding promotional avenues for her books. She compiles long lists of names, addresses and phone numbers of publications and groups that might be interested in her work and gives them to the book's publicist. For her book on father-daughter relationships, for example, she went to the library and looked up men's groups that could be sent a news release. Realizing that *When Madness Comes Home* is hardly light reading for the beach, she became involved with the National Alliance for the Mentally Ill, a group that supports families of people with mental illness. She spoke at the association's national convention and for several local chapters around the country, offering herself as a spokeswoman for the organization on local radio and television shows.

Despite her flair for self-promotion, her first television appearance frightened her. "I hired a coach to teach me how to do television so I could get through the *Today Show* without throwing up on Jane Pauley," she recalls. Secunda learned not to wave her hands or bob her head. She learned to condense her book's theme to one sentence, aimed at an ideal reader, and to expound on that sentence in interviews. She and her coach role-played interviews, taped them and critiqued them. Recalling the first time her media coach asked her how she thought she had performed, Secunda told her, 'I think I was terrific because I didn't pass out.' She said, 'But you were stiff.' So we went over it, and over it and over it."

If a television show invites you to be a guest, never be affronted if the interviewer hasn't read your book. "Just get down on your hands and knees and thank God you're on their show," Secunda advises. Having worked as an associate producer in television, she understands the deadline pressure, the hectic pace and the number of press kits stations receive each day, and she views any airtime as a gift.

While some news organizations have reporters who specialize on particular beats, it's more likely that reporters won't know much about you, your book or even the topic. So help them do their jobs. Secunda once appeared on a radio show that didn't expect her until the next day. Although they weren't prepared, she was. She handed them a list of questions to ask about her book, and the next thing she knew, the hour was up.

Who Else But You?

Promotion doesn't start the minute the presses stop; many authors plan their promotional efforts when their books are still in the proposal stage. Success as a writer often depends upon speeches, book signings, newsletters, television appearances, radio interviews, Web sites, visits to groups, campuses and organizations, and more. Who else but you knows your book better? Who else but you is as dedicated to its success? Who else but you can talk about it as ardently?

In fact, talking is more important than writing for the success of many nonfiction books, says Michael Larsen, an agent and author of several books about getting published, including *Guerilla Marketing for Writers* (Writer's Digest Books, 2000). "We get calls from writers every week who suppose the publisher is going to promote their books," Larsen says. "This is an understandable innocence on their part. It's not information they're born with. But, especially when they approach an agent, they should find out about it." For most nonfiction books with a wide national audience, Larsen believes the author's promotional plan is eight times more important than the book's contents.

While publishers do promote some titles, publicists in many houses are too busy to do much for every book. Even well-known authors go on the road, give talks and do interviews to promote their works. Even fiction writers recognize that promotion is as much a part of writing as knowing the difference between active and passive voice.

Speak Up

Jeanne Dams, whose synopsis for her mystery novel *The Body in the Transept* (Walker and Company, 1995) is reprinted in chapter ten, knew from the first that to be a successful author she would have to promote her books. Her first public speech was at a university, and it sounded as if it would be miserable: The students were required to attend, the scheduled speaker had canceled at the last minute and the organizers called Dams only because they knew she had worked for the university.

"Then I thought, 'I have had a dream come true. That doesn't happen to too many people,'" she says. So Dams built a speech around her dream of becoming an author, wrote out every word and practiced it. When it was over, "they didn't throw anything at me," she says, laughing. Some students even told her they thought the speech was funny, so Dams began to relax and enjoy herself as well. "I have discovered to my absolute astonishment that I'm pretty good at public speaking," she says.

To talk up your work, it can be helpful to think of an interesting angle, or angles, that will appeal to a broader audience than simply people who are interested in its topic. For example, a Florida biomedical scientist who writes as Dirk Wyle offers a workshop, "Using Your Professional Experience to Write a Mystery or Thriller." Most readers believe that their life experiences could furnish material for a novel, he says, and rightfully so. "Professional experience is an important aspect because most readers devote twelve-plus hours' attention per day to their professional lives, and they would like to see that interest reflected in serious fiction," he says. "Or reflected seriously in fiction." Whether he gets forty attendees or two, he considers it a rewarding experience.

The News Release

A news release should be a page or two at most, double-spaced. At the top of the release, include your name and a phone number where you can be reached days and evenings.

The release's goal is to tell people not only what your work is about, but more importantly, why they should care. What's in it for them? It should lead with the most intriguing point of your book or the most useful aspect of your findings. Write it in third person, and include a few strong quotes from yourself.

Make it read like a news story you'd see in your paper, complete with a headline, because smaller, overworked news staffs sometimes simply reprint releases. Larger news organizations may call you for an interview, using your release as a starting point for their own reporting. Either way, you win.

It's a good idea to prepare a list of talking points, questions that a reporter can ask that will highlight important parts of your book, because many reporters must fit such interviews with visiting authors in between covering fires, reporting on car wrecks and sitting through school board meetings. Assume they don't have time to read your book. If you go in person for an interview, bring a copy of your talking points, just in case they've misplaced the one you sent.

Before you mail your releases, verify the names and addresses of editors and producers by phone. If you don't want to mail your own, you can pay the PR Newswire to distribute releases electronically to print and broadcast news organizations across the country. Contact the Newswire at 1515 Broadway, New York, NY 10155, (212) 832-9400 or (800) 832-5533 (www.prnewswire.com).

The Internet has many sites devoted to public speaking (which is, after all, one of the most dreaded of all human experiences). A good site for self-help is from The Pennsylvania State University Department of Speech Communication and written by Sam Walch (www.la.psu.edu/speech/100a/workbook/wrkbk.htm).

If public speaking gives you tremors, enroll in a speech class at a local college for instruction, practice and feedback. Or join Toastmasters International, which offers nationwide clubs to help people improve their speaking skills. Call (800) 9WE-SPEAK (www.toastmasters.org).

Call local bookstores and offer to do a talk and a book signing. Be imaginative about other groups to address. The *Encyclopedia of Associations*, (Gale Research) available at libraries, is a compendium of organizations around the world. It can help you find audiences. If you write about nursing, for example, you can find dozens of nursing associations, each of which may have newsletters for members and meetings where you may be permitted to give a presentation. Look up your topic in the yellow pages to find local businesses, churches and groups that may agree to let you promote your work to their members.

Use visual aids. Whitney Otto created a slide show to promote *The Passion Dream Book* (HarperCollins, 1997), a novel that explores the relationship between art and the lives of artists. The slides also helped her add originality to her tour and broaden it to include libraries and art schools. "Besides, *Dream Book* as a whole is artistically more like a painting, and the slide show allowed me to present an overview, to look at it thematically," she tells *Publishers Weekly*.

Go Visit

Janice Papolos, whose book proposal for *The Virgin Homeowner* (W.W. Norton and Company, 1997) is reprinted in chapter nine, makes a point of visiting local bookstores to meet the staffs and talk about her book. If they know her, they're more likely to put her book in the window when she asks, she notes. When she visited relatives in California, she called the local media and asked for interviews. "People say 'I'm a writer, not a publicist,'" she says. "You can't be one without the other."

Dams used *The Deadly Directory* (Deadly Serious Press), which she calls an indispensable reference for mystery writers, to find mystery bookstores. She visited every store within driving distance to supplement the book tour arranged by her publisher. "Even when I drew very few people, I established a personal relationship with the bookseller," Dams says. "That really matters because mystery bookstores hand sell their books." Today, even the chain stores call her.

Victoria Secunda had met a producer who invited her to be a guest on the *Today Show* for her newspaper column. The publicist for her next book liked how she appeared on the tape. So for her next book, *When You and Your Mother Can't Be Friends*, the publisher wanted to send her on a ten-city tour. "My adorable husband said, 'Let's add five more cities.' We paid for five more cities, which cost a fortune, but it was worth every cent and gave me phenomenal experience." And after that book, the publisher sent her on fifteen-city tours.

If your publisher doesn't spring for book tours, you can plan your own. Some writers have combined book tours with family vacations, hauling the kids and some-times even their dogs along as they traverse the country.

Libraries and bookstores often welcome visiting authors who wish to speak or give readings. To find those outside your telephone book's area, try these directories at the library.

> *American Book Trade Directory* (R.R. Bowker Co.). Lists contact information for more than 30,000 booksellers in the U.S. and Canada, arranged geographically.
>
> *American Library Directory* (R.R. Bowker Co.). Lists more than 36,000 librar-ies throughout the U.S. and Canada, arranged geographically, with names of department heads.
>
> *Directory of Special Libraries and Information Centers* (Gale Research). Includes more than 22,000 places that house special collections.

You also can search for members of the American Booksellers Association by state and zip code at BookWeb.org (www.bookweb.org/bd-bin/search_bd).

Send a news release to media outlets in every city you'll visit, then follow up with a phone call before you arrive. Some newspapers may have a reporter to talk to people who simply walk in, but don't count on it.

Use the Media

If your publisher doesn't do it for you, write a news release and send it to your local media and any other publication or electronic news organization you want to visit. If you've written a speech, it should be easy to adapt it into a news release, focusing on whatever major aspect of your work is most useful to a general audience.

Don't send a release only to book editors, because few smaller news organizations employ such a person anyway. Also send it to the editor of the appropriate department at a newspaper. For example, releases about books on management should go to the business editor; those on relationships go to the features editor. Send your release to the producers of television shows.

A radio "tour" allows you to promote your book without leaving your kitchen. But you may be doing interviews in early morning hours, and late at night to meet deadline cycles of stations in a different time zone.

To let radio and television shows know you're available, you can take out an ad in *Radio-TV Interview Report*, a publication made up completely of ads. It is published three times a month and circulates to more than four thousand radio and television producers looking for people to interview. Call Bradley Communications, (800) 553-8002, ext. 408, for recorded information and to receive a kit. Another publication, *Authors on the Air*, circulates to about six hundred radio and television producers. Call (941) 739-4801.

Directories such as *Talk Shows and Hosts on Radio* (Whitefoord Press, 1995) or *Talk Show "Selects"* (Broadcast Interview Source) also are helpful in finding hosts on radio and television. Television demands different skills than radio or print interviews, because your appearance is critical. If you're going to be on a television show and can't afford a media coach, try role-playing an interview and then watch a tape of it carefully. Are any of your mannerisms distracting? Are your answers clear? Can you speak in sound bites of thirty seconds or so? Is your voice expressive? Are you entertaining? And, despite all those questions, do you seem relaxed?

Television can be an intimidating medium, so it's best to start small, with your local cable station. "I was really afraid of TV, but I was more afraid of failure," says Janice Papolos. Although Papolos is a teacher and was a performer—an opera singer—she hired a media coach to help her learn to do television interviews. She learned how to make a point, give an example, then repeat the point. She bought three "pulled together outfits that travel well." They cost a lot, but, she notes, you get to take them home with you.

What's most important, she says, is for writers to write only what they believe in deeply and will talk about fervently. "When you talk about it, talk about it with passion," Papolos says, "but be passionately sane."

Try these sources for contact information for the media. Don't forget to send a release to wire services, such as the Associated Press, which transmit copy to newspapers and broadcast stations around the globe.

Adweek Major Media Directory (Adweek Directories). Lists about 9,000 contacts in top markets in radio, broadcast and cable television, daily newspapers and magazines.

The Association of Alternative News Weeklies, 1000 Connecticut Ave. NW #822, Washington, DC 20036, (202) 822-1955. Faxes or mails you a list of its publications.

Bacon's Newspaper Directory and *Bacon's Magazine Directory* (Bacon's Information, Inc.). Lists more than 13,000 trade and consumer magazines and daily and weekly publications.

Bacon's Radio Directory and *Bacon's TV/Cable Directory* (Bacon's Information, Inc.). Includes more than 10,000 radio and television stations, including college, public television and cable stations.

Broadcasting and Cable Yearbook (R.R. Bowker Co.). Lists all television and radio stations in the U.S. and its territories and Canada, with names of contact people.

Burrelle's Media Directory (Burrelle's Information Services). Lists 48,000 print and electronic media outlets in North America, with names of key contacts.

Editor and Publisher International Year Book (Editor and Publisher). Lists newspapers in the U.S. and Canada, with names of department chiefs.

Gale Directory of Publications and Broadcast Media (Gale Research). Lists more than 37,000 newspapers, magazines, journals and other periodicals. Markets are arranged geographically and indexed by subject.

Literary Market Place (R.R. Bowker Co.), A fabulous resource for writers. Its huge compendium includes lists of contacts for book reviews, direct-mail specialists, lecture agents and public relations services and more. It is well worth the trip to the library.

Ulrich's International Periodicals Directory (R.R. Bowker Co.). A huge listing of about 165,000 periodicals and newspapers worldwide.

Below is a list of some of the major publications that review books. But don't neglect your local print publications; a book sold in Dayton, Ohio, earns as much profit as a book sold in New York City. Call each publication for the name of the appropriate editor to review your genre or your topic, and send either a galley copy (photocopy of the book's pages before it's published) or the book as early as you can—as soon as four months prior to publication.

The Booklist, American Library Association, 50 E. Huron St., Chicago, IL 60611-2729, (800) 545-2433. Send two copies of the book or galleys.

Chicago Tribune Books, 435 N. Michigan Ave., Room 400, Chicago, IL 60611-4022, (312) 222-3232. Send review copies.

Kirkus Reviews, 200 Park Ave. S. #1118, New York, NY 10003-1543, (212) 777-4554. Send galleys at least two months prior to publication.

Library Journal, 245 W. Seventeenth St., New York, NY 10011, (212) 463-6819. Send the book or galleys four months before publication date.

Los Angeles Times Book Review, Times Mirror Square, Los Angeles, CA 90053, (213) 237-7001. Send review copies.

Midwest Book Review, 278 Orchard Dr., Oregon, WI 53575, (608) 835-7937. Send review copies.

The New York Review of Books, 1755 Broadway, 5th Floor, New York, NY 10019, (212) 757-8070. Send review copies.

The New York Times Book Review, 229 W. Forty-third St., New York, NY 10036, (212) 556-1234. Send galleys as soon as possible, followed by the book when printed.

Publishers Weekly, 245 W. Seventeenth St., New York, NY 10011, (212) 463-6758. Send galleys at least three months prior to the book publication date to PW Forecasts.

USA Today, 1000 Wilson Blvd., Arlington, VA 22229, (703) 276-3400. Send review copies.

The Wall Street Journal, 200 Liberty St., New York, NY 10281-0001, (212) 416-2487. Send review copies.

Washington Post Book World, 1150 Fifteenth St. NW, Washington, DC 20071, (202) 334-7882. Send review copies.

Write

Dams and three other mystery writers, Barbara D'Amato, Hugh Holton and Mark Zubro, started a newsletter to promote their books. They started their mailing list by asking their publishers to slip a postcard for a subscription into their books, and now they mail it to two thousand or more people twice a year. (They also mail it to anyone else they think would be remotely interested, Dams notes.) Into it goes an article by each author, mystery quizzes, even recipes for foods mentioned in their books. The newsletter always includes a list of the authors' appearances and their books in print. It is a time-consuming and expensive promotional tool, but the costs are borne by all four authors and, Dams says, "I've gotten a lot of good feedback from it."

Network

Everyone was a beginner once, and many successful authors remember how difficult it was to become established. These authors are often a tremendous resource for beginners. The book you're reading now wouldn't exist without the generosity of writers, agents and editors who took time to share their expertise.

Joining a writers association and attending writers conferences can help you learn how to write and sell your work, but more importantly, these networks help you meet people who may be able to help you—and whom you also may be able to help. "I do many favors for people in and around publishing, and I ask for favors," Secunda says. "That part takes all my courage, because I hate asking for favors. And I don't do it unless I'm prepared to reciprocate." (See chapter sixteen for help in finding a community of writers.)

Writers groups also can help their members promote their work. C.J. Songer, author of the Meg Gillis crime novel series, used a list published by Sisters in Crime, a group for mystery writers, to reach independent bookstores. Through the group, she also bought a discounted ad in *Publishers Weekly.* "Although it was a fair amount of money, *Bait* was my first-ever book and it was a treat to myself," Songer says. Because she had taken that ad, she also earned a discount on a promotional page for her book on *Publishers Weekly*'s site at www.bookwire.com. "It was very gratifying to be able to go online and see my own book, plus it was so accessible then for family and friends (and acquaintances) all across the country," she says.

Songer, like other writers, believes that promotional costs for early books may not pay off in increased book sales. "I'm taking the longer view that, like any business, you have to plow most of your proceeds back into the business for the first several years in order to establish and grow," she says.

Get Linked

The Internet is becoming a vast shopping mall, virtually as interactive as a real mall. Several authors have figured out ways to capitalize on those facts. Dirk Wyle's Web site (www.dirk-wyle.com) offers brief reviews and excerpts of his books, copies of the books for sale at discounts and his E-mail address for readers. "Scores of readers have written me with their reaction to *Pharmacology Is Murder* (Rainbow Books, 1998). I incorporate their comments and offer information into my 'Discussions With Dirk,'" he says. "My typical reader is interested in science, so my 'Pick of the Month' presents interesting scientific and literary Web sites."

John Kremer, author of *1001 Ways to Market Your Books* (Open Horizons, 1998), offers an electronic and paper newsletter with promotional tips for authors (to subscribe, visit www.bookmarket.com). In one of those newsletters, Kremer mentioned that he noticed that his book had no reviews at Amazon.com other than the one he provided. So he offered a free copy of a book to whoever wrote the best review. And he suggested that other authors do the same for their books.

Think of your Web site as a storefront. Once it's built, you'll need to invite people to come in and browse. But first, you need to tell readers it's open for business.

You can submit your site's URL directly to major search engines and directories by following on-screen directions. Some services, such as The Promoter and Submit-it!, will send your URL to search engines for you. Try Barnes and Noble's Web site (www.bn.com) for help in doing this, which is designed for Barnes and

Noble's affiliates, those people who sell Barnes and Noble books from their site. The promotional advice is nonetheless online for all to see (affiliate.net/affnet/traffic.asp). Of course, it also offers a link to books to help you promote your Web site.

Amazon.com and Barnes and Noble allow authors to submit information about their books, and, important for small presses, provide a distribution network for those books. Amazon notes that a picture of the cover is its "most influential selling point" online.

Some good sites for writers, which include information on promotions and markets, are Inkspot (www.inkspot.com), Inscriptions (come.to/Inscriptions) and Writers Write (www.writerswrite.com). Writers Write offers book promotion services for a fee. All offer E-mail newsletters.

Author L.L. Thrasher shares some useful tips at her Practical Book Promotion for Writers page (www.teleport.com/~baty/promo.html).

In addition to direct promotion, you can learn a lot about writing and promoting your writing by joining a discussion group or mailing list. A good place to start is Deja.com (www.deja.com). Type in *writing* or *publishing* in the Quick Search box and click Search.

LinkExchange Daily Digest is a discussion list in which members ask and answer questions about site promotion (sign up at digest.linkexchange.com). The talk can become a bit technical (one section of the digest is called "Geek Tips"), but the marketing discussion is useful.

Para Publishing (www.parapublishing.com) is full of promotional tips, particularly aimed at self-publishers, and it also sells mailing lists. The Gebbie Press also has some solid advice on promotional strategies (www.gebbieinc.com).

Hundreds of other promotional tactics, ranging from buying mailing lists of potential customers to creating refrigerator magnets, can help you sell your work. While many beginning writers simply want to write, many successful writers know that if you want readers, you'll have to promote yourself. Some have learned it can even be fun. "I never enjoy it in prospect, and I come home from speaking gigs dead tired," says Dams. "But the actual contact with people I just eat up. I love it."

The following resource list can help you find ways to reach more readers.

Resources

An Author's Guide to Children's Book Promotion by Susan Salzman Raab (Raab Associates, 1996).

Book Blitz: Getting Your Book in the News: 60 Steps to a Best Seller by Barbara Gaughen and Ernest Weckbaugh (Best Seller Books, 1994).

Book Promotion for the Shameless: 101 Marketing Tips That Really Work by Lorna Tedder (Spilled Candy Books for Writers, 1999).

Direct Marketing Market Place 2000 (National Register Pub. Co.).

Do-It-Yourself Book Publicity Kit by John Kremer (Open Horizons), (bookmark et.com).

Guerilla Marketing for Authors by Jay Conrad Levinson, Michael Larsen and Rick Frishman (Writer's Digest Books, 2000).

Jump Start Your Book Sales by Marilyn and Tom Ross (Communication Creativity, 1999).

News Releases and Book Publicity by Dan Poynter (Para Publishing, 1997).

1001 Ways to Market Your Books: For Authors and Publishers by John Kremer (Open Horizons, 1998).

The Publicity Handbook by David R. Yale (NTC/Contemporary Publishing Co., 1994).

Publish to Win: Smart Strategies to Sell More Books by Jerrold R. Jenkins and Anne M. Stanton (Rhodes and Easton, 1997).

CHAPTER FIFTEEN

Making and Saving Money

Each year thousands of writers fail in their dream to become freelancers. Sadly, many fail not because they couldn't write well enough, but because they never mastered the business side of the profession.

Though just as important as your creative abilities, the business side of freelancing is a lot less appealing. So it's easy to shove business matters into the bottom drawer, where they slowly kindle into a blaze of uncollected bills and overdue taxes. If you take the right approach, however, the details of business need not consume much of your hard work and talent. A few hours a week keeping your business matters well organized and up-to-date is all it really takes.

This chapter focuses on what you need to know to keep the business side of freelancing from overwhelming you—so that your success as a writer is unfettered by the mundane details of business and taxes.

Part 1: Tax Issues

Becoming a freelancer means saying good-bye to the days you spent thirty minutes filling out your annual tax returns. As soon as you make any money freelancing, you'll have to use Form 1040 (the long one) and Schedule C (business profit or loss). If you plan to deduct car or equipment expenses, you'll have another even more complex form to fill out.

You could hire someone to do your taxes and keep your books. But even then you'll still be responsible for keeping receipts and records. The best strategy is to spend a little time learning the tax rules, then adopt a simple system of keeping records. Even if you do hire an accountant or tax preparer, keeping good records will save time and fees.

Estimated Taxes

Freelancers don't have any tax withheld from their income. Like any self-employed person, they are liable for paying estimated taxes quarterly. You can use IRS Form 1040-ES to calculate and make your estimated payments.

If you can't estimate a year's income accurately, you will usually be safe from penalties if you base your quarterly taxes on what you owed the prior year. Your state and city may also require you to pay estimated taxes. To be safe, you should put aside half of your net earnings to cover your federal, state and local taxes as well as the employer/employee share of Social Security taxes.

Auto Expenses

If you work from your home you can deduct mileage from home and back for interviews, trips to the library for research or travel for business functions. This is true even if you don't qualify for the home office deduction. If you work from an office outside the home, however, you can't deduct mileage for commuting to the office.

You can calculate auto expenses using the standard mileage rate or the actual-cost method. To use the standard mileage rate, multiply the mileage driven by the current mileage rate. The rate frequently changes, but is stated each year in the instructions that come with Schedule C, the IRS form for reporting business income and expenses. Using the standard mileage rate is the easiest method in terms of record keeping.

As the name implies, the actual-cost method uses what it really costs you to operate your car. For this method you'll have to keep receipts for all automobile expenses, including gas, maintenance and repairs, insurance, taxes, loan interest and depreciation of the car's cost.

If you use the car for both business and personal reasons, you must calculate the percentage of business miles each year and deduct only that percentage of your costs. There are limits to how much of your car's value you may write off each year. For details you'll need a current copy of IRS Publication 917.

Home Office Expenses

Qualifying for the home office deduction means jumping through regulatory hoops and increasing your risk of an audit. But the tax savings can be tempting. You may be able to deduct a percentage of your mortgage interest or rent, utilities and upkeep for your home each year.

To qualify for the deduction you must use an area of your home regularly and exclusively for business. Occasional or incidental use of your home office won't cut it, even if you don't use the space for anything else.

"Exclusive use" means just that—no games on your personal computer, no personal calls from the phone in your office, no relatives rolling out sleeping bags there on the weekend. Some furnishings are banned in a home office, such as TVs and sofas. The IRS sees them as signs of personal use. Although it is best to have an entire room set aside for a home office, a portion of a room set aside exclusively for business also satisfies the Internal Revenue Code.

The most accurate way to calculate the business portion of your home is to divide the square feet of the work area by the total square feet of your home. Expenses you can deduct include the business percentage of:

- Mortgage interest
- Utilities and services, such as electricity, heat, trash removal and cleaning services
- Depreciation of the value of your house
- Home security systems
- Repairs, maintenance and permanent improvement costs for your house
- All costs of repairs, painting or modifications of your home office. (Repairs

you can write off in full the first year. Permanent improvements are considered capital expenditures and subject to depreciation over several years.)

One other word of caution—you can't use home office expenses to put you in the red, that is, they can't be used to help create a loss.

Before you take any home office deductions, figure out what the tax savings will be to see if it's worth the risk of an audit. If the savings are minor, you may not want to bother. What you lose in taxes you may gain in peace of mind. You can get more information from IRS Publication 587.

Other Expenses

The IRS applies the "ordinary" and "necessary" rules in judging the validity of a business expense. This means the expenses should be ordinary for your profession and necessary for carrying out your business.

Office equipment is a necessary—and often major—expense for freelance writers. Computers, desks, chairs, shelves, filing cabinets and other office furnishings are deductible expenses if you use them in your business. These can be deducted even if you don't opt for the home office deduction. IRS Publication 534 provides more details on how to depreciate business property.

Among the largest costs for freelancers is phone expense. The IRS prohibits deductions for your personal phone line, even if you use it for business. But you can still deduct the cost of long-distance business calls, even if they're from a personal line. You can also deduct the cost of a second line or other services used exclusively for business, such as distinctive ring or voice mail.

If you entertain sources or clients you can deduct 50 percent of that expense. You must keep a log showing the date, location, person entertained and business purpose of the entertainment for every item you deduct. If you travel in connection with your writing you can deduct the cost of transportation, lodging and meals.

Other deductible expenses include the cost of:
- Dues to professional organizations
- Newspapers, magazines and journals used for your business
- Research, copying services and online databases

- Office supplies
- Postage for business use
- Cleaning supplies for your office
- Legal, accounting and other professional services
- Business licenses

If publishers or clients reimburse you for some of your expenses, remember to keep records of those payments and either report them as income or subtract them from the expenses you report.

Self-Employment Tax

Besides ordinary income tax, freelancers must pay a self-employment tax for Social Security and Medicare. Employees pay Social Security tax, too, but the self-employed pay roughly twice as much (about 15 percent), because they're expected to cover both the "employee" half and the "employer" portion. When you look at your tax bill, you'll find that's one of the strongest motivations for taking every deduction you're allowed.

Keep in mind that the more you cut your self-employment tax, the lower your Social Security check will be once you retire. That said, you'll still likely do better if you take some of your tax savings and put them in a tax-exempt retirement account.

Schedule C Pointers

Schedule C is a catchall form for all businesses, so much of it can be meaningless and mysterious for a freelancer. Here are a few things to remember if you fill out the form yourself:

- You'll probably check the "cash" box for accounting method. That just means you record income when you get the check and expenses when you pay them. Few freelancers will use the more complicated methods.
- Check the "does not apply" box for method used to value closing inventory. You don't have any. Unpublished manuscripts don't count.
- Under the income section such items as returns and allowances and cost of goods sold probably will not apply to you.

- In the expenses section, you can't write off any bad debts (unless you use the more sophisticated accrual accounting method).
- The office expense category is a catchall that includes office supplies, postage, etc. You only fill out the pension and profit sharing portion if you have employees participating in a plan. Your own plan contribution, if any, is reported on Form 1040.
- The tax and license expenses that you can deduct include real estate and personal property taxes on business assets, employee Social Security and federal unemployment taxes.
- Long-distance charges fall in the utilities line. Since long-distance calls can be a big expense, it may be wise to itemize your utility expenses on a separate sheet and attach it.
- A big total in the "other expenses" column can make the IRS very suspicious. Break these items down as much as you can in the space provided.
- Ignore the "cost of goods sold" section because you're not a retailer or manufacturer.
- Your principal business or professional activity code will most likely be 711510 (the category for independent artists, writers and performers) unless you work in advertising or related services (541800) or the publishing industry (511000).

Professional Help

As you've figured out by now, business tax forms are a lot more complicated than ordinary tax forms, so you may want professional help. If so, your options include tax preparation services and accountants. You may also get tax preparer training offered by H&R Block or other services, which can save you money and even allow you to start a sideline preparing taxes.

If you are incorporated or face particularly complex business issues, you may need help from a certified public accountant (CPA). Small or medium-sized CPA firms are most likely to be familiar with issues that concern you. Franchise tax services provide a consistent, mass-produced product. They're the cheapest option. But they may be less familiar with some of the unusual situations of freelancers.

Year-End Tax Strategies

The end of the year presents some opportunities to minimize your taxes.

- Bill late in December so checks won't arrive (and won't be taxed) until the next year.
- Before December 31 buy equipment you're planning to use next year, so you can take advantage of depreciation or deduction this year.
- Before December ends, load up on office supplies and other essentials you'll need for the coming year.
- Pay for next year's subscriptions and professional dues in December.

Publishers and other clients have their own year-end strategies. That means you'll see checks dated in December that end up in your mailbox in January. You aren't liable for taxes on money until you receive it. Just be sure to document when you received the checks. You may even want to attach a note of explanation to your tax return and save the envelope, showing when the payment was postmarked.

IRS Publications and Assistance

Many IRS publications and help guides are available at public libraries. You also may order them by calling (800) TAX-FORM. Be aware, however, that the IRS publications will only detail how the IRS interprets the law. They may not explain all the deductions for which you qualify.

You can also get free help from the IRS in preparing returns. Look under "telephone assistance—federal tax information" in the index of your tax form. The IRS phone numbers in your phone book can guide you to more information about free help available in your area. Also check out the IRS Web site (www.irs.gov).

IRS publications that may be of help to you include the following:

1 Your Rights As a Taxpayer
17 Your Federal Income Tax (a digest of key publications)
334 Tax Guide for Small Business
463 Travel, Entertainment, Gift and Car Expenses

502 Medical and Dental Expenses

505 Tax Withholding and Estimated Tax

520 Scholarships and Fellowships

523 Selling Your Home

529 Miscellaneous Deductions (important if you write as a hobby)

533 Self-Employment Tax

534 Depreciation

544 Sales and Other Dispositions of Assets

551 Basis of Assets

552 Recordkeeping for Individuals

560 Retirement Plans for Small Businesses

587 Business Use of Your Home

590 Individual Retirement Arrangements

910 Guide to Free Tax Services

917 Business Use of a Car

Part 2: Finances for Writers

Setting up a simple budget is not only essential for business, it can make your life easier as well. For our purposes we'll assume you are a full-time freelancer or are about to become one. If this is not the case, you may still benefit from having a more complete understanding of the business side of the trade.

As with any budget, what you're trying to create is only a rough representation of what's likely to happen. As you go through the steps keep in mind that it will get easier each year. Once you are established as a freelancer you'll have the previous year's income and expenses as a basis for planning. You'll also have a regular base of clients to make your income more predictable.

The best way to start the budgeting process is to estimate your costs. Monthly overhead (what you must pay whether you work or not) should be the first category. This includes any payments on your computer or other equipment, office rent, publications, answering service and auto expenses (estimated).

After figuring overhead, look at your household budget and calculate the minimum amount you'll need for living expenses. Include your rent, mortgage, car payment, other consumer debt, groceries and the like. Then, subtract from this amount your spouse's take-home pay and other sources of steady income.

Financial planners recommend freelancers have cash for two to six months of overhead and living expenses available when they start their businesses. Even if you start with as much work as you can handle, you should still count on two to three months for the checks to appear in your mailbox. One survey by the Editorial Freelancers Association found that freelancers waited anywhere from a week to a year to get paid, with one or two months being typical.

Ideally, your capital reserve will be your savings account. Realistically, the start-up costs for a freelance writing business are small enough that most freelancers can get by without borrowing. If you need to borrow money, it makes sense to apply for a separate credit card for business use. (It can still be in your name.) Any interest paid for business purposes is tax deductible and it's a lot easier to maintain your books with a separate business account. If your card has a grace period, and you pay your balance every month, your card works like a rolling line of credit with no interest cost whatsoever.

If you have a good credit record or other assets, such as sufficient home equity, you may have other loan options. To get a bank loan, you may need to develop a business plan. (In fact, it's probably not a bad idea to develop one anyway.) Such a plan should include the following information:

- A description of your business, including your background and why your services are unique
- An analysis of the market, including the characteristics of the publications or clients that will use your services
- Your marketing or sales plan
- An outline of your finances, which will include a balance sheet, cash flow statement and break-even analysis

If you're turned down for a loan—a distinct possibility—you may be eligible for a government-guaranteed loan through the U.S. Small Business Administration

(SBA). Even if the SBA doesn't give you a loan, it can give you something that may be more valuable: The Service Corps of Retired Executives (SCORE) is an SBA service that offers free advice to small businesses. The retired executives who volunteer their time can help steer you through a business plan.

Planning Income

The overhead calculation you did earlier is important in deciding how much to charge for your services. To calculate an hourly rate, figure the amount you hope to earn. That may be what you used to make at your old job or what you'd dream of making at your new one. Then, add in your annual overhead expenses. Divide that figure by the number of billable hours you expect to work in a year. (Count on spending a quarter of your time marketing your services, maintaining your records and reading professional publications.)

Most magazines and clients won't pay by the hour but by the word, inch or article. You can, however, analyze how long an assignment will take and multiply that by your hourly rate. Remember to consider expenses, too. Try to estimate your costs for phone calls, mileage and other expenses. Add these to the fee you negotiate.

Always keep in mind what the market will bear when making your calculations. Check with other freelance writers in your area to find out what they charge. Don't charge more than you can get, but don't underestimate yourself, either. Lowball pricing may get you a few jobs, but it will hurt your image with clients and editors and often your self-esteem.

Records and Accounts

Nobody becomes a freelance writer to do bookkeeping. But freelancers quickly find it becomes an important part of their jobs. Again, it need not be cumbersome. Ideally, record keeping should take no more than two hours each week.

Your record-keeping system can be as simple as a daily log of income and expenses. If you're more comfortable keeping records on your computer, a local computer store should have a wide array of software that fits your needs.

Financial planners recommend that you set up a separate checking account for your business. This will keep you from tapping your business funds for personal needs. It also will provide clearer documentation of your income and business expenses.

You also need some kind of documentation for each business transaction, for example, a canceled check or cash receipt. You should write the business purpose on the receipt or check. Your system for saving receipts can be something as simple as a shoe box.

Since you'll probably deduct auto expenses on your tax form, you'll need a mileage log to substantiate them. The log must show the date of each trip, the beginning and ending mileage and the business purpose.

The IRS strongly recommends you keep expense records for as long as the period of limitations for audits. In most cases, that's three years from the date the return was filed or two years from when the tax was paid, whichever is later.

Keep income records for six years after each tax return is filed. That's the period the IRS has for going after unreported income.

You'll need records for the cost of your home or improvements for as long as you own the home if you take the home office deduction. Also, you must keep records of items for which you claim depreciation, such as cars, for as long as you depreciate them, plus the three years after you file your return.

Though costly and time-consuming, audits are relatively rare. The IRS audits fewer than 1 percent of the tax returns each year. Among businesses and the self-employed the chances are about 4 percent. Even if you're audited you won't necessarily owe money. About one-fifth of those audited don't owe any additional taxes, and some even get refunds.

Tracking Income

Expenses are only half of what you'll be tracking. You'll also need to record income as you receive it and keep pay stubs that document your earnings. Each source that pays you more than $600 a year must report your earnings to the IRS and send you a Form 1099 showing the amount. Income records are important for comparing to the amounts reported on each Form 1099.

If you've been bartering with other businesses (receiving goods or services rather than cash) the law requires you to report as income the fair market dollar value.

Cash Flow

That first big check for your writing will be a thrill. But don't rush out and spend it. You'll have a lean period. With the right strategy you can minimize the ups and downs.

The best way to avoid cash flow problems is to continually work on developing new clients. That means sending out queries or contacting potential clients even when you're busy. Try to set aside a couple days each month for such marketing.

Next, never rely too much on any one source of income. Developing a few key accounts, preferably large and reliable enough to cover your overhead and basic living expenses, is important. But don't become complacent. Nothing lasts forever, so don't let any single account become more than one-third of your business.

Dealing with the choppy seas of cash flow requires discipline. Using your budget, establish a maximum amount that you will spend in any month. Keeping your earnings in a business account separate from your personal savings or checking account is one good way to keep from spending it all.

You should also meticulously track what your clients owe you. Record who owes you money, how much it is and when it's due. To the extent possible, arrange payment on your terms. Remember, book authors are not the only ones who get paid some money in advance. You may be able to get some money up front for copywriting or even for expenses for magazine assignments.

For article writers, publications that pay on acceptance are obviously more desirable than those that pay on publication. If you're getting paid on publication, you could wait months for your article to be published, and at least a month after that to get paid. If paid on acceptance, you should get paid within a month of your final rewrite.

Fast action is the key to good cash flow. To optimize the pace of your receipts:

- Incorporate billing into your weekly schedule.
- Tabulate your phone or other expenses as soon as they come due.
- Bill as soon as payment is due.
- Don't let a new, unproven account run up huge tabs before you get paid. In most cases, you won't know how good a publisher's or client's payment practices are until he owes you money.

Getting Paid

Waiting for checks is one of the most nerve-racking parts of being a writer. Let's face it, as writers we rely heavily on the creative side of our brain. Business and finances are not something most of us enjoy dealing with. So we like to think that our creative efforts will always be rewarded fairly and promptly. Yet even when our rights are carefully spelled out in a contract, there's no guarantee that payment will arrive when it's due.

One skill that writers acquire is patience. But we needn't be too patient. No matter how bad the publisher's cash flow, it's usually better than ours. So when the wait gets too long, here are some steps you can take.

1. If payment is thirty days past due, call and/or write immediately. You need not be confrontational. Simply send a late notice or call to check on the status of payment or to make sure your invoice wasn't lost. If you call, be sure to get a commitment from the editor or accounting office on when the payment will be sent.

2. If payment isn't in your mailbox by the time promised, call and talk to the person in charge of payment. Be polite but firm. If you're told the check is on its way, get specifics about when it was mailed or when it will be mailed. This is a good time to let her know you won't be able to send any more work until payment is received. Your leverage increases greatly if you're working on another assignment that's needed soon.

3. If payment isn't forthcoming after the second time you call or write, and the money you are owed warrants it, send a final notice informing the publisher that you will have to turn the account over for collection or legal action if payment isn't received by a specified date. Take that further action promptly if the deadline passes. It could be a letter from a lawyer, or you may want to hire a collection agency.

If the amount in question does not warrant hiring an attorney or collection agency, you may be able to get help from certain writers organizations if you are a member. Some writers organizations will send letters on behalf of members who have not been paid for published work. A letter from a third party is an attention getter that will sometimes disgorge a check from many slow payers.

4. If your payment dispute is with a book publisher, the expense of a lawsuit may be justified. In other instances small-claims court can be a solution. Filing fees are nominal and lawyers aren't required. Best of all, novices are tolerated.

Although you save considerable money with small-claims court, you should expect to invest some time, which for a writer is often the same as money. You'll have to wait in line to get papers to file, and wait in line again to file them. In front of you will be lots of people who are unfamiliar with the process. Later, you may have to spend the better part of a day in court waiting for your case to come up. This can also work to your advantage. Faced with the prospect of wasting a day in court, the editor may become your staunchest advocate before the accounting department.

Small-claims court won't handle every situation. Depending on the state, the court will have a claim limit of $1,000 to $5,000. Also, you may not be able to sue an out-of-state publisher in your local court. Winning your suit is no guarantee you'll be paid. You may need to follow up by filing a claim against the publisher's assets. And if the bank is out of state, you may not succeed.

5. If all else fails and there's little hope of seeing the money owed you, you can get some sense of satisfaction (and save others from a similar problem) by alerting your fellow writers about the problem publisher. Several organizations will note nonpayments in their newsletters. You can spread the word rapidly through online forums and bulletin boards frequented by writers. The threat of such disclosure can even work in your favor.

If you learned about the publication in a directory, inform the directory's staff of your problem. They may also write on your behalf or at least consider deleting the publication from the next edition of their directory.

Tips for Credit Checking

The following points are not scientific methods but they are certainly prudent steps that can save you from being cheated.

- Look at several copies of a publication before you do any work. Editorial quality is often a sign of business integrity. If a publication cheats its readers, what makes you think it won't shortchange its writers? Some danger signs are headlines that promise what articles don't deliver and articles that are misleading, overhyped and underresearched.

- Try to contact some of the writers to find out about the publication's payment practices.
- Compare the amount of advertising to the same period a year earlier. If the ad pages are slipping seriously, this could be a sign of a failing publication that will have trouble paying its bills.

Should I Incorporate?

Generally when professionals form corporations, only the assets of the corporation are subject to seizure by creditors or potential litigants. Libel is one of the largest litigation traps a writer faces. But because libel may be considered a personal statement, a court could still make your personal assets part of a settlement, even if you are incorporated.

Whether to incorporate is a complex question best handled by an accountant or lawyer who knows your situation. Should you opt for incorporation, ask the state office that oversees corporations, such as the secretary of state, to send you information detailing the steps you need to take.

For further information contact one of the following:

Service Corps of Retired Executives (SCORE), National Headquarters, 409 Third St. SW, 4th Floor, Washington, DC 20024, (202) 205-6762.

Volunteer Lawyers for the Arts, 1 E. Fifty-third St., New York, NY 10022, (212) 319-2787 (www.artswire.org/artlaw/info.html).

Saving for the Future

While you may be able to write in your retirement years, you still will need some other savings if you hope to maintain your standard of living. One great advantage to being self-employed is the ability to set up your own pension plan. Your options include an Individual Retirement Account (IRA), a Simplified Employee Pension (SEP-IRA) or a Keogh plan.

The formulas for setting up a plan can be pretty complicated, so it's a good idea to get help from a financial planner or accountant in the early stages. The following points can give you a general overview and comparison of the different plans.

You may not be able to deduct your contributions to regular IRAs if your spouse is covered by a pension plan or if your earnings exceed certain limits. But a SEP-IRA isn't so restricted and provides the same benefits. Even if you have a pension from another job, you can set up a SEP-IRA for your earnings from self-employment and deduct your contribution from your taxes. Each year you can effectively deduct up to 13 percent of your taxable self-employment income through SEP-IRA contributions, but your yearly contribution can't exceed $30,000.

Under a Keogh plan you have two options. A money-purchase plan requires you to contribute a fixed percentage of your income every year—up to 25 percent. With a profit-sharing Keogh you can put in as much or as little as you want each year. But you're limited to the same 13 percent of self-employment income as with a SEP-IRA. With either Keogh setup, you're also subject to the $30,000 annual limit.

The major advantages of these plans are that you can both deduct your contributions from current taxable income and accumulate interest tax free. All this money is taxable when you take it out at retirement. But if you're in a lower tax bracket at that time you'll come out ahead. Plus, tax-free interest accumulation will leave you with a lot more money than you'd have had saving the money without the plan. There are, of course, drawbacks:

- If you withdraw money from the plan before you reach age 59½, you may be subject to a 10 percent penalty as well as the tax due on what you withdraw.
- You can't reduce self-employment taxes (Social Security, etc.) with these plans, only federal income tax. You may not get any deduction from state and local taxes for your contribution, either.
- You may have to pay fees or commissions for administration of your plan.
- If you hire employees someday, you'll have to cover them with whatever plan you've established for yourself.

Health Insurance

Health insurance is one of the biggest expenses you'll face as a freelancer. If you're leaving a job with health benefits, federal law requires employers to allow you to continue your coverage for up to eighteen months (at your expense). Beyond that you can choose from other group plans or individual coverage. Whatever route you choose, expect it to cost no less than $2,000 a year and as much as several thousand dollars.

Many writers organizations and business organizations offer group health insurance. Some even offer choices, including major medical plans with a range of deductibles and health maintenance organizations (HMOs). But membership in one of these organizations may not guarantee you'll be accepted for coverage.

You should check with the organization or its insurance carrier for details of the plan. Most are perfectly acceptable. But some organizations provide only a fixed amount of coverage based on the number of days in the hospital and cover no expenses for physician treatment outside a hospital.

Depending on your state, an individual plan may leave you vulnerable to cancellation or steep rate increases should you develop a lengthy illness. Also, most independent coverage will have a waiting period of several months.

A less costly approach is to opt for an individual plan with relatively high deductibles and co-payments. It will still do what insurance is supposed to do, which is to keep you from getting wiped out by a huge medical bill. If you ask, most hospitals and doctors will let you pay off what you owe over time.

One of the best cheap insurance options, if you can find it, is an HMO that will offer you a high deductible in exchange for low premiums. This way your deductible may still be cheaper than the premiums charged for traditional coverage.

Other Insurance

Going into business for yourself should not mean forgoing disability insurance. To the contrary, you should seek out a plan that covers the highest percentage of income for as long as possible. No insurance company will underwrite a policy that pays 100 percent of your income, because that would provide no incentive for you to go back to work. But policies may go as high as 80 percent and last as long as ten years or to age sixty-five.

Many writers organizations offer group disability coverage. The groups may also offer relatively inexpensive group life insurance that can cover such items as your mortgage. But it's important to look at disability plans closely. Some plans cover only a fixed period, so you'd be out of luck and money in the event of a long-term disability.

If you work from your home, you should also check with your home or tenant insurance carrier to make sure your business equipment is covered. Professional liability is another coverage to consider. Your largest liability exposure is for libel. If your work seems likely to involve you in libel litigation somewhere down the road, you may want to take out a separate policy through a group such as the National Writers Union.

Here are some national groups for writers and small businesses that offer insurance to their members.

> Co-Op America, 2100 M St. NW, Suite 403, Washington, DC 20036, (202) 872-5307 or (800) 424-9711.
>
> Editorial Freelancers Association, 71 W. Twenty-third St., Suite 1910, New York, NY 10010, phone: (212) 929-5400, fax: (212) 929-543 (www .the-efa.org).
>
> National Association for the Self-Employed, P.O. Box 612067, Dallas, TX 75261-9968, (800) 232-6273.
>
> National Small Business United, 1155 Fifteenth St. NW, Suite 710, Washington, DC 20005, (800) 345-NSBU.
>
> National Writers Union, 113 University Place, 6th Floor, New York, NY 10003, phone: (212) 254-0279 or (800) 417-8114, fax: (212) 254-0673 nwu@nwu.org (www.nwu.org)
>
> Small Business Service Bureau, P.O. Box 1441, 544 Main St., Worcester, MA 01601, (508) 756-3513 or (800) 343-0939.
>
> Support Services Alliances, P.O. Box 130, Schoharie, NY 12157, (518) 295-7966 or (800) 322-3920.

CHAPTER SIXTEEN

Finding a Community

High on a ridge overlooking southern California's Temecula Valley, the Dorland Mountain Arts Colony attracts dozens of writers each year. Besides its pristine setting on a three-hundred-acre nature preserve, Dorland is perhaps most noted for its lack of electricity and the scarcity of modern conveniences. All cooking, refrigeration and water heating are fueled by propane. Visitors reside in individual cabins that are heated by woodstoves and lit by kerosene lamps.

The goal is for writers and artists to detach themselves from the outside world—allowing the sounds and rhythms of nature to become a vital part of their creative experience. Despite its primitive conditions, Dorland is one of the most renowned havens for writers, visual artists and composers worldwide.

While far more primitive than most, Dorland is very representative of what writers look for at dozens of colonies across the U.S. Far from the distractions of home, colonies can provide an intensive creative experience lasting several weeks or even several months.

A colony is just one way writers can break out of their creative and physical confines—to find a new sense of community among other writers. Writers conferences, university programs and correspondence schools are three other options. Which if any of these you choose depends on where you are in your career and your needs at the time.

If your goal is to pick up skills from top professionals or expand your contacts in the business, conferences can be an excellent investment of time and money. A writers colony is a great place to finish a project, start a new one or reassess a stalled piece of work. University programs and correspondence schools require a long-term commitment, but are especially useful for those just getting started in the business of writing.

Is a Writers Colony Right for You?

Writers colonies (sometimes called retreats) offer a wonderful change of pace—providing an opportunity to get the most out of your creative powers in a short time. The ways in which colonies are set up to do this can be as varied as a writer's imagination.

Some allow you to work virtually uninterrupted. Others provide space for quiet work but also encourage participants to interact and learn from each other during breaks or through critiques, readings and workshops. Some even bring together creative people from different disciplines—painters, writers, musicians—believing you can learn more about your own art by talking with others about theirs. At some retreats the interaction takes place randomly throughout the day as different people gather informally.

Most colonies require that you submit an application, including samples of your work and a description of how you will utilize your time. All of this is reviewed by a selection committee, whose goal is to make sure applicants are serious about their work. To get accepted you must demonstrate how you will use your time to begin or complete a project.

Few if any colonies enforce a regimented schedule or keep tabs on your progress. Writers respond to this freedom differently. Some overwork and burn out in a short period of time. More commonly, writers need several days to adjust to their new-found freedom before they can develop routines for their work.

Some colonies select writers with substantial professional credentials. Others cater to emerging talent. Still others try to foster a mix of better-known and lesser-known talent. Some colonies are highly competitive—receiving dozens of applications for every position they have open. One way to improve your chances is to consider going in the off-season when there are fewer applicants.

The typical stay at a colony lasts from a couple of weeks to three months, although some last several months. The cost of most colonies is relatively inexpensive. Most programs charge a small application fee, then $75 to $200 per week. The majority of colonies stress that payment is voluntary and no qualified applicant will be turned away simply because he cannot pay. Many require that you bring along whatever equipment you plan to use.

Before you select a writers colony, consider the following information:

- Most colonies schedule visits six months in advance, so make sure you assemble your writing samples and apply at least eight months before you would like to attend.
- Look for a colony that fits your lifestyle. Some writers thrive in a rural atmosphere; others find the peace and quiet uninspiring. Some writers like to cook their own meals at their convenience. Others prefer to have their meals prepared for them on a regular schedule. Compare all aspects of the colony before applying.
- Some colonies offer weekend programs, but the majority want you to stay two weeks to two months. Since most writers work more quickly at a colony, plan your work ahead of time, even if the colony doesn't require it. If possible, talk to other writers who've been to colonies to find out how they used the experience.

Locating Writers Colonies

Several sources offer information on writers colonies, including *The Guide to Writers Conferences* published online by Shaw Guides. As a service to its members, The Authors Guild compiles a list of colonies. *Poets & Writers* magazine frequently carries advertisements and notices of colonies. The Alliance of Artists' Communities is another good source. To reach any of these organizations use the information below. You may also want to check with your state arts council.

Alliance of Artists' Communities, 2311 E. Burnside, Portland, OR 97214, phone: (503) 797-6988, fax: (503) 797-9560, aac@eleport.com (www.artist communities.org).

The Authors Guild, 330 W. Forty-second St., 29th Floor, New York, NY 10036, phone: (212) 563-5904, fax: (212) 564-5363, staff@authorsguild .org (www.authorsguild.org).

Novel and Short Story Writer's Market, Writer's Digest Books, 1507 Dana Ave., Cincinnati, OH 45207, (513) 531-2690 or (800) 289-0963, (www.writers digest.com).

Poets and Writers 72 Spring St., New York, NY 10012, phone: (212) 226-3586, Fax: (212) 226-3963, subs@pw.org (www.pw.org).

Shaw Guides, P.O. Box 1295, New York, NY 10023, phone: (212) 799-6464, fax: (212) 724-9287, info@shawguides.com (www.shawguides.com).

Getting the Most From Writers Conferences

Whether you are just starting in the business or are already a professional writer, attending writers conferences can be very beneficial. Beginners can learn a lot about the creative and business sides of writing. Established writers can gain added insights into all aspects of the trade.

Writers—whether beginners or seasoned—have many different goals when they attend a conference. Some want to explore a new writing area or learn from a particular instructor. Others are interested in making contacts with writers, editors and agents. Still others like the inspiration of spending time with fellow writers.

If you are thinking of attending a writers conference, consider the following:

- Your chances of individual meetings or instruction are greater at a small conference, but smaller conferences are less likely to attract prominent speakers. Instead of focusing on the total number attending, ask about the number in each session. If the number is thirty or less, you'll have more opportunities to ask questions and discuss your work with the instructor.
- Money is a key consideration for almost any writer. But don't choose a confer-

ence solely on the basis of cost. Attending a conference is an investment in your future success. The least expensive option may not be the best for you. A one- or two-day workshop can cost up to $200. Conferences that last up to a week can cost $800 or more, which usually includes the cost of lodging and some meals. One way to work a conference into your budget is to combine it with a vacation.

- The caliber of the conference faculty is usually the most important criterion when evaluating a conference. Look for writers who have credentials in the particular areas they will be teaching.

- Some conferences offer individual consultations with instructors, editors or agents for an additional fee. Such personal feedback must be arranged ahead of time. If you are paying for an appointment, you have every right to know what to expect from the meeting. Don't go in expecting to find an editor who will want to publish your work or an agent who will want to represent you. Such overnight success stories are few and far between.

- Most conferences attract writers of a variety of skill levels and are geared accordingly. Check the program for clues as to whether sessions are geared toward beginners or professionals. You should avoid sessions that seem too far below or above your level of experience.

- A conference's format can make a big difference. The best conferences are set up to provide interaction between the attendees and the instructors/speakers, rather than just lectures. Also look for panel discussions where writers, editors and agents offer their opinions on subjects of interest to you.

Locating Writers Conferences

One of the most comprehensive and readily available lists is found on the *Writer's Digest* Web site (www.writersdigest.com). Thanks to information supplied by Shaw Guides, you can browse more than four hundred conferences and workshops by location, date and subject matter. You can even identify conferences by the authors, agents and publishers attending.

The Guide to Writers Conferences lists hundreds of workshops, seminars, residencies, retreats and organizations for writers. The guide is indexed by month, region and specialty. The May issue of *Writer's Digest* magazine also has conference listings by state. *Writers Conferences*, available each March from Poets & Writers Inc., lists dates, addresses, fees, deadlines and workshop leaders for two hundred conferences.

Choosing a College Program That Suits Your Needs

For young people a college environment is a great way to develop their skills and immerse themselves in the writer's world. Yet attending a college or university writing program is expensive and requires a large commitment of time. So if you're already earning a decent living as a writer, or if you have a full-time job and can find the time to pursue a writing career, a degree may not be a wise investment of time or money. Agents have been known to scout the well-known programs for talent, but there are other ways to attract attention that cost far less than a degree.

There may be other reasons to enroll in classes, however, including the opportunity to study with a writer whom you admire or to develop specific skills. Universities also support more experimental writing and have literary magazines that will publish students' work.

Consider the following guidelines in making your decision:

- Programs are almost as varied as the number of schools. Some schools offer small programs where students receive individual attention. Others offer larger programs with prestigious faculties. Some are conducted in a straight classroom setup. Others take a workshop approach in which you bring in work to be critiqued by the teacher and fellow students. You can tell a lot about a program by the type of degree it confers. A master's degree (M.A.) usually requires more reading while a master of fine arts (M.F.A.) requires more writing. Each program has its own focus and requirements; try talking to past graduates to decide which approach is best for you.

- Besides investigating the program itself, inquire about the caliber of the visiting writers, the faculty and the literary publications affiliated with the program.

The community surrounding a program can be just as important to your creative development as the program.

- Reading the program's literary publications and the works of its faculty is a great way to evaluate the program. It can also help you select the best submissions from your own writing. (A sample poetry submission will have ten to twenty poems, and a fiction or nonfiction sample typically includes three stories.)

- If cost is a major consideration—and when isn't it—be sure to check out financial aid options at different schools as well as the availability of assistantships. In addition to the cost of instruction, be sure to compare the cost of living in various areas. And since you're going to be there a while, choose a place where you feel comfortable.

- Weigh the benefits of several programs and be flexible in your choice of institutions. It's not unusual for more renowned programs to receive hundreds of applications for only a few dozen openings.

Locating Writing Programs

The best source for locating a writing program is *The AWP Official Guide to Writing Programs* published by Associated Writing Programs at George Mason University. The guide has information on more than three hundred programs in North America both at the undergraduate and graduate level. Contact Associated Writing Programs, Tallwood House, MSN 1E3, George Mason University, Fairfax, VA 22030, phone: (703) 993-4301, fax: (703) 993-4302, awp@gmu.edu (www.gmu.edu/departments/awp).

Picking the Best Correspondence School

A correspondence course is a good choice if you lack easy access to a college or if your schedule prevents you from attending classes. Most home study courses can be finished in less than a year, and most offer one-on-one instruction with the same teacher for the length of the course. But choose your course wisely. You cannot always adapt the course to your needs if you require specialized instruction.

Correspondence programs also allow you to work at your own pace, but only up to a point. If you have difficulty meeting deadlines, a correspondence course is not for you. Most courses have deadlines, and getting an extension usually costs extra.

Evaluate correspondence courses with the following points in mind:

- Some courses offer a range of topics covering everything from newswriting to fiction. Others focus on a single subject, such as poetry or short stories. Be careful to pick a course that suits your specific goals.

- The cost of a correspondence course can vary from a few hundred dollars to a few thousand dollars. Compare different courses against each other, because the most costly do not always offer what is best for you. Ask what payment plans are available. Look for a course that allows you to return the materials for a refund if you are not initially satisfied.

- Any reputable school will share information about the caliber of its instructors. Look for instructors who not only know the subject but have recent sales in their chosen genres. Of course feedback from the instructor can make or break your learning experience, so it's important to get a good match. Look for a school that is willing to assign you another instructor if things don't work out.

- Inquire about the level of feedback that you can expect from your instructor. Ideally you want frequent detailed critiques of your work—not just overall evaluations.

Locating Correspondence Programs

For listings of correspondence programs check *The Correspondence Educational Directory and Alternative Educational Opportunities* (Racz Publishing, 1984). Also check with your local university to see if it offers correspondence or independent study courses. Groups such as the National Writers Association also offer correspondence instruction.

WRITERS COLONY APPLICATION FORM: SAMPLE #1

The Millay Colony for the Arts

Name: _____

Date: _____

Permanent Address: _____

Telephone: _____

Present Address and Telephone (if different): _____

Art Form: _____

Age (optional): _____

Period of Residence Requested

Residencies are for one month and cover a period from approximately the first to the 28th of each month. Please choose months within the same review period.

First choice: _____

Second choice: _____

Please describe your work in the past year and how you visualize using your time at the Millay Colony (attach another sheet if necessary).

Please submit examples of your work with this application. Writers can submit up to 30 pages in manuscript form. If you are applying in two separate disciplines (for example, poetry and fiction), please submit two copies of your application form and resume. You may also submit a resume and any documents that you consider will be helpful to the admissions committee in making its decision. Unless you include an SASE we can not return your work. Return envelopes without sufficient postage will be sent postage due. If you enclose a self-addressed, stamped postcard we will acknowledge receipt of your application.

The committee requires one professional letter of reference, which can be sent either with your application materials or directly to us, in which case it must arrive within one week after the deadline date.

Application Deadlines

On May 1 we will review applicants for the following October–January. On September 1 we will review applicants for the following February–May. On February 1 we will review applicants for the following June–September.

Complete applications must be in the Millay Colony office on the deadline date. Our deadlines are not postmark deadlines. We will return your materials and notify you of the results of your application approximately two months after the deadline date. The February applicants for summer spaces will be notified at the end of April.

WRITERS COLONY APPLICATION FORM: SAMPLE #2

Yaddo

P.O. Box 395 (Union Avenue), Saratoga Springs, NY 12866, (518) 584-0746

Application Deadlines

The August 1 deadline is for visits requested from late October of the same year to May of the following year. The January 15 deadline is for visits requested from mid-May of the same year through February of the following year. Completed applications must be postmarked by these deadlines to be considered in these judging periods. Notification of results will be mailed April 1 and October 1. Yaddo is closed from the end of August to the third week of September.

Yaddo encourages artists of all backgrounds to apply for admission. Yaddo does not discriminate in its programs and activities against anyone on the basis of race, creed, color, religion, national origin, sex, age, sexual orientation, marital status, ancestry, disability, HIV status or veteran status.

Application Materials

In order to be processed, your application must include all the following materials:

- Three copies of the application form.
- Three copies of a professional resume.
- Work samples, as specified below, with a self-addressed, stamped return envelope when appropriate.
- Two letters of support, sent directly to Yaddo by the sponsors on the enclosed form. Applicants are responsible for sending the forms to sponsors and for providing them appropriate information. Artists who have either been to Yaddo within the past five years or submitted two sponsoring letters within the past three years need not have additional letters sent. Application deadlines also apply to sponsor letters.
- A nonrefundable application fee of $20 made payable to "The Corporation of Yaddo."
- A stamped, self-addressed postcard for notification of the receipt of the completed application.

Two or three persons wishing to be considered as a single collaborative artistic unit should indicate that fact but submit separate application forms. Preference is normally given to persons who did not visit Yaddo the previous year.

Work Samples

Samples should be of representative work, preferably recent. They may take the form of typescripts, slides, scores, audiocassettes and/or videocassettes, according to the medium in which the applicant works. Please send only the materials requested below.

Literature: Three copies of a typescript of no more than 30 pages, consisting of a short story, a one-act play or a portion of a novel, play or other work, accompanied by a synopsis if necessary. Poets should send 10 short poems or an appropriate excerpt from a longer poem. Do not send published books: Photocopies of selected pages are acceptable. Do not bind manuscript pages. It is helpful if writers who work in languages other than English submit typescripts in both the original and English translations.

Today's Date: _____

Application Deadline (check one):

- ☐ August 1
- ☐ January 15

Type of Application (check where appropriate):

- ☐ First visit
- ☐ Reapplication for first visit
- ☐ Return visit
- ☐ Individual
- ☐ In collaboration with

Name: _____

Mailing Address: _____

Telephone (home & work): _____

Optional Information (voluntary):

Birth Date: _____

Birthplace: _____

Medium/Genre (you may check more than one):

- ☐ Drama
- ☐ Fiction
- ☐ Nonfiction

Collaborators: Do you share a studio?   ☐ yes   ☐ no

Preferred Visit Times: Indicate preferences of months of availability. Be specific about other times when you are able to come. Specify dates or length of visit (2 weeks to 2 months). Please apply for the longest visit you expect to be useful, and keep Yaddo advised of changes in availability.

Aug. 1 Deadline: Nov., Dec., Jan., Feb., March, April, Early May

Dates Available/Length of Stay: _____

Jan. 15 Deadline: mid-May, June, July, Aug., Late Sept./Early Oct., Nov., Dec., Jan., Feb.

Dates Available/Length of Stay: _____

1. Brief biographical highlights. Summarize training, performances, publications, exhibitions. Please attach a complete resume as well.
2. Briefly describe the work you plan to do at Yaddo and the place of this work in your professional development.
3. Except for those who have either been to Yaddo within the past five years or submitted sponsoring letters within the past three years, Yaddo requires two letters, sent directly to Yaddo by the sponsors on the enclosed form, discussing the applicant's professional capacity and temperamental suitability for a residency in a working community with other artists. Sponsors' letters should include the applicant's full name and the genre in which he or she is applying at the top of the letter. Name the two sponsors from whom you have requested letters.

Sponsor Letter Form

To the sponsor: Please answer the following questions about the above-named applicant. Please attach additional sheets of paper or use the reverse if necessary.

A. What is your opinion of the work this person has done and is presently doing?

_____

_____

_____

_____

_____

_____

B. Do you know of any reason why this person could not function well and live harmoniously in a working community of artists?

_____

_____

_____

_____

_____

_____

Please sign, date and return this document as soon as possible.

Sponsor letters will not be considered confidential unless applicant instructs Yaddo otherwise.

CHAPTER SEVENTEEN

Finding More Money

Several thousand organizations exist throughout the U.S. to award money to writers in the form of grants, fellowships or prizes. Publicly or privately funded, many operate on a national level. Many more exist on the state and local levels.

Grants are a way to stay solvent through lengthy projects. Fellowships offer opportunities for career-enhancing education that freelance writers may not otherwise get, since they have no chance at paid leaves of absence. Contests and awards can offer not only recognition for a job well done, but also money to do the next job well, too.

While thousands of organizations offer financial support, anyone who has ever applied for it knows that these programs are anything but a free ride. It takes hard work and skill to be accepted. Much like selling an article or a book, getting a grant, fellowship or award means having a good idea, doing superior work and then searching for the appropriate market. You'll need to find catalogs and directories, then study the listings to find ones whose funding interests match your creative interests.

Many grants have strict eligibility requirements. Some organizations require simply an application. Others require nominations from a member of the organization. Grants from state and local arts councils, for instance, require recipients to live in the state or locality.

The more money in question, the tougher the competition for it. Some of the biggest present rather high hurdles to face even before you apply, such as having a number of years of professional experience, a book previously published or a set number of articles published in literary magazines.

Every organization approaches the application process differently. Generally, the process of applying for a grant or fellowship involves these steps.

1. Call or write to get details or any changes concerning the deadline, eligibility and application process. Be sure to follow exactly any details as far as manuscript preparation or display of published works. And find out if the deadline is when the application must be postmarked or when it must be at their door. You may need to send your application by overnight delivery to ensure on-time arrival.

2. Send in your application, which usually will include samples of your published work and may include an essay or letter of explanation about your plans for future work.

3. Wait for your application to be screened by a committee that chooses finalists. (In some cases there are multiple screening levels, or semifinals.)

4. Finalists will often be interviewed before the final decision, especially for higher-paying awards and fellowships.

Grant application is often framed as a mysterious art best left to experienced practitioners. But in many cases, all the bells and whistles you can muster in a grant application won't make much difference. The quality of your work as viewed by the judges is the primary criterion.

In many cases, selection committees must wade through hundreds or thousands of applications for a handful of awards. Other more specialized programs may have only a handful of applicants.

Like submitting your work for publication, applying for foundation grants and fellowships means getting your share of rejections. Program administrators advise writers not to be discouraged by an initial rejection. Many writers go on to find acceptance elsewhere or even from the same program in later years.

The following list will give you an idea of some of the grants and awards available to writers. For a more comprehensive list, look for the volume entitled *Grants and*

Awards Available to American Writers, published by the PEN American Center, 568 Broadway, New York, NY 10012, (212) 334-1660.

Academy of American Poets Raiziss/de Palchi Translation Fellowship. The $20,000 Raiziss/de Palchi Translation Fellowship is given for a translation into English of a significant work of modern Italian poetry. The annual fellowship enables a U.S. citizen to travel, study or otherwise advance a significant work in progress. Deadline: November 1. Contact: Academy of American Poets, Raiziss/de Palchi Translation Fellowship, 584 Broadway, Suite 1208, New York, NY 10012 (212) 274-0343, academy@dti.net (www.poets.org).

Academy of American Poets Walt Whitman Award. This $5,000 award is open to any U.S. citizen who has not published a book of poems in a standard edition. Deadline: Entries must be postmarked between September 15 and November 30. Contact: Academy of American Poets, 584 Broadway, Suite 1208, New York, NY 10012, (212) 274-0343.

American Antiquarian Society Visiting Fellowships for Historical Research. The $1,200 fellowship includes a monthlong residency at the American Antiquarian Society in Worcester, Massachusetts. Fellowships allow creative writers and artists to research pre-1876 American history and culture. Deadline: October 5. Contact: American Antiquarian Society, Visiting Fellowships for Historical Research, 185 Salisbury St., Worcester, MA 01609-1634, (508) 755-5221.

Arizona Commission on the Arts Creative Writing Fellowships. These $5,000 creative writing fellowships are awarded to Arizona residents who are at least eighteen years old and not enrolled full-time at a college or university. The fellowships alternate between fiction and poetry. Deadline: September 16. Contact: Arizona Commission on the Arts, Creative Writing Fellowships, 417 W. Roosevelt St., Phoenix, AZ 85003, (602) 255-5882, general@ArizonaArts.org (www.az.arts.asu.edu/artscomm).

ArtServe Michigan Creative Artist Grants. Grants ranging from $2,500 to $7,000 are given to writers working and living in Michigan. Deadline: June 17. Contact: ArtServe Michigan, Creative Artist Grants, 17515 W. Nine

Mile Rd., Suite 250, Southfield, MI 48075, (248) 557-8288, ext. 14, artists @artservemichigan.org.

The Cleveland Foundation Anisfield-Wolf Book Awards. Awards of $5,000 are given annually to recognize a book of poetry or fiction and a scholarly book that shed light on racism. Deadline: January 31. Contact: The Cleveland Foundation, Anisfield-Wolf Book Awards, Suite 1400, Hanna Building, 1422 Euclid Ave., Cleveland, OH 44115, (216) 861-3810.

Colorado Council on the Arts Artist Fellowships. Annual $4,000 fellowships for Colorado writers alternate between poetry/playwriting and fiction/creative nonfiction. Deadline: September. Contact: Colorado Council on the Arts, Artist Fellowships, 750 Pennsylvania St., Denver, CO 80203, (303) 894-2617, coloarts@artswire.org (www.aclin .org/code/arts).

Connecticut Commission on the Arts Artist Fellowships. Fellowships ranging from $2,500 to $5,000 are given to poets and fiction writers who have lived in and demonstrated a history of professional activity in Connecticut for at least four years. Deadline: September. Contact: Connecticut Commission on the Arts, Artist Fellowships, 755 Main St., One Financial Plaza, Hartford, CT 06103, (860) 566-4770.

Fine Arts Work Center in Provincetown Fellowships. Writing fellowships for emerging poets and fiction writers include a seven-month stay at the center from October 1 to May 1 and a monthly stipend of $600. Deadline: December 1. Contact: Fine Arts Work Center in Provincetown, 24 Pearl St., Provincetown, MA 02657, (508) 487-9960 (www.capecodaccess.com/ fineartsworkcenter).

Glimmer Train Press Very Short Fiction Award. Submit a short story of 2,000 words or less. Winning entries are published in *Glimmer Train Stories*. Deadline: January 31. Contact: Glimmer Train Press, 710 S.W. Madison St., Suite 504, Portland, OR 97205, (503) 221-0836 (www.glimmertrain.com).

Heekin Group Foundation Writing Fellowships. Fellowships ranging from $1,500 to $3,000 are given annually to unpublished fiction, nonfiction and essay writers or those who are beginning their careers. Deadline: December 1. Contact: Heekin Group Foundation, Writing Fellowships, P.O. Box 1534, Sisters, OR 97759, (541) 548-4147.

Helicon Nine Editions Literary Prizes. Awards of $1,000 are given for unpublished manuscripts of fiction and poetry. Winning entries are published by Helicon Nine Editions. Deadline: May 1. Contact: Helicon Nine Editions, Literary Prizes, 3607 Pennsylvania Ave., Kansas City, MO 64111, (816) 753-1095.

Institute of International Education Cintas Fellowships Program. Annual fellowships of $10,000 are offered to poets and fiction writers of Cuban descent. Deadline: March 1. Contact: Institute of International Education, Cintas Fellowships Program, Arts International, 809 United Nations Plaza, New York, NY 10017.

The Iowa Review Literary Awards. The annual Iowa Review Award of $1,000 is given for the best work in any genre published in *The Iowa Review*. The Tim McGinnis Award of $500 is given on an irregular basis for the best piece of humorous writing (either poetry, fiction or nonfiction) published in *The Iowa Review*. *The Iowa Review* accepts manuscripts from September through January. Contact: *The Iowa Review*, Literary Awards, 308 EPB, University of Iowa, Iowa City, IA 52242, (319) 335-0462 (www.uiowa.edu/~iareview).

Kalliope Sue Saniel Elkind Poetry Contest. The prize of $1,000 is given annually for a poem by a woman. Deadline: November 1. Contact: Kalliope, Sue Saniel Elkind Poetry Contest, Florida Community College at Jacksonville, 3939 Roosevelt Blvd., Jacksonville, FL 32205 (www.fccj.org/kalliope).

Kentucky Arts Council Fellowships and Professional Assistance Awards. Fellowships of $5,000 and professional assistance awards of $1,000 are awarded biennially to poets and fiction and creative nonfiction writers who have been Kentucky residents for one year prior to application and are not currently enrolled in a degree program. All writers who apply for fellowships are also considered for professional assistance awards. Deadline: Fall. Contact:

Kentucky Arts Council, Fellowships and Professional Assistance Awards, 31 Fountain Place, Frankfort, KY 40601-1942, (502) 564-3757.

Leeway Foundation Grants for Excellence. The foundation makes grants of up to to $30,000 annually to individual women artists who are at least twenty-five years old and who have resided in the Philadelphia area for at least two years. Applications are available from the foundation in September. Contact: Leeway Foundation, Grants for Excellence, 123 S. Broad St., Suite 2040, Philadelphia, PA 19109, (215) 545-4078, info@leeway .org.

Mid-List Press First Series Awards. Awards are given to writers who have not published a book. Winners receive $1,000 and their manuscripts are published by Mid-List Press. Deadline: July 1. Contact: Mid-List Press, First Series Awards, 4324 Twelfth Ave. S., Minneapolis, MN 55407-3218, (www.midlist.org).

The Missouri Review Editors' Prize Contest. Prizes ranging from $1,000 to $1,500 are given annually for a group of poems, a short story and an essay. Deadline: October 15. Contact: *The Missouri Review*, Editors' Prize Contest, University of Missouri, 1507 Hillcrest Hall, Columbia, MO 65211, (573) 882-4474.

Money for Women/Barbara Deming Memorial Fund Individual Artist Grants for Women. Grants of up to $1,000 are given twice yearly to feminist writers. Contact: Money for Women/Barbara Deming Memorial Fund, P.O. Box 630125, Bronx, NY 10463.

New Issues Press Poetry Prize. The $1,000 prize is given to a poet who has not published a collection of poems of more than forty-eight pages in an edition of five hundred or more copies. Winning works are published by New Issues Press. Deadline: November 30. Contact: New Issues Press, Poetry Prize, Department of English, Western Michigan University, Kalamazoo, MI 49008-5092, (616) 387-2592.

North Carolina Arts Council Residency Program. The Arts Council provides grants of up to several thousand dollars to pay for residency programs for writers. The grants are matched by various residency centers to cover the cost of travel, food and lodging. Deadline: November 1. Contact: North Carolina Arts Council, Residency Program, Department of Cultural Resources, Raleigh, NC 27601, (919) 733-2111, ext. 22 (www.ncarts.org.)

North Carolina Writers' Network Randall Jarrell Poetry Prize. The $1,000 award is given annually for an unpublished poem in any form. Deadline: November 1. Contact: North Carolina Writers' Network, Randall Jarrell Poetry Prize, P.O. Box 954, Carrboro, NC 27510, (919) 967-9540.

Northeastern University Samuel French Morse Poetry Prize. The annual prize of $1,000 is awarded for a first or second book of poetry by a U.S. poet. Winning entries are published by Northeastern University Press. Deadline: September 15. Contact: Northeastern University, Samuel French Morse Poetry Prize, English Department, 406 Holmes Hall, Boston, MA 02115 (www.casdn.neu.edu/~english/morse.htm).

Ohio State University Press Journal Award in Poetry. The $1,000 award is given annually for a collection of unpublished poetry of at least forty-eight pages. The winning manuscript is published by the Ohio State University Press Poetry Series. Deadline: Poetry must be postmarked during the month of September. Contact: Ohio State University Press, The Journal Award in Poetry, 180 Pressey Hall, 1070 Carmack Rd., Columbus, OH 43210, (614) 292-6930.

Passaic County Community College Paterson Poetry Prize. The $1,000 award is given annually for a book of poetry published in the preceding year. Books must be at least forty-eight pages in length, with a minimum press run of five hundred copies. Deadline: Publishers may submit three copies of books by February 1. Contact: Passaic County Community College, Paterson Poetry Prize, One College Blvd., Paterson, NJ 07505, (973) 684-6555.

PEN American Center Martha Albrand Award for the Art of the Memoir. The $1,000 prize is given for a U.S. author's first book-length memoir. Deadline: December 15. Contact: PEN American Center, 568 Broadway, New York, NY 10012, (212) 334-1660.

PEN American Center PEN/Book-of-the-Month Club Translation Prize.
The $3,000 prize is given for a book-length literary translation from any
language into English published in the U.S. Deadline: December 15.
Contact: PEN American Center, 568 Broadway, New York, NY 10012,
(212) 334-1660.

Poets' Prize Annual Award. A prize of $3,000 is awarded for a book of poetry
published in the previous year. Deadline: August 15. Contact: Poets' Prize,
Annual Award, Nicholas Roerich Museum, 319 W. 107 St., New York,
NY 10025, (212) 864-7752.

Potato Eyes Foundation William and Kingman Page Poetry Book Award.
The annual award of $1,000 is given for a poetry collection of no more
than forty-one pages. Deadline: November 15. Contact: Potato Eyes
Foundation, William and Kingman Page Poetry Book Award, P.O. Box
76, Troy, ME 04987, (207) 948-3427, potatoeyes@uninets.net.

Pushcart Press Editors' Book Award. Any book-length manuscript of fiction
or nonfiction that has been submitted to but not accepted by a commercial
publisher is eligible for this $1,000 prize. Manuscripts must be nominated
by an editor at a U.S. or Canadian publishing company and accepted from
May 15 to October 15. Winning manuscripts are published by Pushcart
Press. Contact: Pushcart Press, Editors' Book Award, P.O. Box 380,
Wainscott, NY 11975, (516) 324-7449.

Radcliffe College Bunting Fellowship Program. The Bunting Fellowship
Program supports women who wish to pursue independent study in creative
writing, the arts, academia or professional fields. Each recipient receives a
stipend of $40,000 and will spend the year in residence at Radcliffe College.
Deadline: October 1. Contact: Radcliffe College, Bunting Fellowship
Program, Mary Ingraham Bunting Institute, 34 Concord Ave., Cambridge,
MA 02138, (617) 495-8212.

Ragdale Foundation Frances Shaw Fellowship. The fellowship is given
annually to a woman who began writing seriously after the age of fifty-five.
Fellows are flown to Ragdale from anywhere in the continental U.S. and
receive a free two-month residency. Deadline: February 1. Contact: Ragdale

Foundation, Frances Shaw Fellowship, 1260 N. Green Bay Rd., Lake Forest, IL 60045, (847) 234-1063, ragdale1@aol.com.

Salmon Run Press National Poetry Book Award. The annual prize of $1,000 is given for a poetry manuscript of sixty-eight to ninety-six pages. Winning collections are published by Salmon Run Press. Deadline: December 31. Contact: Salmon Run Press, National Poetry Book Award, P.O. Box 672130, Chugiak, AK 99567, (907) 688-4268.

Shenandoah Literary Prizes. Annual prizes ranging from $500 to $1,000 are given for the best short story, poem and essay published in *Shenandoah*. Contact: *Shenandoah*, Literary Prizes, Washington and Lee University, Troubadour Theater, 2nd Floor, Lexington, VA 24450-0303, (540) 463-8765.

South Carolina Arts Commission Professional Artist Fellowship in Literature. The commission awards one literature fellowship to a South Carolina resident annually. The $7,500 Professional Artist Fellowship alternates between prose and poetry. Deadline: February 15. The South Carolina Fiction Project awards $500 annually to South Carolina writers of short fiction. The annual award includes publication in the Charleston *Post and Courier*. Deadline: January 15. Contact: South Carolina Arts Commission, 1800 Gervais St., Columbia, SC 29201, (803) 734-8696.

The Sow's Ear Poetry Review Poetry Prize. The $1,000 prize is given annually for an unpublished poem of any length. Submissions are accepted during September and October. Contact: The Sow's Ear Poetry Review, Poetry Prize, 19535 Pleasant View Dr., Abingdon, VA 24211-6827.

State University of New York at Farmingdale Paumanok Poetry Award. The award is given annually by State University of New York (SUNY) Farmingdale's Visiting Writers Program to an outstanding poet. Prize includes $1,000 and travel expenses to SUNY Farmingdale to give a reading. Deadline: September 15. Contact: SUNY Farmingdale, Paumanok Poetry Award, Visiting Writers Program, Knapp Hall, Route 110, Farmingdale, NY 11735, (516) 420-2645.

Story Line Press Nicholas Roerich Poetry Prize. The $1,000 prize is given to a poet who has not published a full-length volume of poetry. Winning manuscripts are published by Story Line Press. Deadline: October 31. Contact: Story Line Press, Nicholas Roerich Poetry Prize, Three Oaks Farm, P.O. Box 1240, Ashland, OR 97520-0055, (541) 512-8792 (www .storylinepress.com/roerich.htm).

University of North Texas Press Vassar Miller Prize in Poetry. The $1,000 award is given annually for an original poetry manuscript. The winning manuscript is published by the University of North Texas Press. Deadline: November 30. Contact: Vassar Miller Prize in Poetry, English Department, Old Dominion University, Norfolk, VA 23529, (757) 683-4042.

University of Pittsburgh Press Drue Heinz Literature Prize. The $10,000 award is given to a writer who has published a book-length fiction manuscript. Winning entries are published by the University of Pittsburgh Press. Deadline: Manuscripts must be mailed only during May and June and must be postmarked no later than June 30. Contact: University of Pittsburgh Press, Drue Heinz Literature Prize, 3347 Forbes Ave., Pittsburgh, PA 15261, (412) 383-2456.

University of Wisconsin Fellows of the Institute for Creative Writing. The nine-month fellowships provide time, space and an intellectual community for writers working on a first book. Each fellow receives $22,000. Fellows teach one creative writing workshop per semester and give one public reading. Applicants must have an M.F.A. in creative writing or a comparable graduate degree and must not have published a book. Applications will only be accepted in February. Contact: University of Wisconsin, Institute for Creative Writing, English Department, 600 N. Park St., Madison, WI 53706.

University of Wisconsin Press Poetry Series, The Brittingham/Felix Pollak Prizes in Poetry. The prizes are given annually by the University of Wisconsin Press and the university's creative writing program. Winning manuscripts are published by the University of Wisconsin Press. Manuscripts are accepted during September only. Contact: University of Wisconsin Press Poetry Series, The Brittingham/Felix Pollak Prizes in Poetry, University of Wisconsin Press, 2537 Daniels St., Madison, WI 53718-6772.

Unterberg Poetry Center/The Nation, Discovery/The Nation Prize. This award is open to poets who have not yet published a book of poems. Winners receive $300, publication in *The Nation* and an expenses-paid trip to read at the 92nd Street Y in New York City. Deadline: January 29. Contact: Discovery/The Nation Prizes, 92nd Street Y Unterberg Poetry Center, 1395 Lexington Ave., New York, NY 10128, (212) 415-5759.

Utah State University Press May Swenson Poetry Award. The $1,000 award is given annually for a poetry collection and includes publication by Utah State University Press. Deadline: September 30. Contact: Utah State University Press, May Swenson Poetry Award, 7800 Old Main Hill, Logan, UT 84322-7800, (801) 797-1362 (www.usu.edu/~usupress/poetcomp.htm).

Virginia Commission for the Arts Individual Artist Fellowships. Writers' grants of up to $5,000 are given on a rotating basis with other artistic disciplines. Deadline: October 1. Contact: Virginia Commission for the Arts, Individual Artist Fellowships, Lewis House, 2nd floor, 223 Governor St., Richmond, VA 23219, vacomm@artswire.org (www.artswire.org/~vacomm).

Virginia Quarterly Review Emily Clark Balch Prizes. The annual prizes of $500 are given for the best fiction and poetry published in the *Virginia Quarterly Review* in the preceding calendar year. Contact: *Virginia Quarterly Review*, Emily Clark Balch Prizes, One West Range, Charlottesville, VA 22903, (804) 924-3124.

Whetstone Literary Journal Whetstone Prize. The $500 award is given for the best poetry, fiction or creative nonfiction published in *Whetstone* each year. Contact: *Whetstone Literary Journal*, Whetstone Prize, Barrington Area Arts Council, P.O. Box 1266, Barrington, IL 60011, (847) 381-9467.

Writers at Work Poetry, Fiction and Creative Nonfiction Fellowships. Awards of $1,500 are given each year to writers of poetry, fiction and creative nonfiction who have not published a book-length work. Each winner is published in *Quarterly West* and receives free tuition at the Writers at Work Conference in Park City, Utah. Deadline: March 15. Contact: Writers at Work, Poetry, Fiction and Creative Nonfiction Fellowships, P.O. Box 1146, Centerville, UT 84014-5146, (801) 292-9285.

The YMCA National Writer's Voice Writers Community Residencies. The residencies are given to midcareer writers in recognition of literary achievement. Residents conduct master-level workshops and give public readings at YMCA-based Writer's Voice centers. Each resident receives $6,000. Centers have different deadlines. Contact: The YMCA National Writer's Voice, Writers Community Residencies, YMCA of the USA Arts and Humanities Office, 101 N. Wacker Dr., Chicago, IL 60606, (800) USA-YMCA, ext. 515.

SAMPLE AWARD ENTRY GUIDELINES

The Missouri Review Annual Editors' Prize in Fiction & Essay and the Editors' Prize in Poetry

$1,500 Fiction/$1,500 Poetry/$1,000 Essay

Deadline

Entries must be postmarked by 15 October 1999.

One winner and three finalists will be chosen in each category. Winners will be published and finalists announced in the following spring's issue of *The Missouri Review*. Finalists in all categories will receive a minimum of $100 or consideration for publication at regular rates.

Complete Guidelines

(No other information is needed to enter.)

- Page restrictions: 25 typed, double-spaced, for fiction and nonfiction. Poetry entries can include any number of poems up to 10 pages. Each story or essay constitutes one entry.
- Entry fee: $15 for each entry (checks made payable to *The Missouri Review*). Each fee entitles entrant to a one-year subscription to *MR*, an extension of a current subscription or a gift subscription (a $4 savings from the regular subscription price). Please indicate your choice and enclose a complete address for subscriptions.
- Entries must be clearly addressed to: Missouri Review Editors' Prize, 1507 Hillcrest Hall, UMC, Columbia, MO 65211. Outside of the envelope must be marked "Fiction," "Essay" or "Poetry." Each entry in each category must be mailed in a separate envelope.
- Enclose an index card with author's name, address and telephone number in the left corner—and the work's title in the center of the card if fiction or essay. This information should also be included on the first page of the submission.
- Entries must be previously unpublished and will not be returned. Enclose a #10 SASE for announcement of winners only.

SAMPLE GRANT FORM GUIDELINES

North Carolina Artist Fellowships

The North Carolina Arts Council provides fellowships to support artists in the development and creation of art because their work is essential to our cultural heritage and the creative vitality of the state. Artists are eligible to apply if they have been residents of North Carolina for at least one year immediately prior to the application deadline. Artists who receive fellowships must maintain their North Carolina residency status during the grant period. Artists may not receive grants while they are pursuing academic or professional degrees.

Deadline and Project Period

Applications must be received in our office by 5 P.M. on November 2, 1998. All fellowship activities must take place between July 1, 1999, and June 30, 2000.

Who May Apply

This program operates on a two-year cycle. Composers, playwrights, screenwriters, songwriters and writers are eligible to apply this year. Choreographers, film/video artists and visual artists will be eligible to apply in the fall of 1999.

Artists who received a fellowship in the last six years are not eligible to apply. Artists may submit only one fellowship application per year.

What We Fund

Fellowships in the amount of $8,000 are awarded to support the creative development of North Carolina artists and to generate the creation of new work. Artists may use these funds to:

- Set aside time to work
- Pursue projects that further artistic development and support the realization of specific creative ideas
- Purchase supplies and equipment

Grant funds may be used for expenses related to the proposal. These may include costs related to studio construction or improvements. Grant funds cannot support academic research or formal study toward an academic or professional degree.

How We Make Funding Decisions

Applications will be reviewed by one of three discipline panels made up of a combination of in-state and out-of-state arts professionals. The primary evaluation criterion will be artistic excellence based on work samples. The panel will also review the proposal narrative in making final decisions.

How to Apply

Please read and follow the specific instructions for your art form and the instructions on the application form.

Writers Fellowship Eligibility

- Writers of fiction, poetry, literary nonfiction and literary translation
- Writers whose work crosses genres or art forms
- Writers of work for children

APPLICANTS SHOULD SUBMIT THE FOLLOWING:

Application Form and Narrative

5 copies of the completed application form and 5 copies of the narrative. In the narrative, explain how you plan to use the fellowship, how it will affect your artistic development and why it's important that you receive a fellowship at this time.

Work Sample

5 copies of 10 single-spaced poems, 20 double-spaced pages of fiction or nonfiction, or work in a combination of these genres no longer than 20 pages. The work must have been written in the past 5 years.

The manuscript must be typed or printed on letter-quality equipment. If you submit an excerpt from a novel or a long nonfiction work, include within the 20 pages a one-page synopsis of the work as a whole. Work that has been published must be submitted in typewritten rather than published form.

Title Page

One copy of a page listing the title(s) of the piece(s) submitted. Your name should appear only on this title page, not on the manuscript.

Resume

5 copies of a typewritten resume with information about your education and/or important learning experiences. Include any other pertinent biographical details. You may also include information about your employment, commissions, honors, performances and lists of recently created works.

Return Envelope

A stamped, self-addressed envelope if you wish to have your work samples returned. Please don't send metered stamps for return envelopes.

For More Information

Call (919) 733-2111.

Application Form Instructions

- Provide answers to all questions on the application form. Refer to the glossary behind the form for listings of codes.
- Carefully follow the instructions in the guidelines to prepare your narrative, resume and work samples.
- Assemble your application package in the following order. Collate these materials into sets, each bound with a paper clip. Make sure you submit the number of copies requested in the guidelines.

  1. Cover Page
  2. Summary Page
  3. Application Narrative
  4. Resume
  5. Work Sample

- Call the staff contact listed if you have questions.
- Make sure your application is received by 5 P.M. November 2. We don't accept late applications or fax transmissions.

For postal-service-delivered applications, our mailing address is:

Grants Office

North Carolina Arts Council

Department of Cultural Resources

Raleigh, NC 27601

For hand-delivered or express-delivered applications, our street address is:

221 East Lane Street

Raleigh, NC 27601-2812

We'll send you a notice acknowledging receipt of your application a few weeks after the deadline. If you wish to be notified sooner, enclose a self-addressed, stamped postcard on top of your application package and we'll mail it back as soon as your application arrives. You'll be informed of the results of your application in July or August, once the legislature adjourns and our budget is confirmed.

CONGRATULATIONS!
You've now got the ultimate "how-to" guide for publishing success...

Double your potential with the ultimate "where-to"

(OVER)

2000 Writer's Market
$27.99, pb (CAN $41.99) 0-89879-911-2

The ultimate writer's resource, 2000 Writer's Market gives you the contacts to get published and get PAID for it. Included are more than 4,000 up-to-date leads, featuring consumer and trade magazines, book publishers, script buyers and more. You'll also receive valuable how-to information on writing query letters, formatting submissions and much more. It's all here, ready and waiting to help make your writing career happen. #10609

Available NOW at bookstores everywhere.
For information call 1-800-289-0963 or go to
www.writersdigest.com

And don't miss these other great resources:

2000 Writer's Market—The Electronic Edition
$49.99, pb w/CD-ROM (CAN $74.99) 0-89879-916-3

The same great information as 2000 Writer's Market and more! Use easy-to-customize search settings to target your most promising market opportunities. Also includes Submission Tracker, a built in program to keep track of all your correspondence. #10614

2000 Novel & Short Story Writer's Market
$24.99, pb (CAN 38.99) 0-89879-934-1

This is the single most important tool for fiction writers—unlike any other resource on the market! Within, you'll find over 2000 places to publish your fiction, screenplays and short stories. #10625

2000 Guide to Literary Agents
$21.99, pb (CAN $34.99) 0-89879-936-8

The most current source of literary and script agents available! Includes contact information for more than 500 agents who sell what you write. #10627

2000 Children's Writer's & Illustrator's Market
$21.99, pb (CAN $34.99) 0-89879-935-X

Up-to-date information on hundreds of publishers of children's books, magazines, games, puzzles, poetry and more. #10626

2000 Poet's Market
$23.99, pb (CAN $35.99) 0-89879-915-5

Publish your poetry! 2000 Poet's Market provides you with more than 1,800 editors representing book publishers, literary journals, university quarterlies, magazines and more. #10613

And don't miss out on our other titles in the Writer's Market Library:

Formatting & Submitting Your Manuscript
$18.99, pb (CAN $28.99) 0-89879-921-X

Covering every part of the manuscript submission package, this guide shows you the dos and don'ts for creating persuasive and professional correspondence and submission materials. Features full-size examples. #10618

ARTIST'S/INDIVIDUAL'S GRANT APPLICATION—COVER PAGE

North Carolina Arts Council, Department of Cultural Resources
   Raleigh, NC 27601-2807

Name of Individual: _____

Mailing Address: _____

City, County (NC): _____

State: _____

Zip Code: _____

Artist Type: _____

Work Phone: _____

Home Phone: _____

Fax Number: _____

E-mail: _____

Web Site Address: _____

☐ If you have never applied for a Council grant before, check here.
Please complete the Applicant Data below. You will be sent a complete mailing list form but we need several codes now in order to process your application.

Application Category:
Check the one Grant Category in which this application is submitted:
☐ Composers/Songwriters Fellowship
☐ Playwrights/Screenwriters Fellowship
☐ Writers Fellowship
☐ LaNapoule Residency for Writers
☐ Both Writers Fellowship and LaNapoule Residency
☐ Folklife Documentary Project
☐ Folklife Internship
☐ Community Arts Administration Internship

INDIVIDUAL'S GRANT APPLICATION— SUMMARY PAGE

Applicant Name: _____

Grant Category: _____

Application Summary: _____

_____

Grant Amount Requested: $ _____

Project Start Date: _____

Project End Date: _____

Applicant Race/Ethnicity: _____

Discipline Code: _____

Type of Activity Code: _____

International Activity: _____

Project Race/Ethnicity: _____

Certification:

I have been living in North Carolina since _____. I certify that the information contained in this application, including all attachments and supporting materials, is true and correct to the best of my knowledge. If this application is for a fellowship or residency grant, I certify that I have been a full-time, year-round resident of North Carolina for the past 12 months.

Typed Name of Applicant: _____

Signature of Applicant and Date: _____

Applicant Social Security Number: _____

Pricing Guide

Why Write?

Before you can figure out how much to charge for your work, first figure out why you are writing: Do you want to make writing your full-time occupation? Do you want to write, but are you holding onto your day job? Do you want to earn enough with your writing to break even, meeting all the expenses of setting up an office? Or do you want only to earn enough to pay for your computer, your rent, your food or a really good dinner?

The answers to those questions will help you decide how to set prices in this business of writing. If writing is your livelihood, you may well have to pay for your own IRA, Social Security taxes and health insurance, in addition to office expenses, food, shelter and clothing. If you're writing to scratch an itch, any payment you receive may seem like play money.

Or maybe your goal is to practice your art—to write poetry or the Great American Novel. If this type of writing is more your idea of success, you may want to structure your freelance career in a way that affords you time for your art. Many writers spend half their week churning out freelance work or technical writing so that they can use the rest of their time in more creative pursuits.

As a group writers are underpaid. Surveys by such organizations as the Authors Guild and the National Writers Union show that income growth for most writers lags behind that of most other professions. Even so, there are still a substantial number of writers in the United States—at least 15 percent—making more than $30,000 a year. Many make $50,000 or more annually.

The question for you, then, is how to maximize your earning potential either as a full-time or a part-time writer. The decision you have to make is whether you will approach your writing as a hobby, or whether you will tackle it as a profession. In actuality, freelance writing is similar to other creative fields, such as art, photography and music. You can either earn hobby rates or you can earn a professional wage. The difference is in how seriously you take your work.

Freelancers who command top dollar are experienced professionals who have spent years perfecting their skills as writers employed in journalism, advertising, public relations or publishing. Beyond being talented writers, they are reliable professionals who respect deadlines and have mastered the fine details of running an independent business. They are especially good at marketing themselves.

A freelancer, like any independent business person, must also set goals and develop a business plan. The plan doesn't have to be as formal as those for bigger businesses, but at the very least you have to decide what writing skills you have to sell, who might buy them and how you will prove that you are the best person for the job.

While producers of other products can check out the competition's prices at malls and markets, writers are lonely souls, left to negotiate individually with publishers and clients. Joining a writers group can broaden your perspective on pay rates, particularly a national group, such as the Editorial Freelancers Association or the National Writers Union, which publish data about how much their members earn for jobs. Reading books such as *Writer's Market* (Writer's Digest Books), which annually publishes lists of pay scales for dozens of types of writing, can also help you determine what to charge. Joining an E-mail list allows you to simply post your rates and ask plugged-in counterparts, "Am I charging enough?" Brenner Books (www.brennerbooks.com) publishes books and articles on pricing for writers, editors, graphic designers and other publishing professionals.

Many freelancers find most of their work by networking with other writers, editors and potential clients. Other good leads come through E-mail and hard-copy queries or networking through Chambers of Commerce and similar organizations. But the best referrals come from satisfied clients who tell others about your work.

Newspapers are the most accessible medium for young writers to break into. But writing for newspapers (either full-time or part-time) is not typically a good way to build a professional income. Newspapers can be useful, however, as a source of initial clips or publicity.

Frankly, beginners will earn less in this profession, as in most others. In addition, asking for more money is never easy. Some clients may be more willing to negotiate with writers who have already produced materials that meet their needs, but many are not willing to do so when dealing with a new freelancer. To get your feet wet, you may have to settle for less—at first. The trick is to raise your prices as your reputation grows. Remember: The best client is one who is willing to pay you more than once.

If you don't wish to merely accept whatever pay scale is offered, you can use the formulas on these pages to help determine an hourly rate that can cover your bills and earn you a profit as a writer.

Calculating Your Expenses

Any business has to make enough money to cover expenses. The following worksheet will help you figure out your overhead costs and other expenses. Overhead for a writing business typically includes a computer, office supplies, fax, telephone and office space.

This formula assumes you "expense" your computer equipment in one year, meaning you will write the total off as a business expense in one year. If you plan to use the equipment several years, you can depreciate its value over several years. For example, if you plan to keep your $1,600 computer three years, then your expense for one year would be $1,600 divided by 3, or $534. Divide this figure by 12 to find the monthly cost.

Taxes are high for freelancers, because you pay both your and the employer's portion of Social Security taxes. Estimate 50 percent of your income going to the government; the figure may be a bit high, but it's better to have too much than too little money ready to send the government at the end of each quarter. In the table below, we estimated an annual income of $30,000, so the tax bill would be about $15,000. That divided by 12 is $1,250 of taxes each month.

You may have other expenses—renting an office, for example. In the table below, "other" expenses can include dues for professional associations, seminar fees, subscriptions, advertising/promotion, travel and licenses.

Monthly Expense Calculation (example)

Computer ($1,600/12 months)	$ 134
Printer ($200/12 months)	$ 17
Telephone	$ 35
Office Supplies	$ 25
Postage	$ 15
Taxes	$ 1,250 (estimate)
Other ($144/12 months)	$ 12
TOTAL	$ 1,488

Monthly Expense Worksheet

Computer (divided by 12)	$
Printer (divided by 12)	$
Telephone	$
Office Supplies	$
Postage	$
Taxes (50 percent of gross)	$
Other	$
TOTAL	$

Hourly Rate Calculation

1. Covering Expenses. To figure out how much you'll have to earn per hour to pay for expenses, first decide how much time you'll have to devote to writing per month. To calculate the break-even hourly rate, divide your monthly expenses by the number of hours you plan to work. In the example above, if you can work 160 hours each month on your writing, the hourly rate would be $1,488/160 = $9.50 per hour.

Consider this your bare minimum hourly rate, because it does not include any remuneration for your expertise or any profit. If you use this figure to give an estimate for a job, you'd be valuing your time and talent at zero.

2. Setting Fees. One way to make sure you are paid market rates is to estimate how much a company would pay an employee to do similar work. But remember that a company also may pay for health insurance, retirement funds, unemployment insurance, vacation time, holidays, etc. These costs can range from 25 to 45 percent of an employee's annual salary, depending upon which perks the employee gets and where he lives. You can call companies to find actual costs for each of the benefits you need, or just use a 35 percent estimate.

> Estimated yearly salary: $30,000 divided by 2,000 (40 hours per week for 50 weeks) equals an hourly pay rate of $15. (This formula assumes you will take two weeks of vacation a year.)
>
> Adding fringe benefit costs of 35 percent ($5.25) gives you an hourly rate of $20.25.
>
> Add to this amount your minimum rate to cover overhead ($9.50) and you have a total hourly rate of $29.75.
>
> In addition, you might want to add another 10 to 20 percent of profit ($3.50) for a total hourly fee of $32.25.

A rate of $30 or more an hour may be high for a particular type of writing or may be quite reasonable, depending on your level of experience, the perceived value of your work and the prevailing rates available to the client. In determining the prices you will charge for various types of work you must first conduct research. This includes talking to other writers about what they charge.

When calculating the hours you invest in your work you also need to consider the time spent writing queries and making calls to find jobs, billing, filing tax returns, driving to the post office, shopping for office supplies and maintaining your computer. To be successful, at least one-fifth of your time should be spent marketing yourself. Your hourly rate for all these activities needs to be recouped somewhere—either in higher fees or additional hours that you bill your clients.

Fee Worksheet

Employee's estimated yearly salary	$
Divide by hours worked (2,000 for 40 hours week for 50 weeks)	÷ 2,000
Estimated employee hourly rate	$
Fringe benefit costs (add 30 percent)	+ $
Your minimum rate to cover overhead	+ $
Profit (.10 to .20 × hourly rate)	+ $
Your hourly rate	$

It's best to have a written contract spelling out what work you are expected to do at what rate. None of the above calculations includes reimbursement for expenses for specific jobs, such as travel, overnight mail or long-distance telephone calls. These should be added to the bill and paid by the client.

Project Rates

An alternative way of pricing is to charge by the project. The advantage of project pricing is that if you work quickly, you can earn a high hourly rate. If you quote a price of $300 for a piece, and manage to turn it around in three hours, well, you do the math. If you decide to work more slowly, that's your option, too. But with an hourly rate, you've set your ceiling and a client probably won't pay you more.

The disadvantage of accepting a project price is that if you estimate too low, you may discover you could have earned better wages at McDonald's. You can always try negotiating for more, but you'll have to convince your client why your original estimate was wrong, which is difficult and, if it's your fault, embarrassing.

Some clients will tell you their pay rates up front. Others may ask what you charge. If asked, don't be evasive. It's not very professional to show uncertainty about something as basic and important as your price. Since they're asking, feel free to quote your full fee. Remember, you can always adjust downward but you probably cannot negotiate upward after you have already quoted a price.

Seasoned writers have an easier time figuring out an acceptable price for a project. Almost by instinct they can discern the amount of time and effort that will go into a project. Beginners typically fare better by focusing on an hourly fee. This way they not only learn which types of projects are best suited for them, they can also keep better track of the gains they make in skill and efficiency. Unfortunately most clients want a fixed price, especially if they are not familiar with your work. The solution is to negotiate a set price based on the number of hours you expect to spend on the project. If you are going to earn a set fee it is important to detail up front precisely what the work will entail. Once you have talked this over with the client or editor, estimate how many hours you expect to spend on the project, including research, interviews, editing and proofreading. (It helps to look at similar projects completed for the client in the past.) Then multiply the number of hours by your hourly rate to get the amount of money you expect to earn.

When starting out as a freelance writer you won't be able to command the same fee as someone with several years of experience. This does not mean, however, that you are at the mercy of the client. If you are qualified as a writer, then you are producing a professional product and should be compensated fairly. Decide early on the lowest figure you will accept and stick to it.

Early in your career you might not make out as well charging by the project. But as you gain experience—enabling you to work faster and to estimate your time better—you will do quite well. Publications and most other businesses are time sensitive. To your pleasant surprise, clients and editors will be willing to pay you more for getting work done more quickly. As your proficiency and efficiency improve you will, in effect, earn more money for less work.

Keep Track of Time

Keeping track of how long it takes to finish a project might feel as if you're attaching a meter to your mind. But it is vitally important whether you are charging by the hours or by the project. By keeping good records for specific types of projects you will eventually discern patterns. You can use the insight you gain to improve your work flow, cut out unnecessary steps and set fees that maximize your income while still keeping you competitive. Even so, many writers do not closely track how much time they spent on a project. Even if they know how much time they spend at the keyboard, they often underestimate the hours spent researching, interviewing, billing and corresponding with their clients.

It need not be this way, because keeping track of your time is not as much effort as you might think—and the payoff far outweighs the investment of time you put into it. The insight you gain into your work habits can help you better use your time in the future—giving you more free time down the road. You will also improve your ability to accurately bid your services.

One easy method is to watch the clock and keep a log book by your computer or in your briefcase. Some people even use a stopwatch. They simply start the watch when they begin work, turn it off whenever they step away and turn it on again when they resume work. The watch keeps an accurate tally of their cumulative time.

Ironically it's sometimes the small projects that reveal the most about our work habits. Bigger projects get spread over weeks or even months, making it harder to get a clear picture of all the work involved. A small project that lasts just a couple days is easier to track and analyze. You might be surprised by what you learn.

Joe spends a good deal of his freelance time managing large projects of 15 to 30 articles involving several writers. Only when he handled a smaller project of a couple stories did he realize just how much time he spent overseeing, editing and proofreading each story. When he multiplied that time for bigger projects, he realized he was working many more hours than he realized.

With a record of time invested in a job, you can examine hard data to estimate how much you think you ought to earn on a project. You can use the data in asking for more money on the next project. Use the chart below to track your hours per project. In the column labeled "Notes," include anything that made the job easier or harder than expected.

Job name	Date	Notes	Hours of work	Project payment	Hourly rate

Negotiating for More

Few of us like to haggle over the price of goods or services. When you land a writing job, however, you are in a good negotiating position: You have something that your client wants.

A good rule to consider in wrangling over fees is to consider the three points on the triangle (see the following diagram). Most people want things good, inexpensive and fast. But most times, they will only get two of the three. For example, you might be able to write something inexpensively and fast, but you probably won't be able to do it well. Or you can do it fast and make it good, but it won't be cheap. By this reasoning, if a client asks for a quick turnaround time, you should expect to be paid extra for it.

Once you work with a client or editor, and prove you can deliver, it will be easier to negotiate for more money. While many editors are understandably reluctant to invest large amounts in unknown writers, they may be able to find more in their budgets for someone they have come to know and trust.

It may be easier for beginning writers to quote a range of pay they would like to earn. You could tell the client the job would cost between $100 and $200, for example, depending on how much time it involves. If you can do it for less, they may be grateful for a smaller bill and be more willing to give you another assignment. But never undervalue your work, for if you do, you can be sure that others will, too.

Negotiation doesn't have to be confrontational. After all, an editor often doesn't hold the purse strings, and may be sympathetic to polite requests for more money. Before you ask for more (or ask to retain certain rights to resell your work), decide which things you sincerely want and which you can give up. First, state everything that you would like. Then be prepared to adopt a position that gets you most of what you want. If you've kept of log of how long previous projects have taken and what types of work they entailed, your arguments will be more persuasive. Be realistic, however. A publication that pays a penny a word is hardly likely to increase that ten fold.

Simply saying nothing or repeating the project price might prompt the client to increase it. Here's a true story: A young woman from Kentucky moved to New York City and was offered a job working in the computer department of a large publishing firm. When she was asked what salary she wanted, she paused. They offered $45,000. She accepted. Used to working for minimum wage, she was delighted. But just two days later, she was offered a promotion and a raise to $50,000. She couldn't believe it "Fifty-thousand dollars?" she repeated incredulously. Whereupon the company increased the offer to $55,000. While most writers don't make the wages that computer specialists do, repeating the pay may be a successful negotiating ploy.

Keep in mind that business people talk money all the time, and writing is a business. If you ask for more, usually the worst that could happen is being told no. At that point it's up to you to decide whether you'll take the job or move on.

Raising Your Rates

Like any businessperson, you, as a freelancer, will eventually face the day when you need to raise prices. Maybe it is because inflation has cut into your profit margin or your living standard. Perhaps you feel the value of your services has increased. Or maybe you have discovered that you have been pricing your services below the market value. In any of these cases don't be reluctant to ask for what you think is fair and justified.

Other businesses consistently raise their rates. Consider the cost of concerts and professional sports tickets. Price increases are a fact of life. So don't keep your prices artificially low when an increase is justified. Underpricing your services can produce an impression that you lack the skill and experience to command professional fees. It can also suggest that your work is of lower quality.

If you do decide to raise your price, avoid being erratic. If you change prices often—whether raising or lowering them—you may create the impression that you have no basis for your fee. When you do raise your price, make the increases small and base the change on a sound business decision that you can justify. Keep in mind that an increase of just a few percent in your overall price can raise your profit margin substantially.

Of course you don't always have to raise your rates to bring in extra income. If you really can't justify a rate increase, examine your work for instances where you give services to clients for free. While you don't want to "nickel and dime" your clients with petty fees, neither do you want to give away vital services, especially when they receive a direct benefit.

You can also base your price on speed of delivery. If you are asked to turn a project around in half the time, charge extra for this value-added service. Chances are you have to put other projects on hold and work extra hard to accomplish a last-minute request. Be fair, but charge extra for the added effort. Most businesses and consumers realize the added value of convenience, which is why we pay more for quick oil changes, overnight shipments and lenses that are ready "in about an hour."

If you are questioned about a price change, explain how you have incorporated extra value into your services, how your work has helped the client win business or helped a publication gain readership. Explain how your fee is a bargain given the benefits provided or the service received.

As a final word, consider this: A client who does not want you to earn a fair wage is not a client worth having. Is it worth losing some low-profit clients in return for earning extra income from your more profitable clients? Raising your prices may be a way to do a profitable business in a forty-hour week—to work smarter instead of working longer hours.

Sample Fees

The following prices are culled from the 1999 *Writer's Market* survey and represent a range of prices charged by freelance writers across North America. Use the prices only as general guidelines because the fees writers charge can vary greatly depending on location, size and complexity of the project and the writer's own experience or expertise. Many writers charge far less or far more than the prices shown here. Prices listed do not include additional fees or expenses that are typically paid by the client.

- Advertisement for print: $200-$500 per project
- Advertisement for radio: $50-$125 per hour or $400-$2,000 per spot
- Advertising copyediting: $25-$35 per hour
- Advertising copywriting: $400-$2,000 per full-page ad
- Advertorial: $25-$35 per hour, $300 for 700 words or $1,000 per printed page
- Annual report: $35-$100 per hour, $300-$600 per page or $3,000-$6,000 per project
- Audiovisual: $250-$350 per scripted minute or $1,500-$2,000 per job
- Brochure writing: $30-$100 per hour or $1,000-$2,500 for four-page project
- Computer documentation: $35-$100 per hour
- Copyediting a book: $30-$50 per hour or $3-$5 per page
- Copyediting for business: $20-$40 per hour
- Copyediting for a magazine: $25-$50 per hour
- Copyediting for a newspaper: $10-$40 per hour
- Direct-mail copywriting: $25-$45 per hour, $75 or more per item or $400-$800 per page
- Editing a book: $35-$65 per hour
- Editing for an individual client: $10-$50 per hour or $2-$7 per page
- Editing a legal or government document: $25-$65 per hour
- Editing a magazine: $30-$60 per hour
- Editing a medical or science document: $60-$85 per hour
- Fact checking for a magazine: $50-$75 per hour
- Film script for business: $85-$200 per hour or $100-$175 per minute of script
- Ghostwriting a book: $15,000-$25,000 per project or $25-$85 an hour
- Ghostwriting a magazine article: up to $2 per word or $300-$3,000 per project
- Grant proposal: $30-$100 an hour
- Indexing: $25-$40 per hour or $2-$6 per indexable page
- Legal/government writing: $30-$65 per hour
- Letter for business: $65-$100 per hour, $25-$30 per letter or $2 per word

- Letter for sales or promotion: $70-$125 per hour, $2 per word or $750-$2,000 per project
- Magazine column: $250-$2,500 per piece
- Magazine feature: $150-$2,750 per 1,500-word article
- Newsletter writing or editing: $25-$100 hour or $200-$500 per issue
- Newspaper article: $45-$200 per piece
- Press kit creation: $70-$125 per hour or $1,000-$5,000 per project
- Press release: $70-$150 per hour or $350-$500 per project
- Product information: $30-$60 per hour, $400-$500 per day or $100-$300 per page
- Promotion for tourism: $20-$50 per hour
- Proofreading a book: $30-$55 per hour or $4-$6 per page
- Proofreading for business: $15-$50 per hour
- Proofreading for a newspapers or magazine: $15-$25 per hour
- Radio documentary: $260 per sixty-minute local broadcast
- Radio editorial: $10-$30 per two-minute spot
- Research for business: $35-$50 per hour
- Research for magazine: $20-$25 per hour
- Slide presentation: $150-$600 for fifteen-minute presentation
- Speechwriting: up to $80 per hour or $400-$800 for thirty-minute speech
- Technical writing: $30-$75 per hour or $20-$30 per page
- TV commercial: $950-$1,500 per thirty-second spot
- TV news feature: $60-$140 per feature
- TV script: $15,000 per thirty-minute sitcom
- Web page writing or editing: $50-$125 per hour or $200-$500 per page

Resources

WEB SITES

Brenner Books (www.brennerbooks.com). Brenner Books publishes books and articles on pricing for writers, graphic designers and other publishing professionals.

National Writers Union (www.nwu.org/). In a section for members, site includes a database of magazine rates paid to NWU members.

The Society for Technical Communication (www.stc-va.org). The Society for Technical Communication has posted a survey showing salaries and benefits of members in the U.S. and Canada.

Anne Wallingford, Wordsmith (www.aw-wrdsmth.com). Anne Wallingford's Freelancer's FAQs includes detailed calculations showing that freelancers must make $77 per hour to make the equivalent of a full-time $45,000 annual salary.

Writer's Digest (www.writersdigest.com). Site includes a standing link to rates, called "What should I charge?"

BOOKS

Guide to Freelance Rates and Standard Practice by the National Writers Union (Writer's Digest Books, 1995).

Writer's Market (Writer's Digest Books). Includes typical pay rates for a variety of writing and publishing work.